THE CHURCH OF THE EAST

The Church of the East is currently the only complete history in English of the East Syriac Church. It covers the periods of the Sassanians, Arabs, Mongols, Ottomans, and the twentieth century, with information about the Syriac, Iranian, and Chinese documentation of this unique and almost forgotten part of Christendom.

"This is an important book. It tells the story concisely of the 'Church of the East' ... established in east Syria but principally in Parthia beyond Rome's eastern frontier. ... It was associated with the doctrinal view of the deposed patriarch of Constantinople, Nestorius, and was known as the Nestorian Church. ... Today, it has survived as a small minority in parts of Persia and Iraq, and it has more adherents in the US than in its ancient homeland. ... This is the best short history of the Church of the East to date ... a fine, scholarly work, bringing to the notice of students the wealth of the spiritual and theological legacy as well as the sheer missionary drive of this now half-forgotten Church. As a book it will not easily be replaced, and it is a credit to its authors and publishers alike."

W. H. C. Frend, University of Cambridge

"There has long been a need for a reliable book in English on the history of the Church of the East which also gives good coverage to the position of this ancient Syriac Church in the context of modern ecumenical discussion. It is most welcome that this need is now met by Baum and Winkler in this translation of their German book."

Sebastian Brock, University of Oxford

"Baum and Winkler have done us good service in providing this easily accessible account of the Church of the East ... the first full history of the Church of the East since the work of Cardinal Tisserant."

Munro-Hay

The authors

Wilhelm Baum is Associate Professor and teaches Medieval History at the Universities of Graz and Klagenfurt, Austria. He is the author of *The Transformation of the Myth of Prester John* (1999) and *Ethiopia and Europe in the Middle Ages* (2001).

Dietmar W. Winkler is Associate Professor and teaches Patristics and Ecumenical Theology at the University of Graz and the Cistercian School of Theology Heiligenkreuz, Austria.

THE CHURCH OF THE EAST

A concise history

*Wilhelm Baum and
Dietmar W. Winkler*

RoutledgeCurzon
Taylor & Francis Group
LONDON AND NEW YORK

Transferred to Digital Printing 2010

First published 2000 as *Die Apostolische Kirche des Ostens*
by Verlag Kitab, Klagenfurt

English translation published 2003
by RoutledgeCurzon
2 Park Square, Milton Park, Abingdon, Oxon, OX14 4RN

Simultaneously published in the USA and Canada
by RoutledgeCurzon
270 Madison Ave, New York NY 10016

RoutledgeCurzon is an imprint of the Taylor & Francis Group

© 2000 Verlag Kitab Klagenfurt
English translation © 2003 Verlag Kitab Klagenfurt
English translation by Miranda G. Henry

Produced with the support of the Foundation Pro Oriente (Austria)

Typeset in Sabon by RefineCatch Limited, Bungay, Suffolk

British Library Cataloguing in Publication Data
A catalogue record for this book is available from the British Library

Library of Congress Cataloging in Publication Data
Baum, Wilhelm
The Church of the East: a concise history/Wilhelm Baum
& Dietmar W. Winkler.
p. cm.
Includes bibliographical references and index.
1. Nestorian Church–History. 2. Nestorians. I. Winkler, Dietmar W.
II. Title.

BX153.3 .B38 2003

281'.8'09–dc21   2002036712

ISBN 978-0-415-29770-7 (hbk)
ISBN 978-0-415-60021-7 (pbk)

CONTENTS

CONTENTS

CONTENTS

ILLUSTRATIONS

ILLUSTRATIONS

PREFACE

It is still the case that the Orient is commonly regarded as belonging to Islam. Western consciousness is not very much aware of the facts not only that Christianity has its roots in the Middle East, but that it is still alive in the various Oriental Christian churches, which have a troubled and eventful history as well as a rich theological, spiritual, and liturgical heritage.

We have followed the track of one of those apostolic churches: the "Church of the East" which spread outside the Roman empire and is today the smallest among the Oriental churches. However, in the European Middle Ages, it was geographically far larger than any Western church, with followers along the Silk Road, in Central Asia, China, and of course in India.

This book aims to provide a concise history of this remarkable church. It is based on the current state of research and covers the periods of the Sassanians, Arabs, Mongols, Ottomans, and the twentieth century. It also describes the Syriac, Iranian, and Chinese literature of this unique part of Christendom. However, our intention was to present the history of the Church of the East in a comprehensive manner, not only for students of church history or Syriac scholars, but also for a wider public and the general reader, in an understandable language. Those who are interested in culture, religion, and theology can gain access to an almost forgotten part of Christianity with a marvellous literary and spiritual heritage. This is even more important since many (East) Syriac Christians found a new home in Europe, America, and Australia.

As the volume was written with a non-specialist audience in mind, we refrained from using scholarly transcription of names with diacritical signs, and there are no footnotes. For the most part we follow the style of the *Encyclopaedia Britannica*, and the bibliography at the end enables the reader to find more detail than the present account is able to provide.

PREFACE

We would like to thank Prof. Manfred Hutter (Bonn, Germany) for his contribution on the Iranian literature of the Church of the East. Prof. Wolfgang Hage (Marburg/Lahn, Germany) provided valuable comments on the German first edition, Prof. Herbert Franke (Gauting, Germany) on the chapters concerning China. We would also like to thank Helga Anschütz (Reinbeck, Germany) for the pictures from Kotchannes, Aleksander Naymark (Indiana, USA) for the ones of the coins from Bukhara, and Christoph Baumer (Switzerland) for the photographs of the copper plates from India.

Last but not least, we would like to thank Miranda Henry (Pittsburgh, USA) for the translation into English, and the Foundation Pro Oriente (Austria) for their support.

Dietmar W. Winkler, Wilhelm Baum
Graz and Klagenfurt, Austria
October 2002

THE "APOSTOLIC CHURCH OF THE EAST"

A brief introduction to the writing of church history and to terminology

Dietmar W. Winkler

The "Apostolic Church of the East" is, in the West, the least-known church of Christendom and is currently the smallest of the Eastern churches.

Until the present day, little consideration was shown in church history and theology for the fact that early Christianity spread not only within the Roman empire – i.e. Europe and the Mediterranean region – but also beyond the imperial boundaries. Already in the first century there were Christian communities in Mesopotamia, which was part of the empire of the Parthians, superseded by the Persian Sassanians in the third century. As early as the fifth century the Oxus had been crossed, and Sogdians and Turks, as well as the South Indian Malabar coast, had been reached. East Syriac Christianity gained a foothold on the Arabian Peninsula and, in the seventh century, reached the Chinese imperial court of the Tang Dynasty. In the eleventh century, those Turkish-Tartar tribes in Central Asia which eventually formed part of the Mongol kingdom were won, entirely or in part, for Christianity. Thus the "Church of the East" achieved the greatest geographical scope of any Christian church until the Middle Ages. For reasons of historical and political circumstance, the church has become a minority today and is represented in the countries of Iraq, Iran, and India, as well as in the diaspora in North America, Australia, Syria, the Caucasus, and Lebanon. The Apostolic Church of the East has preserved an important heritage of theology, history, and spirituality, which has

1

been rejected as heretical – "Nestorian" – by the rest of Christendom.

Deficiencies of church history

Knowledge of this branch of Christendom is slight, although Syriac Christianity constitutes its third strand, alongside the Latin-Western and Greek-Byzantine traditions. Today several churches belong to this tradition: in the so-called West Syriac tradition stand the Syrian Orthodox Church of Antioch and the Malankara Orthodox Church of India, as well as the Maronite, Syro-Malankara, and Syriac Catholic Churches. The East Syriac tradition includes two branches of the Apostolic (Assyrian) Church of the East and the Chaldean and Syro-Malabar Churches, which are in union with the Catholic Church.

Although the gospel has its origin in a Syro-Aramaic setting, and there has been continually throughout history a Christian Aramaic tradition – which we encounter in the various Syriac churches – this has moved to the background and has been largely forgotten in theological discourse. In many cases the discussion addresses only the "Latin West" (including the churches of the Reformation and the Anglicans) and the "Greek East" (including Slavic Orthodoxy), while the third important tradition, the "Syriac Orient" receives no consideration. Sebastian Brock, of the Oriental Institute at Oxford University, traces this narrow historical viewpoint to several factors, including the following:

1 First of all, there is the *Ecclesiastical History* of Eusebius of Caesarea († 339), whose perspective became the model for nearly every subsequent foray into church history until the twentieth century. Eusebius concentrated on an account of Christianity in the Roman empire, which led him to pay heightened attention to Europe. This Eurocentrism, including Byzantine Orthodoxy as well as the Latin Church, overlooked the fact that a large part of Christianity – above all those variations of Syro-Aramaic provenance but also the Armenian, Coptic, and Ethiopian branches – took hold outside of the Roman empire and spread across all of Asia and parts of Africa. As the third branch, the "Syriac Orient," encompassing India and China, represents an authentic Asian Christianity, while the Greek-Slavic East and the Latin West demonstrate the way Christianity developed in Europe.

2

2 On the basis of the fifth-century controversies over Christology, those churches which accepted the definition of faith established by the Council of Chalcedon (451) – the fourth "ecumenical council" – judged Syriac Christianity, i.e. the "West Syriac" ("Monophysite") and "East Syriac" ("Nestorian") traditions, as schismatic at best but in most instances as heretical. Thus this branch of Christianity soon became marginalized in Western church history and disappeared from common ecclesiastical awareness.

3 Within European academic theology the Syriac tradition continued to be disregarded, on the one hand because the Council of Chalcedon led to a concentration on the Latin West and Greek East and on the other hand because Oriental languages such as Syriac were studied more often in academic programs at institutes of Oriental studies and philology than in theological schools. Syriac literature is comprised of religious texts, yet the study of Syriac Christianity was almost totally ignored by the other Christian traditions.

In the twentieth century the Eurocentric perspective of Eusebius was occasionally rejected, and the present ecumenical dialogue has renewed interest in the churches of the Orient. Nevertheless, the Syriac tradition is making its way only fitfully into the awareness of Western academic theology.

Terminology

It is appropriate here to offer a few remarks on terminology, that is, on the various names by which the "Apostolic Church of the East" has been known.

From the perspective of Christendom in Late Antiquity, the name refers to those churches which lay outside the Roman empire. Regarding these, the sources speak of the "Church of the East," that is to say, the "Apostolic Church of the East" whose patriarch (catholicos) had his see at the Persian capital Seleucia-Ctesiphon. The patriarchates of the Roman empire – Rome, Constantinople, Alexandria, Antioch, Jerusalem – are considered "Western" by the Church of the East. The term "Apostolic Church of the East" is regarded by ecumenists and historians well-versed in the area, as well as by scholars of Syriac and Oriental Studies, as the most useful and accurate.

A second, equally correct term is the "East Syriac Church." This

3

name refers to the liturgical tradition and the Syriac-Aramaic language which has been maintained to the present day in the Apostolic Church of the East.

Naturally, appropriate names are also "Holy Apostolic Catholic Assyrian Church of the East" and "Ancient Church of the East," favored by the two jurisdictions of the church itself. In early East Syriac sources the preferred term was for the most part simply "Church of the East." Under the influence of Anglican missionaries in the second half of the nineteenth century the term "Assyrian" was retrieved from the ancient Orient. In the course of the Assyrian nationalist movement arising in the early twentieth century, this attribute was eventually adopted as a self-description and was added to the name officially in 1976.

An additional designation, found from time to time in the literature and sources, is only partially correct: "Persian Church." Since the Persian empire of the Sassanians was conquered by the Arabs in the seventh century, and the missionary efforts of the Church of the East extended as far as Central Asia, China, and India, this term is too narrow both chronologically and geographically.

Further, there are those terms which are familiar in the West but are also incorrect or valid only in a very limited sense. Until the present time, the most common designation in theological and church-historical literature has been the "Nestorian Church." In this way, the rest of the Christian world attributed to the Church of the East a heterodoxy dating back to the fifth century. At that time, Christendom was rent by the difficult theological question of whether Jesus Christ can be both true God and true man while remaining a single subject. How should one conceive of the relationship between God the Son made man and God the Father? In this bitter debate, some were of the opinion that the patriarch of Constantinople, Nestorius, supported the doctrine of two sons, two persons, that is, two subjects. Christ is both fully God and fully man, united only morally but not ontologically. According to the position of currently available sources, one can conclude that Nestorius did not support this doctrine, that Nestorius was himself no "Nestorian." Nevertheless, the term "Nestorian" has found a secure place in theological history, to denote a Christology which understands the one Savior made man as two subjects. Indeed, even up to now scholars have been of the opinion that the Apostolic Church of the East adopted this heterodoxy in the fifth century. As we will see in the following pages, the designation "Nestorian Church" is incorrect in a formal theological sense, although the

4

theologian Nestorius is honored by the Church of the East as a teacher and saint.

In this context, the Church of the East is also referred to as the "Pre-Ephesian Church" because the aforementioned conflict over Nestorius found its first highpoint in the Council of Ephesus (431), the third "ecumenical council." In its synods, the Church of the East formally accepted only the decisions of the first two councils (Nicaea, 325, and Constantinople, 381); nevertheless, a name based on the rejection of a synod of the Roman empire is of limited value, especially since the Church of the East extended beyond its borders.

Finally, another term is used, referring to the part of the ancient Church of the East which since the sixteenth century has been in communion with the Roman Catholic Church: the "Chaldean Catholic Church." It is the Catholic counterpart of the "Church of the East" in the Near East and the Diaspora. The part of the Church of the East in India which is in communion with Rome is called the "Syro-Malabar Church." All these Christian churches share a common East Syriac liturgical, linguistic, spiritual, and theological heritage.

1

THE AGE OF THE SASSANIANS
Until 651

Dietmar W. Winkler

The Apostolic Church of the East first surfaces in ecclesiastical and dogmatic history only in the fifth-century debates in the Roman empire over orthodox Christology. In nearly all reference books one finds information about this branch of Christianity under the heading "Nestorian Church." Thus a heresy is attributed to the East Syriac Church, a heresy the church itself has rejected as incorrect since at least the sixth century. In 1298 the distinguished East Syriac theologian and canonist Abdisho bar Brika († 1318) wrote in his *Book of the Pearl* (Margarita) that East Syriac Christians "never changed their faith and preserved it as they had received it from the apostles, and they are called Nestorians unjustly, especially since Nestorius was not their patriarch, and they did not understand his language."

Theological use of the epithet "Nestorian" has persisted even into the present day. Many historical accounts begin with the events of the Council of Ephesus (431) and with the controversy between Cyril of Alexandria and Nestorius of Constantinople. This also suggests that the Church of the East separated itself on account of the council's events or that it found its beginning with this council.

In this first section, the beginnings of the Apostolic Church of the East until the entrance of the Arabs into its history will be traced, and we will inquire whether a heretical theology, the so-called "Nestorianism" was adopted.

The beginnings of Christianity in Persia

While Christianity in the Roman empire was subjected to persecutions prior to 313, it could for a time develop in peace on the other

7

side of the Euphrates in the Iranian kingdom of the Parthians (until 224). Presumably Christianity found its way into the regions east of the Tigris – Adiabene and Khuzistan – as early as the beginning of the second century. However, the sources are scanty, and the origins of Christianity are shrouded in legends of apostolic foundation. In contrast, beginning with the early third century, Christianity can be well explored in both literary and archeological sources. In the final chapter of the "Book of the Laws of the Countries" written by Philippus, a pupil of the Aramaic philosopher Bardaisan, mention is made of Christians in Parthia, Kushan, Persia, Media, Edessa, Hatra, and Fars, among other places. On the island of Kharg, third-century Christian graves testify with Syriac inscriptions from Christian communities around the Persian Gulf.

One can assume that Christianity spread from Osrhoene and its capital Edessa (Urfa) and from the region surrounding Nisibis (Nusaybin) – where Christianity is evidenced by the second-century epitaph of Aberkios – into the Parthian empire. The chronicle of Edessa offers a series of dates from the earliest history of Christianity in that city. This source allows us to conclude that Christianity gained a foothold in Osrhoene in the second century. Before the historically well-established flood in the year 201, the faith was already being shaped by Marcion († 160), Bardaisan († 222), and finally Mani († 276), all of whom the great Syriac poet-theologian Ephrem challenged as heretics. Only at the beginning of the fourth century, with Bishop Qune, did Christianity become orthodox in the normative sense known to church history. Since early Christianity in Edessa presented itself as extremely diverse, only conjectures can be put forth regarding the first Christians in Persia.

Very probably, the first Christian congregations emerged in the Jewish communities of the Parthian empire, which, like the inhabitants of Osrhoene and the Roman province of Syria, were Aramaic-speaking. Judaism had been present in Mesopotamia and across the Tigris at least since the Babylonian exile. At the time of the Parthians, the silk trade with China was under Jewish control. The first to bring Christianity to the East were the merchants who traveled the trade routes from the Mediterranean to the Persian Gulf and across Central Asia to China. As Edessa occupied a position where significant trade routes intersected, and Antioch on the Mediterranean was the most influential metropolis of the Roman province of Syria, the gospel traveled a route from Jerusalem through Antioch and Edessa to Mesopotamia. Edessa's significance for Syriac Christianity extends finally to the fact that the Aramaic dialect of this city (i.e.

"Syriac") became the definitive biblical and liturgical language of this branch of Christianity.

An additional factor contributing to the development of Christianity in Persia was the expanding movement of refugees. Wartime deportations are reported up to the sixth century. With the strengthening of the Persian empire under the Sassanians (224), a state of perpetual conflict arose between the Persians and the Roman empire. This situation had consequences for the spread of the gospel above all during the reign of Shapur I (240–72). Shapur I and his army advanced far into Roman territory and finally reached Antioch in 260. Many Christians from Antioch, Cappadocia, Cilicia, and Syria were deported to Persian provinces and established as tradesmen and artisans in Babylonia, Persia, Parthia, and Susiana. Among them was Bishop Demetrius of Antioch, who subsequently served as the first bishop of Beth Lapat (Gundeshapur). These deported Christians, to the extent that they belonged to Greek-speaking communities, appear not to have integrated themselves into the local Christian population before the fifth century, since separate churches and two hierarchies, with Greek and Syriac-Aramaic as liturgical languages, are reported. The inscription of the Zoroastrian magician Kartir (Kerdir) – who occupied an important position under Shapur I, Hormizd I († 273), Bahram I († 276), and especially Bahram II († 293) – speaks of "Nazarenes" (nasraye) and "Christians" (krestyane). This could be a significant indication of the double community. Although an exact interpretation of the inscription of Kartir remains to be determined, it can be assumed that the first term denotes the local Aramaic Christian congregation and the second designates those Greek-speaking Christians deported from Syria under Shapur I.

In the time of Shapur I, i.e. the second half of the third century, Christianity in Persia already had an episcopal structure, as evidenced by the conflict over Papa, who as bishop of Seleucia-Ctesiphon should have held a position of primacy over the other bishops. The sources, however, exhibit contradictions. Seleucia-Ctesiphon probably became a diocese only in the third century. As early as the end of the third century or beginning of the fourth, Papa attempted to gain supremacy, in the face of opposition from the other bishops. According to the (disputed, possibly fabricated) account of the Chronicle of Arbela, this claim was founded on the fact that he was bishop of the royal residence. Besides this purely political argument, also of interest is the fact, preserved in the chronicle, that Papa, because of the continued opposition, turned to the bishops of the "West" (i.e. the Roman empire) and especially Sada, bishop of Edessa. The *Chronicle of Arbela* makes Papa, with Western help, the first supreme head of the Persian Church. It is striking that Papa appealed to the bishop of Edessa rather than that of Antioch. The *Chronicle of Arbela* appears here actually to be more historically reliable that the lists and biographies of the patriarchs, which locate the origins of the episcopal see of Seleucia-Ctesiphon in the apostolic era. Over and above that, the conflict and the intervention of the Western fathers are also mentioned in the speech of Agapet, recorded in the acts of the Synod of Dadisho (424), which are included in the collection of East Syriac synodical documents (*Synodicon Orientale*).

Nevertheless, certain questions remain open: Why is this undoubtedly noteworthy Western intervention mentioned in no historical source of the Church of the Roman Empire? Additionally, is it possible that a "patriarchate" of the East was supported by the Western bishops even before the time of the Council of Nicaea (325), where the prerogatives of Rome, Alexandria, and Antioch were first recognized? The questions surrounding the first catholicos-patriarch of Seleucia-Ctesiphon seem impossible to answer satisfactorily with the currently available sources. In any case, one can nonetheless conclude from the opposition to the claim of primacy made by the bishop of the capital city that already at the dawn of the fourth century a series of independently organized dioceses existed in the Persian empire.

Persian martyrologies provide further clues to the ecclesiastical structure of the time. While in the times of the Parthians, because of their liberal religious policies, Persia was a refuge for Christians persecuted by the Roman empire in its outlying provinces, Christians at times also endured various forms of repression under the succeeding Sassanians and the dominance of Zoroastrian religion. Among others we find the *Acts* of the Persian Martyrs an extensive account of the life and execution of Mar Shimun I (+ 341), who was the successor of Papa in the see of Seleucia-Ctesiphon.

Violent persecution tormented Christians most notably between 339 and 379 under Shapur II (309–79), and these events are reflected in the Syriac writings of a contemporary witness, the theologian Aphrahat († 350), called the "Persian Sage." Causes of the persecution included not only the increasing strength of the Zoroastrian religion but also the political circumstances. The Roman ruler Constantine considered himself a Christian emperor and true lord of the Church. In a 337 letter preserved by Eusebius, he wrote to

Shapur II that the Christians ought to be protected. The undiplomatic demand of Constantine, who as earthly leader of the Church considered all Christians his subjects, could attract little sympathy in Persia. Moreover, the Roman–Persian conflict also involved Armenia, which had been a Christian state since 301. Thus the Sassanian rulers of the time, recognizing that Christianity in the Roman empire was on its way to becoming the state religion, saw the Christians of Persia as a threat to their interests.

The major developments of the Church of the Roman Empire since the Edict of Milan, such as the Arian controversy at the Council of Nicaea (325), had no impact whatsoever on the Persian church. On the contrary, while under the Parthians the attitude toward the Christians was tolerant, and under the first Sassanians there were only isolated, localized persecutions for apostasy from Zoroastrianism, the reign of Shapur II brought, in response to developments in the Roman empire, the first systematic persecutions of the region's Christians. These persecutions, as well as the destruction of churches in the fourth century, are described in detail in the Persian martyrologies. Even if they include legendary characteristics and tend toward exaggeration, they nonetheless offer sufficient material to grasp the scale of the persecutions. Furthermore, references are made to bishops, priests, deacons, and monks from various towns and provinces, attesting to the extent of Christianity and so providing information about the Church of the East.

Besides Aphrahat, another outstanding theologian of the time, Ephrem the Syrian, was eyewitness to the Persian–Roman clash. He lived through the fall of his native city Nisibis, which after three futile sieges (338, 346, 350) was peacefully ceded to Shapur II in 363 during negotiations with the Roman emperor Jovian (363/4). Bishop Abraham fled the city with his Christian community, and many educated Christians went to Edessa, the nearby capital of Osrhoene. Among them was Ephrem himself, with whom the founding of the school of the Persians in Edessa would later be associated.

The question of apostolic foundation

The sources regarding the origins of Christianity in Persia do not suffice to enable one to draw a reliable picture. As we have seen, Christianity may have been spread in the Persian empire first by traders, then by refugees from the Roman empire, and eventually through what is called the deportation. Christian names testify also to conversions among the Iranian population. Nomadic Arab tribes around Hatra also came into early contact with the gospel. Nevertheless, the majority of Christians arose from the Aramaic population, which gradually absorbed the congregations of the deported Greek population as well.

However, the tradition of the Apostolic Church of the East traces its origins back to the apostle Thomas and to Addai and his disciples Aggai and Mari. In this regard, the sources are conflicting and complex.

The best-known and most widely disseminated version of this missionary tradition appears to be the one transmitted by the patriarchal chronicle of Mari b. Suleiman (twelfth century). This tradition can be verified as early as the ninth century and has been preserved in East Syriac literature (Elias Damascenus, c.893; Abdisho bar Brika) as well as West Syriac (*Chronicon anonymum*, 846; *Doctrina Apostolorum*, ninth century; Barhebraeus, *Chronicon Ecclesiasticum*). According to these, the East was evangelized by Thomas from the circle of the Twelve and by Addai, Mari, and Aggai from the Seventy. Edessa, Nisibis, Mosul, Arbela, Beth Garmai, and Babylonia are credited to Addai and his disciples. Following Addai's return to Edessa, Aggai continued on to Gibal (Media), al-Ahwaz (Khuzistan), and to the border of India, as well as to the neighboring regions of Gog and Magog (China). The East Syriac canonist Ibn at-Taiyib († 1043) designated the East as a whole the missionary territory of Addai, Aggai and Mari, while India and China belonged to the territory of Thomas.

In particular, the Mari tradition views this student of Addai as the missionary of Persia, as well as founder and liturgical organizer of the Church of the East. According to the East Syriac historian Amr b. Matta (fourteenth century), it was Mari who established the patriarchal see at Seleucia-Ctesiphon, thus serving as the first catholicos. Beforehand he also appointed a bishop of Kashkar, who because of this apostolic foundation served as vicar to the patriarch. With this, Amr portrayed in his missionary account an ecclesiastical organization corresponding to that of the sixth century, because only at the Synod of Joseph (554) was the function of the patriarchal vicar explicitly assigned to the bishop of Kashkar.

According to the *vita* of Mari, Papa was personally ordained by Mari as his successor. However, Papa is historically verifiable only in the early fourth century. Therefore the account of his primacy and the placement of the See of Seleucia-Ctesiphon in apostolic succession is historically difficult to comprehend.

Why is the connection to Mari or Aggai – and thus to their

teacher Addai – of such import? The answer to this question requires a look at the evangelization tradition of Edessa, the mother city of Syriac Christianity. This tradition is preserved in the *Ecclesiastical History* of Eusebius, produced between 311 and 325, and above all in the *Doctrina Addai* (*c.*400). According to these reports, the king of Edessa, Abgar Ukama, suffered from a serious illness and learned of the work of Jesus in Palestine. Through his secretary Hannan, he sent a letter to Jesus, with the request that he come to Edessa and heal him. He also offered Jesus protection from his persecutors. In his response, Jesus praised Abgar as blessed, for he believed without seeing (cf. John 20.21), but he did not accept Abgar's invitation, for he had to return to his Father in fulfillment of his mission. In a dictated letter, he promised Abgar that after his death and resurrection he would send him one of his apostles. This apostle was Addai, who was chosen by Thomas after the Ascension. Addai healed Abgar, preached the gospel, and founded the church in Edessa. After Addai's death, his disciple Aggai was selected as his successor.

The Abgar legend has been interpreted many times. The historical kernel within the story is believed to be that Christianity was adopted as the state religion under King Abgar VIII the Great (177–212); this was then conflated with the historically unsubstantiated Abgar V (13–50). That Abgar VIII was the first Christian king of Edessa cannot be verified. This missionary account is definitely historical fiction. Eusebius of Caesarea provided the first version of this story around 303 or 312; before, it was unknown. The *Chronicle of Edessa*, a reliable source, says nothing about an apostle Addai, the correspondence with Jesus, or Abgar's conversion. According to this, a Christian apostle Addai is purely legendary. Eusebius called Addai in his *Ecclesiastical History* "Thaddeus," because Addai was unknown to him, and he included him in the circle of the seventy-two commissioned apostles (cf. Luke 10.1). However, Addai was the best-known Manichean missionary of the Syriac-Mesopotamian region, whom the *Doctrina Addai*, as an anti-Manichean document of Edessan orthodoxy, wove into the Abgar legend (Han J. W. Drijvers). The intention of the fourth-century *Doctrina Addai* is the defense of an orthodoxy going back to Jesus, in opposition to other sects, such as those of Mani, Bardaisan, or Marcion.

In the diary of her pilgrimage through the Holy Land, Egeria also reports letters from Jesus kept in the archives of Edessa. In 384 she spent three days in Edessa. According to Egeria, in addition to Jesus' letter to Abgar, the grave of the apostle Thomas, whose corpse was brought back to Edessa from India, was also venerated in the city. A later insertion into the *Doctrina Addai* added that the famous Mandylion, a portrait of Jesus which Hannan made for Abgar, was also venerated in Edessa. However, the Mandylion is first mentioned only by Evagrius Scholastikos in 593. Because of the letters from Jesus, the grave of Thomas, and the portrait of Jesus, Edessa was one of early Christianity's most important sites.

The legends of Addai, Mari, and Aggai, which developed later, projected the founding of the episcopal see at Seleucia-Ctesiphon back into the apostolic era. Through the correspondence of Jesus with Abgar, the missionary activity of Addai was traced back through the apostle Thomas finally to Jesus himself. This assures not only the apostolic nature of the church but also its directly divine origins. In other sources, the ordination of the bishops of Kashkar and Seleucia-Ctesiphon is attributed directly to Mari.

In the East Syriac synods, the attribute "apostolic" appears in reference to the see of the bishop of Seleucia-Ctesiphon for the first time in 497. Interestingly, there is no reference to the missionary tradition in the records of East Syriac synods, known as the *Synodicon Orientale*. Mari and Aggai are never mentioned; Addai is named but once and not until 612.

The centralization of the Church and the reception of the faith of Nicaea

As a consequence of the deaths of Shapur II (379) and his successor Ardeshir (Ardaschir) II († 383), the situation of the Christians improved toward the end of the fourth century. Above all Yazdgird I (399–421) sought to ease political tensions with the Roman empire and began to integrate Christians into imperial politics. Thus began the period of diplomatic exchanges between the two great empires of Late Antiquity, exchanges in which the Christian hierarchy of Persia played an essential role. Several Persian diplomatic missions to the neighboring Christian empire were led by bishops and patriarchs of the Church of the East. Likewise the Roman empire was represented by delegates at Persian courts. Under the influence of one of the Roman delegations, led by Marutha, the respected bishop of the border city Maipherkat, Yazdgird permitted the release of Christians and the rebuilding of churches.

Christianity had spread as far as Merv, which had been a diocese since the second half of the fourth century. The individual dioceses were still not collectively organized. The diplomatic skills of the

14

Aramaic bishop Marutha contributed, however, to the first East Syriac council documented in the *Synodicon Orientale*. This synod, held under the "Grand Metropolitan" Isaac in 410, reorganized the church after the persecutions and provided an essential contribution to the establishment of the East Syriac Church and the primacy of the bishop of Seleucia-Ctesiphon.

The impulse for the first recorded synod came from Marutha of Maipherkat, a bishop from the Roman empire. However, the synod was convoked by the Sassanian king Yazdgird I. In the first session of the forty assembled bishops, a letter from the "Western" fathers was read, which Marutha had brought. The letter, signed by bishops Porphyry of Antioch, Akakios of Aleppo, Pakida of Edessa, Eusebius of Tella, Akakios of Amid, and others, was translated from Greek into Persian and had been brought to Yazdgird's attention earlier. The letter included three demands or recommendations, which were eventually adopted by the synod and defined more precisely in the canons: (1) in each city and its surrounding region there should be only one bishop, ordained by three bishops, who possess the full authority of the metropolitan and head of bishops, i.e. the bishop of Seleucia-Ctesiphon; (2) liturgical feasts should be celebrated together and on the same days; Epiphany, Lent, and Easter were mentioned explicitly. Calendrical evidence indicates that at the time there was in this regard still no unity in the Persian church; (3) the creed and canons of the Council of Nicaea (325) should be adopted.

The first demand was intended to oppose the persistent double hierarchy of genuine Aramaic Christians and those Greek Christians deported from the Roman empire. Thus the twenty-one canons of the Council of Nicaea were not simply reproduced but rather were adapted to the specific situation of the Church of the East. Final authority over ordination was granted to the bishop of Seleucia. With this the bishop of the imperial capital became the definitive head of the Church of the East – with the approval of the king who had called the synod. The bishop of the imperial capital was thus granted primacy over the other bishops, following the model of the patriarchal structure of the Roman empire. Later the order of succession of the metropolitans was established, with the bishop of Seleucia-Ctesiphon named first, followed by the metropolitans of Beth Lapat (Khuzistan), Nisibis, Prat de Maishan (Basra), Arbela (Irbil), and Karka de Beth Slokh (Kirkuk).

The East Syriac church was at the Synod of Isaac in Seleucia-Ctesiphon (410) on the way to becoming centrally organized. Maintaining that the bishop of Seleucia was already being addressed as Catholicos in the acts is considered anachronistic and reflects a later projection. The characterization presented in Canon 21, "Grand Metropolitan and Head of Bishops," is surely more accurate.

Through this synod the Church of the East was to be not only reorganized and centralized, however, but also brought into harmony with the faith of the West. In the *Synodicon Orientale* the creed of the Council of Nicaea (325) appears before the synodical canons as adapted for the Persian church. The problem now encountered is that the Syriac text of the creed adopted in 410 has been transmitted in two distinct versions, a West Syriac and an East Syriac. The first version includes theological elements from early East Syriac theology, which were combined with the Nicene confession of faith. The second offers an exact translation of the Nicene creed into Syriac. There has been a continuing debate over which of the two versions was actually accepted in 410. The research of André de Halleux has demonstrated that the West Syriac version is the older original and that the East Syriac form, preserved in the *Synodicon Orientale*, is not the original one. Conformity with the beliefs of the Church of the Roman Empire was firmly established at the Synod of Seleucia-Ctesiphon in 410, though the canons *and* the creed were not simply assumed. The canons were adjusted to meet the needs of the Church of the East, and the creed was altered on the basis of a local Persian creed:

> We believe in one God, Father, who in his Son made heaven and earth; and in him were established the worlds above and that are below; and in him he effected the resurrection and renovation for all creation.
>
> And in his Son, the Only-Begotten who was born from him, that is, however, from the essence of his Father, God from God, Light from Light, true God from true God; he was born and was not made; who is of the same nature as his Father; who for the sake of us human beings who were created through him, and for the sake of our salvation, descended and put on a body and became man, and suffered and rose on the third day, and ascended to heaven and took his seat at the right hand of his Father; and he is coming in order to judge the dead and the living.
>
> And we confess the living and holy Spirit, the living Paraclete who (is) from the Father and the Son;
>
> And in one Trinity and in one Essence and in one will.
>
> (Trans. S. P. Brock)

16

This creed is a wonderful historical example of an agreement of faith despite differing formulations. The conformity with the Council of Nicaea is expressed in words the Persian fathers deemed adequate for their church.

Like the councils of the Roman empire, the first synod of the Church of the East was called and supported by the state authorities. The impulse came from outside, and communion with the Church of the Roman Empire was accomplished through the co-moderation of Grand Metropolitan Isaac of Seleucia-Ctesiphon and Bishop Marutha of Maipherkat, as well as by the acceptance of Nicene orthodoxy and the adoption of a standardized calendar. The establishment of the primacy of the bishop of the imperial capital was based on purely political grounds. In the synodical acts of 410 there is no evidence or mention of an apostolic origin for the see.

The letter from the Western fathers was signed by the bishop of Antioch and his suffragans, but he signed in the name of the Church of the Roman Empire. In their letter the Antiochene bishops made no claim of jurisdiction over the Persian church. There is no indication in the synodical acts of a historical dependence upon the patriarchate of Antioch. The Persian church made decisions autonomously following their own synodical procedures. It understood itself as an autonomous and autocephalous church standing in communion with the Church of the Roman Empire.

The acceptance of other Western synods (420)

The decisions of the synod of 410 did not take effect everywhere at once, as is indicated by the acts of the next council, under Grand Metropolitan Yahballaha I (420), which was again held with the co-moderation of a Western bishop, Akakios of Amid, who had signed the letter addressed to the synod of 410.

In 418 Yahballaha I was the leader of a diplomatic delegation of the Persian king to Constantinople, where, according to the *Chronicle of Seert*, the common faith of the churches of the Roman and Persian empires was confirmed. When Akakios traveled to the Sassanian capital as head of the Roman delegation, he supported Yahballaha and his synod. Reasons for the synod included not only internal church difficulties but also the unease among Zoroastrians regarding the growth of Christianity, especially in the higher levels of society. These nobles, in turn, occasionally influenced the leadership of the church or the appointment of bishops. The twelve bishops of the synod therefore recognized Yahballaha as "head and regent over us and all our brother-bishops in the whole of the empire." The unity of the Church of the East under the leadership of the bishop of Seleucia-Ctesiphon was strongly emphasized at the synod. The decisions of 410 were confirmed, the Council of Nicaea was again accepted, and additional synods of the West, those of Ancyra (314?), Neocaesaria (between 314 and 325), Gangra (343), Antioch (341), and Laodicea (c.365), were accepted.

The process of accepting the Council of Nicaea and the other synods is significant insofar as one bears in mind that the ecumenical councils were at first limited to bishops of the Imperium Romanum. In each case they were called by the emperor there, who had no power outside the Roman empire. Claims the Roman emperor had made to "Christian subjects" in the Persian empire had resulted in bloody persecutions. During periods of open conflict between the Roman and Persian empires, such as the reign of Shapur II but also the first half of the fifth century under the shahs Yazdgird I (399–421), Bahram V (421–39), and Yazdgird II (439–57), the situation of the Christians deteriorated. This means that regarding the synods of the Roman empire, the creeds and canons had significance only for the *oikoumene* of the Roman imperial church, even though the Church of the East – with Western assistance – later adopted some of them. Despite this process of acceptance, one cannot assume a priori that a synod which has achieved "ecumenical" validity in the history of the Christianity of the Roman empire is necessarily an ecumenical council for the Church as a whole. After all, as imperial synods, even these councils had first a local character, that is, they were reacting to political and theological events within the Roman empire.

In this way, one can reflect on the causes and meaning of the adoption of a corpus of Western synods, as happened in the Church of the East in 420. In Laodicea, for instance, Novatianists, Photians, Quartodecimans, and Montanists were condemned, and in Ancyra the local sect of Eustathians. None of these groups existed in Persia, nor was any of them relevant to the Church of the East. These synods, without exception, reflected a specific context in the Roman empire. It can thus be assumed that their acceptance took place under the influence of the legate Akakios of Amid. However, in the acts of the synod of 420, canons and particulars were not selectively adopted, rather, the Western synods were simply accepted as a whole; there is no recorded reflection on this process. This places beyond doubt the unity with the Church of the Roman Empire; otherwise the acceptance would appear strange and senseless. Only in the later East Syriac canonical tradition were these synodical decisions examined in detail. The work of Ibn at-Tayib is one example. The situation was entirely different at the synod of 410, where the creed was specifically cited and each canon adapted to the needs of the Persian church.

Declaration of independence of the Church of the East in 424?

The persecution of Christians which had begun anew toward the end of the reign of Yazdgird I († 421) continued under Bahram V (421–38). The reasons for this lay in doubts about the loyalty of Christians during the war with the Roman empire and in conflicts with Zoroastrianism. Christianity was no longer limited to the Syriac-Aramaic-speaking population and could point to conversions particularly in the Persian upper class. At this time there were internal disputes in the church over the see of Seleucia-Ctesiphon. Bishop Dadisho was slandered as a Roman sympathizer and placed in prison. Around 422 a peace treaty was concluded between Emperor Theodosius II (408–50) and Bahram V. Bishop Dadisho was released and returned to his monastery, and wanted to resign. At the Synod of Markabta the bishops – all six metropolitans as well as thirty-one bishops participated – persuaded him to resume his office in order to reorganize the church after the persecutions. This time no "Western" bishop from the Roman empire was present to direct or influence the fate of the synod, as had happened in 410 and 420.

The synod of 424 is widely regarded as the occasion on which the Church of the East stated its claim to autocephaly through the rejection of the "right of appeal" to the West. It has been assumed that in this year the Church of the East declared itself independent of the patriarch of Antioch. One must realize, however, that such a declaration of independence from the patriarch of Antioch need not have taken place, as this presupposes an earlier dependence. The Church of the East can be considered to have been autocephalous since the Synod of Isaac in Seleucia-Ctesiphon (410).

The acts of the Synod of Dadisho in Markabta (424) show that the resolutions of the Synod of Isaac (410) could not be entirely carried out. That is why the primacy of the bishop of Seleucia-Ctesiphon deserves special emphasis. After the introductory speech of Dadisho, that of Metropolitan Agapet of Beth Lapat has been preserved in the *Synodicon Orientale*. In this address, the metropolitan established that while in the past the Western fathers had been "supporters and helpers in a shared fatherhood" with the Church of the East, now "persecution and afflictions [prevent] them from caring for us as they did before." Consequently, the primacy of the bishop of Seleucia-Ctesiphon again came to the fore, as it had in 410. This time, however, it was undergirded by stronger arguments: the head of the Church of the East is head in the same sense that Peter was head of the apostles. It was thereby expressed that no further Peter – the patriarchal thrones of Rome and Antioch each serve as a *cathedra Petri* – was necessary. Since the head of the Church of the East occupies the same level as Peter, there can be no other earthly authority over him. It follows that the outrage of supervision or intervention by bishops of the Roman Empire should cease. In the past – Agapet continues – it was always conceded that the head of the Church of the East is right and that any who turned against the patriarch and appealed to a patriarch in the West acknowledged his own guilt and was punished for his transgression. Thus an appeal to the Western patriarchs against the catholicos of the Church of the East is neither necessary nor allowed.

The synod stressed the unity of the Church of the East under its own single head, who was subsequently called "Catholicos"; the title Patriarch is, for this time, still anachronistic, though it was added before the end of the fifth century. According to the synod of 424, disputes internal to the church, especially those concerning its head, should not be settled by calling upon other patriarchs from outside but rather solved within their own sphere. None of the earlier documents included in the *Synodicon Orientale* mentions a "right of appeal." One cannot absolutely rule out the possibility of such a right to call upon ecclesiastical heads of the Roman empire. However, it is at least interesting that the possibility of such a canonically significant appeal is not mentioned in the Greek and Latin sources.

The autonomy of the Church of the East was without doubt established by 410. The Synod of Markabta reiterated this explicitly. The political necessity of such a clear formulation is evident in the historical context, especially in the fact that a Western appropriation of influence would have been viewed with anger by Persian authorities. A definitive statement that bishops of the Roman empire should not interfere in the affairs of the Church of the East could have only positive results and is entirely understandable.

Concerning relations with the patriarch of Antioch, no claim of

Antiochene jurisdiction over the Church of the East during the synods of 410, 420, and 424 can be found. In fact, none of the ancient ecclesiastical sources claims a dependence of the East Syriac church upon Antioch as mother church. Certain texts of the Middle Ages (e.g. Ibn at-Taiyib; the lists of patriarchs of Mari b. Suleiman and Amr b. Matta) are the first to present the idea of the ordination of the catholicos of the Church of the East in Antioch or Jerusalem.

The school of the Persians in Edessa and the Council of Ephesus (431)

Through the synods of 410, 420, and 424, the Church of the East was reorganized, and the primacy of the bishop of Seleucia-Ctesiphon was established and secured. The intervention of the Western bishops, i.e. the bishops of the eastern provinces of the Roman empire, ceased with the decision of 424. Contact with the Roman imperial church was in no way broken off, however, and Western theological developments found another way into the Church of the East, through the school of Edessa and later through the school of Nisibis.

In 363 the city of Nisibis fell into the hands of the Sassanians. Among the many Christians who fled to Edessa was Ephrem the Syrian. In Nisibis at the time of the first bishop known to us, Jacob of Nisibis († 338), who was one of the fathers of the Council of Nicaea (325), Ephrem offered exegetical instruction at a kind of school. The Persian conquest brought an abrupt end to this "first school" of Nisibis.

Ephrem is also associated with the founding of the school of the Persians in Edessa. Tradition traces the origin of the school all the way back to the legendary Addai. Neither is historically accurate, and the date of the founding of this educational institution is unknown. It may be assumed that as an important intellectual center, Edessa had long had a variety of teacher–student circles for the transmission of theological and philosophical instruction. This can be indirectly inferred from the diversity of Edessan Christianity. However, a school in the sense of a theological academy first acquired stable organization in the fourth century, and it eventually achieved renown through Ephrem.

Even after the death of the great teacher from Nisibis, the school stood in full flower. Its theological training and scholarship attained an excellent reputation. Many Persian students, who during the Sassanian persecutions of the first half of the fifth century had found in Edessa an intellectual refuge, were educated there. Edessa was the gate through which theological developments of the Roman imperial church entered the Church of the East.

In the first half of the fifth century Christological conflicts in the Roman empire had severe consequences for Edessa. Where previously the theology and teachings of Ephrem and the early Syriac writings had been authoritative, now – on the basis of a massive translation effort from Greek into Syriac accomplished by theologians of the school of the Persians – new Christological trends came into favor.

Since about 430 the school had stood under the influence of Theodore of Mopsuestia († 428). Even during his lifetime, under the guidance of Qiore († 437), an excellent and ascetical leader of the school of Edessa, virtually all of Theodore's works – as well as those of his teacher Diodore of Tarsus – were translated into Syriac. Through this translation, Antiochene theology became influential in Edessa. Above all, the exegetical and theological works of Theodore of Mopsuestia were enlisted for instruction at the school. In this way, graduates of the school, who during peaceful times returned to the Persian empire, spread a Diphysite (two-nature) theology in the Sassanian empire even before the Council of Ephesus (431).

Since Theodore stands as the classic representative of the Antiochene theology, who opposed Arianism and Apollonarianism, and since his work was studied intensively at the school of Edessa, it is hardly surprising that the delegates from Edessa opposed Cyril of Alexandria at the Council of Ephesus (431). Together with John of Antioch, Ibas of Edessa († 457), the most prominent teacher of the Persian school and his bishop Rabbula († 435) spoke up against Cyril.

The debate at the Council of Ephesus was provoked by the central question of Christianity: How can the One who, according to the Council of Nicaea, is of the same nature as the Father, be both perfect God and perfect man, and, at the same time, the one Jesus Christ?

Two theological approaches competed: the Antiochene and the Alexandrian. For the Antiochene theology, which tended in its exegesis toward literary, literal, and historical interpretations, the precise differentiation of the divine and human natures (Diphysitism or two-nature doctrine) was important. The divinity of the Word as well as the integrity of Christ's humanity had to be preserved. Because of this, the Antiochene theologians opposed above all the teachings of Apollonarius of Laodicea, who de-emphasized the humanity of Christ because he believed that the Logos occupied the place of human reason (Gr. *nous*). The fundamental Antiochene concern is soteriological: salvation is attainable for humanity only by Christ's taking on a perfect human nature. If complete humanity is a soteriological prerequisite, then it is also necessary to emphasize its distinction from the incomprehensible Godhead. This differentiation between divinity and humanity aroused the suspicion that the Antiochenes (Theodore of Mopsuestia, Nestorius of Constantinople, Diodore of Tarsus, Theodoret of Cyrus) saw in Christ two subjects, two persons, or two Sons (classical Nestorianism).

The Alexandrian school with its allegorical exegesis and under the influence of Platonism began theological reflection with the Logos; in this view, emphasis on the unity of divinity and humanity in Christ, the "one nature (*mia physis*) of the Word incarnate" is central. From an Antiochene perspective this concept of unity gave the impression that divinity and humanity are mingled and that the divinity absorbs the humanity (classical Monophysitism).

The feud between Nestorius, patriarch of Constantinople (428–31), and Cyril, patriarch of Alexandria (412–44), over the unity of the perfect divinity and perfect humanity of Christ involved the entire Mediterranean region. Cyril stressed the ontological unity of Christ as a physical or hypostatic union. The primary concern of Nestorius, a student of Theodore of Mopsuestia, was to emphasize both complete natures of Christ, the divine and the human. The debate came to a head over a theological tangent, the disagreement concerning the title *theotokos* (God-bearer). Nestorius believed that the expression *theotokos* should be replaced by *christotokos* (Christ-bearer) because the Virgin could only have borne the human nature. Nestorius's concern escalated into a serious altercation, because of his own unfortunate conduct, the mercilessness of Cyril, and the interests of contemporary church politics.

As patriarch of Alexandria, Cyril, like his predecessor Theophilus, took little pleasure in the fact that the second ecumenical council (381) had placed the church of Constantinople, as the "new Rome" in second position ahead of Alexandria. Earlier, at the Council of Nicaea (325), the order of the patriarchates had been established as Rome, Alexandria, and Antioch. Since then, arguments over pre-eminence in the east of the empire had been a smoldering source of conflict and had contributed greatly to the controversy.

During the summer of 430 Cyril informed Pope Celestine of Nestorius's teachings from his special Alexandrian perspective. In response, Celestine called together a synod in Rome, which condemned Nestorius and entrusted Cyril with the privilege of speaking with the authority of the Roman apostolic see. For his part, Cyril held a synod in Alexandria, which reiterated the judgment of Rome, and wrote a letter to Nestorius, demanding that he agree. This letter included twelve anathemas, which unwisely sought to impose the terminology of Alexandrian theology upon Nestorius.

The Emperor Theodosius II (408–50) was concerned about the peace of the empire and called a council at Ephesus. However, there were actually two synods at Ephesus: the council could not open as planned on June 7 because John of Antioch and the Roman delegates had not yet arrived. John wrote to Cyril that he and the Antiochene bishops had already been traveling for thirty days, and their arrival would be delayed a few days because of difficulties. Nevertheless, Cyril opened the council on June 22, 431. Sixty-eight of the 153 bishops present protested in writing, and the imperial representative Candidian objected. Thus Cyril's synod began with several defects. Nonetheless, Nestorius was summoned before the assembly by Cyril, acting without imperial authority. Understandably, Nestorius refused and did not appear. They decided to settle the divisive questions of the creed of Nicaea. The creed was solemnly confirmed, and after that they read the second letter from Cyril to Nestorius, written in June 430, and its response. The correspondence of Cyril's letter with the Nicene creed was established, while they determined that Nestorius's letter deviated from orthodoxy. Mary could properly be called God-bearer because she had received, carried, and borne the already unified Christ. Cyril's theology was accepted as the true expression of Christian belief and as the faithful explication of the creed of Nicaea (325), while Nestorius, following the testimony of a few witnesses, was deposed.

Although they tried to make up for the illegality of the summoning by following an orderly process, there were serious weaknesses: Cyril was simultaneously head of the synod, prosecutor, and judge. Additionally, the theological positions of Nestorius were not discussed, and the judgment was handed down in the absence of the accused and without his testimony.

After John of Antioch arrived in Ephesus, he – along with the bishops accompanying him, a part of the sixty-eight bishops who had protested against Cyril, and the imperial legate Candidian – called another Ephesian council. Ibas and Rabbula also took part in this council. It resolved to depose Cyril and break from communion with the participants in Cyril's synod. The papal delegates, who had finally arrived, although too late, remained in union with Cyril, following Pope Celestine's orders. They examined the acts and agreed with Cyril's decision because Nestorius had not recanted his teachings as the 430 Synod of Rome had demanded. Nothing was asked regarding the circumstances. The council ended with a schism between the church of Antioch, which remained loyal to Nestorius, and the church of Alexandria. Emperor Theodosius sought in vain to summon a new council and annul everything that had happened at Ephesus.

About a year after Ephesus, Bishop Rabbula of Edessa changed sides, turning from the Antiochene theology to Cyril's position. As a consequence, there followed a serious controversy with the school of the Persians, which maintained its Antiochene stance. Rabbula had the writings of Theodore of Mopsuestia burnt and sent the respected translator Ibas into exile. The writings of Cyril were then translated into Syriac, and thus the foundation for a Syriac Miaphysite (later anti-Chalcedonian, Syrian Orthodox) literature was laid.

The struggles after the council brought the Antiochene and Alexandrian parties closer together and led to a Christological agreement, the so-called Formula of Union (433) between John of Antioch and Cyril of Alexandria. This agreement was based on the council John had led at Ephesus (431), with substantial contributions from the important Antiochene theologian and opponent of Cyril, Theodoret of Cyrus († c.466). Theologically, the Formula of Union was the real result of the Council of Ephesus, and it built a bridge between the councils of Constantinople (381) and Chalcedon (451). Nestorius was a victim of this alliance – although he could have agreed to its substance – as the Antiochene bishops also approved his dismissal. He was banished to Egypt. Several bishops, who could not accept the Formula of Union and were consequently dismissed from the dioceses of the Roman empire, emigrated and, along with their clergy, joined the East Syriac church in Persia.

After the death of Rabbula (435) things changed again in Edessa. Ibas became his successor as bishop, and in 437 the Persian Narsai became head of the theological school. Edessa turned once again, for one final time in its history, to the Antiochene Diphysite theology. Ibas was strongly opposed and condemned at the Second Council of Ephesus (449), for which Pope Leo the Great coined the term "Robber Synod" (*Latrocinium*). The Council of Chalcedon (451) rehabilitated Ibas but dismissed Cyril's successor Dioscorus of Alexandria, which led to the loss of the Egyptian (Coptic) church during the debates surrounding the council.

The Antiochene position could no longer be maintained in the Roman empire, and the Persian school in Edessa was in dire straits. During the episcopacy of Bishop Qurâ (471–98), the school of Edessa was severely suppressed. Presumably on account of an attempt to murder him, Narsai fled to Nisibis.

In 489 Emperor Zeno, under the influence of Bishop Qurâ, had the school closed and the teachers expelled. The Persian school was transformed into a church, characteristically dedicated to the Mother of God (Theotokos). The removal of the school of Edessa by Emperor Zeno was a significant step toward the development of the theology of the Roman empire in a certain direction. The elimination of the Antiochene Christology, which had presented a legitimate counterweight to the Alexandrian legacy, could not be reversed by the Council of Chalcedon (451). Through the condemnation of the so-called "Three Chapters" – the person and writings of Theodore of Mopsuestia, the writings of Theodoret of Cyrus, and the letter of Ibas of Edessa to the Persian Mari – by the imperial synod of Constantinople (553), the fifth "ecumenical" council, the displacement of the Antiochene theology reached its final conclusion.

The school of Nisibis

At the time of Narsai's flight from Edessa, Barsauma († 496), a former student of the school of the Persians, was bishop of Nisibis. Barsauma offered Narsai sanctuary and made the former head of the school of Edessa the founder of the famous school of Nisibis. Actually the politician Barsauma functioned as organizer of the school, while Narsai's theological genius shaped the content of instruction and the reputation of the school in Nisibis for four decades.

The school of Nisibis was modeled on the example of Edessa and furthered its tradition. When Emperor Zeno closed the school in Edessa, many teachers and students fled over the border into the Persian empire and joined Narsai. Nisibis developed into an intellectual center and became the theological power station of the East Syriac church in the Sassanian empire. In its heyday, it numbered about 800 students. It was there that, until the seventh century, almost every great East Syriac church leader and theologian received his education in reading, writing, rhetoric, philosophy, and above all exegesis in a carefully regulated three-year program of study.

Narsai, the Persian poet, preacher, exegete, and theologian, called "the harp of the Spirit," was perhaps the most important poet-theologian of the East Syriac church – as Aphrahat the "Persian sage" († *c.*350) and Ephrem the Syrian († 373) belong to the common West and East Syriac heritage. Over 300 verse homilies (*mêmrê*) have been attributed to Narsai, of which about eighty have been preserved. He stood in the tradition of Ephrem and was furthermore a vehement supporter of the Antiochene theology as elaborated by Diodore of Tarsus and Theodore of Mopsuestia. That he also held Nestorius in high regard is indicated by a verse homily on the three Greek fathers Diodore, Theodore, and Nestorius. It can be argued, however, that Nestorius had no theological significance for Narsai. Rather Narsai was responsible for the authoritative position Theodore's biblical commentaries held in exegetical instruction at the school of Nisibis. For the East Syriac church Theodore's work was therefore the most influential of all the Greek fathers.

Likewise, Narsai's Christology also grew out of that of Theodore of Mopsuestia. Despite the distinction of natures, which the totality of divinity and humanity in Christ ensured, Narsai denied the idea of two *prosopa* (persons) in Christ: "And we call (them) one person, the two who are distinct from one another: the Word is the nature of the (divine) substance and the body the nature of the humanity. One is the Begotten and one the Begetter. They are one in a single unity" (from Homily 81).

Primarily because he was the founder of the school of Nisibis and a Persian theologian, Narsai was accused of being a "Nestorian," that is, denying the unity of Jesus Christ. He was held responsible for the influx of Nestorianism into the Persian church. Even a passing glance at Narsai's verse homilies shows that this is unjustified. He emphasized the unity of the two distinct, concrete natures and vehemently rejected a two-person doctrine.

The comparison of Narsai's homilies with the writings of Theodore of Mopsuestia shows how closely Narsai followed Theodore's arguments. Narsai's work is pervaded by Theodore's exegesis, doctrine of creation, Christology, soteriology, and eschatology. The speed with which Theodore's work was integrated is demonstrated by homilies written while Narsai was still in Edessa. Beginning as early as 420, the school of Edessa had a Diphysite, Antiochene and, from 430 on, a specifically "Theodoran" character. This orthodox tradition lived on in the school of Nisibis, which contributed substantially to the elaboration and dissemination of an Antiochene

Christology in the East Syriac church, modeled on the work of Theodore of Mopsuestia.

Acceptance of Nestorianism at the synods of 484 and 486?

The synods of Beth Lapat (484) and Seleucia-Ctesiphon (486) have been and are still seen as those at which the Church of the East officially adopted the Nestorian faith and thus the schism with the Church catholic took place. The Synod of Beth Lapat (484) is reputed to have accepted Nestorianism at the instigation of Barsauma of Nisibis, and this acceptance is further reputed to have been confirmed at the Synod of Seleucia-Ctesiphon (486). However, the sources in no way allow this conclusion; though it has been tirelessly disseminated.

The synod of Barsauma at Beth Lapat (484) is not included in the official records of East Syriac synods. It was the result of a serious conflict between Catholicos Babowai († 484) and the metropolitan of Nisibis. Barsauma had the support of the Persian shah Peroz (459–84), who first imprisoned Babowai for two years as a Zoroastrian apostate and finally had him executed. However, in the same year, Peroz also died. His successor Balash (484–8) appointed as the new catholicos not Barsauma but rather Aqaq, likewise a former student of Edessa. Soon Barsauma's opposition seemed to crumble. In six recorded letters from the metropolitan of Nisibis to Aqaq it becomes clear that Barsauma regretted the synod of 484 and subordinated himself to Aqaq. At a small synod in Beth Adrai (485), unity was restored, and the Synod of Beth Lapat was annulled. Barsauma officially recognized Aqaq as catholicos, and they decided to hold a synod in the capital of Seleucia-Ctesiphon (which eventually took place in 486). The peace and restored communion were celebrated with a shared Eucharist.

The acts of the Synod of Beth Lapat have not been preserved for us, and only a handful of fragments are available as sources. A few canons against simony, the buying of offices, and invalid ordinations, which clearly indicate abuses during the catholicate of Babowai, are cited in the writings of Elias of Nisibis († 1046) and Abdisho bar Brika. The writings of the canonist Ibn at-Tayib suggest further that because of the misconduct of the catholicos, Barsauma did not consider the centralized primacy established by the synods of the early fifth century as appropriate. He insisted, for instance, that the catholicos not ordain the metropolitan, but rather that the bishops of each metropolitanate do so, and that this required no confirmation by the catholicos.

The only remaining theological fragment is a citation in the acts of the Synod of Gregory (605), which states positively that the Synod of Beth Lapat emphasized the authority of the commentary and homilies of Theodore of Mopsuestia. This comes as no surprise, as Barsauma had co-founded the school of Nisibis with Narsai. The gradual turning away from the Antiochene theology in the Roman empire forms the background of this explicit defense. Had the Synod of Beth Lapat composed a Christological creed, it would most probably have expressed Antiochene concepts based on the theology of Theodore of Mopsuestia. However, we have no evidence to support this. There is de facto no indication that the Christological definition of the Council of Seleucia-Ctesiphon (486) repeated or confirmed an earlier, now lost, creed of 484.

The officially recognized synod of 486, in which Barsauma was supposed to have participated but, for reasons unknown to us, did not, produced the first preserved Christological creed of the Church of the East after the imperial synods of Ephesus (431) and Chalcedon (451):

> Further, let our faith in the dispensation of Christ be in the confession of the two natures, of the divinity and of the humanity, while none of us shall dare to introduce mixture, mingling or confusion into the differences of these two natures; rather, while the divinity remains preserved in what belongs to it, and humanity in what belongs to it, it is to a single Lordship and to a single (object of) worship that we gather together the exemplars of these two natures, because of the perfect and inseparable conjunction that has occurred for the divinity with respect to the humanity.
>
> And if someone considers, or teaches others, that suffering and change have attached to the divinity of our Lord, and (if) he does not preserve, with respect to the union of the prosopon of our Saviour, a confession of perfect God and perfect Man, let such a person be anathema.
>
> (Trans. S. P. Brock)

Until the present day, this profession was unjustly condemned as heretical. Here, in Diphysite terms, the necessity of the existence-in-itself of each complete nature, without mixing or change, is set forth. Nevertheless, there is an inseparable bond between divinity and humanity, a union of the person. As with Narsai, here the theology of Theodore of Mopsuestia and the position of the Antiochenes, each of which excludes Theopaschism (the suffering of the divinity), is determinative. This Christology respects the integrity of divinity and humanity and admits no hint of "Nestorianism."

After the preceding expositions of the schools of Edessa and Nisibis, the spread of the Antiochene theology prior to the Council of Ephesus (431), and the significance of Theodore of Mopsuestia in the East Syriac church, it is hardly surprising that at the Synod of Seleucia-Ctesiphon (486), the Church of the East composed their profession of belief in Christ along Antiochene-Diphysite lines. Over the course of the sixth century, nearly all the synods of the Church of the East included Christological creeds displaying essentially the same character: a strict but orthodox Antiochene Christology, strongly opposing any theopaschism. In these synods it was again established that the correct biblical and Nicene faith is maintained especially in the writings of Theodore of Mopsuestia.

Interestingly, the Council of Ephesus is not mentioned in the East Syriac synodical records. Since it was a synod outside the Persian empire, the Church of the East presumably did not find it necessary to react. Nevertheless, it should also be emphasized that the Church of the East did not condemn the Council of Ephesus. Likewise, the theological decisions of the Council of Chalcedon had no direct impact on the synods, although some canons were adopted at the Synod of Aba (543). Through the two-nature doctrine of Chalcedon and the rehabilitation of Ibas, this council could certainly have aroused the sympathies of the Church of the East. However, the Chalcedonian terminology was unclear for the Church of the East.

Indeed, the authority of Theodore of Mopsuestia is emphasized in the synods of the fifth and sixth centuries, while Nestorius is never mentioned. This patriarch of Constantinople, deposed at Ephesus, appears for the first time in the religious disputation of 612 and only in 680 in the acts of an official East Syriac synod. The teachings of Nestorius seem to have had no significance for the official Church. The earliest East Syriac document to make mention of Nestorius is Narsai's *Homily on the Three Greek Doctors*. However, this very homily demonstrates that Nestorius was insignificant for the theological discussions of the Church of the East. Narsai knew quite a lot about Diodore and of course much about his model Theodore but hardly anything about Nestorius. Nestorius is above all the symbol of a martyr of Antiochene Christology. However the teachings of Nestorius might be judged, the term "Nestorian" in a

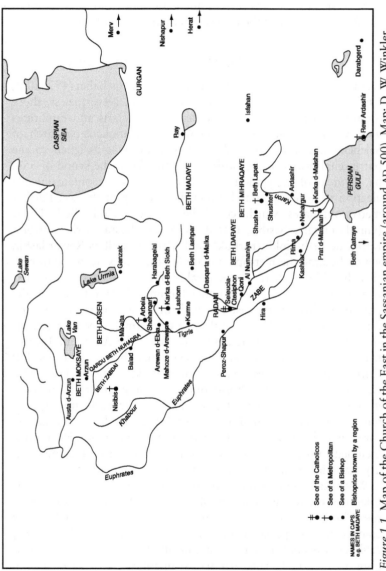

Figure 1.1 Map of the Church of the East in the Sassanian empire (around AD 500). Map: D. W. Winkler.

heretical sense is inaccurate for the Church of the East. Christianity in the Persian empire of the Parthians and Sassanians did not begin with Nestorius nor was there a dogmatic split from the Church of the Roman Empire in the fifth century named after him.

The Church of the East in the sixth century

At the start of the sixth century, under Catholicos Babai (497–502), Christianity had spread across Mesopotamia. Nevertheless, those metropolitanates lying in the valleys of the Tigris and Euphrates were the best organized. Along with the catholicos-patriarch of Seleucia-Ctesiphon, the bishop of Kashkar was assigned to the patriarchal province. According to canon 21 of the synod of 554, he, as vicar of the catholicos, was responsible for organizing the election of a new patriarch upon the vacancy of the see. Further metropolitanates which could be named include Beth Lapat (Gundeshapur), Nisibis, Prat de Maishan (Basra), Arbela (Irbil), Karka de Beth Slokh (Kirkuk), and Merv, as well as Rewardashir, which became the metropolitanate for the Persis in the sixth century. In addition there were several bishoprics independent of metropolitan control that were under the immediate authority of the patriarch. This was the case especially in those regions lying outside the Persian empire. However, the sources permit no definite conclusions regarding this matter, especially since the Arab and Turkish tribes were nomadic or at least semi-nomadic. As early as 410 Christianity was represented in Arabia by the bishop of Hira, who was placed under the authority of the metropolitan of Rewardashir in the sixth century. Christianity came to Turkestan through the temporary flight of King Kawad I (488–531), the legitimate successor of Balash, on account of usurper Djamasp (496–8). His retinue included Christians, who until 498 successfully carried out missionary activities among the local Central Asian population.

When Kawad I was able to regain his throne, a period of religious tolerance began. As members of a Persian church independent of the Christianity of the Roman empire, East Syriac Christians enjoyed relative peace. With canon 3 of the Synod of Aqaq (486) celibacy was abolished and consequently the influence of monasticism was curbed. This aroused sympathies particularly among Zoroastrian Persians, for whom marriage was imperative. Nevertheless, there were occasional conflicts with this religion.

Both Catholicos Babai and his successor Silas (503–23) were married. Before his death, Silas designated his son-in-law Elisha as his successor. Because no consensus could be reached regarding his appointment, he was uncanonically installed as catholicos under the direction of the bishop of Merv. An opposing candidate, Narses, a man from Khuzistan, was nominated and ordained. Though Narses soon died, the tiresome matter nonetheless resulted in a fifteen-year schism within the church. At a synod in 539 it was proclaimed that neither Elisha nor Narses had been, nor continued to be, a legitimate patriarch. Elisha stepped down, and Paul of Khuzistan was selected as the new catholicos. Paul enjoyed great favor with King Chosroes I, and there was hope that he would heal the wounds of the patriarchal schism. However, Paul died just two months after his election. The Church of the East then chose Aba I (540–52), one of the most outstanding figures of the sixth century, as its new patriarch.

Mar Aba I was once a high-ranking Zoroastrian and secretary to the governor of the province of Beth Garmai. He converted to Christianity and studied at the school of Nisibis. It was written that he traveled to Jerusalem, Alexandria, Constantinople, Athens, and Corinth. Cosmas Indicopleustes reported that he received his great knowledge of Holy Scripture from this "exceedingly holy man and great teacher." Following his return to Persia, this far-ranging traveler taught in Nisibis, wrote biblical commentaries, and translated Greek texts into Syriac. After his election as catholicos, he founded his own theological school in Seleucia-Ctesiphon and began energetically to reform the church. He summoned a synod in 544, clarified the hierarchical structure and diocesan boundaries while on a visitation trip through the Persian empire, and annulled unlawful ordinations. However, he fell victim to the new political situation. Danger always threatened Christians during conflicts with the Roman empire, and the Persian–Roman war (540–5) was a good opportunity for the Zoroastrian magicians to slander the apostate who sat upon the patriarchal throne. Aba had to go into exile for several years and was placed under house arrest. Nevertheless, he seemed to have succeeded in consolidating the Church and giving it inner cohesion during the renewed persecutions of Christians under Chosroes I.

The aforementioned synod under Mar Aba (544) sought above all to restore the unity of the Church under the patriarchal See of Seleucia-Ctesiphon, which had been destroyed by the schism of the preceding fifteen years. Mar Aba settled the patriarchal election in the *epistola pragmatica* of the 544 synod. It is established therein that the bishops of the patriarchal province would assemble the metropolitans of Beth Lapat, Prat de Maishan, Arbela, and Karka de Beth Slokh, each of whom would travel to Seleucia-Ctesiphon with three of his bishops, in order to elect an incontestable catholicos-patriarch.

A letter of Catholicos Aba on the "orthodoxy of faith" is also included in the acts of the synod. In it he described the economy of salvation, beginning with the creation, through the life, death, and resurrection of Jesus, the sending of the Holy Spirit, and the end of the world. The avoidance of any technical Christological terminology is astonishing, especially since the highly educated Aba undoubtedly had knowledge of theological developments in the Roman empire and brought various works of Nestorius back with him when he returned to the Persian empire after his travels. Presumably it was he – or his pupil Cyrus of Edessa – who translated the *Book of Heraclides* into Syriac in 539–40.

Despite Aba's opposition to simony and other external influences on the regulation of the patriarchal election, the Persian shah interfered once again. Chosroes I intervened, so that Joseph (552–67), a man of dubious character who was apparently his physician, was elected as the next catholicos. The synod which took place under him established – contrary to the appointment of Joseph himself – that the catholicos should be chosen from among the metropolitans (Canon 13). The professions of faith in Christ produced by the synod confirmed the councils of Nicaea (325) and Constantinople (381), and rejected teachings of two persons in Christ. Each nature maintains its characteristics, though they are one without confusion, mixing, transformation, or change. The text recalls the well-known four adverbs of the Council of Chalcedon, which, like the Synod of Joseph, opposed any Christology involving mixing or division. However, no direct relationship between the two synods is indicated.

Since the displeasure regarding the appointment and installation of Catholicos Joseph endured, he was finally removed from office. Not much is known about his successor Ezechiel (570–82), who was a student of Aba. He held a synod in 576, and his time in office was marked by plague and a new Persian–East Roman war (572–91). Perhaps this explains the dearth of sources. During Ezechiel's period, the expansion of the Persian empire reached well into the Arabian peninsula, where the Ethiopians were besieged and Yemen was captured. Bishops could now be found in Sana and on the island of Sokotra, indicating the spread of Christianity among the pre-Islamic Arabs.

With Ezechiel's successor Ishoyahb I of Arzun (582–96), another former student of Nisibis became catholicos of the Church of the East. At the synod held under him the hierarchy of the Church of the East was given a theological foundation. The ecclesiastical structure was placed parallel to the heavenly one. By this reasoning, church order was set forth as divine, the patriarch equated with the apostles Peter and Paul, and the patriarchal see placed on an apostolic footing.

In canon 29 of the same synod one reads further that the Holy Spirit "designated four patriarchs in the West, and he chose a fifth patriarch for the Orient." The Church of the East thus considered itself one of the five patriarchates of the universal Church. The four Western patriarchates were those established at the Council of Constantinople (381) in alignment with Roman provincial administration: Rome, Constantinople, Alexandria, and Antioch. Since the Church of the East accepted only the first two Roman imperial synods – the Councils of Nicaea (325) and Constantinople (381) – the decision of the Council of Chalcedon (451) that the bishop of Jerusalem be removed from the jurisdiction of the patriarchate of Antioch and granted autonomy had no significance for it. If Rome, Constantinople, Alexandria, Antioch, and Jerusalem formed the pentarchy of the Church of the Roman Empire, the Church of the East also had a "pentarchy" including the patriarchate of Seleucia-Ctesiphon. The East Syriac canonist Ibn at-Taiyib saw the bishop of al-Maidan (Seleucia-Ctesiphon) as the fifth patriarch of the Church.

In addition, the Synod of Ishoyahb strongly emphasized the importance of the writings and tradition of Theodore of Mopsuestia with a separate apology. Occasionally various scholars have sought to identify here evidence of a reaction to the condemnation of Theodore at the Council of Constantinople (553) and the Three Chapters Controversy. However, this cannot be verified. The Church of the East had offered no response to the Council of Ephesus (431) and did the same in the case of the posthumous condemnation of the person (!) and writings of Theodore of Mopsuestia in the Roman empire.

The emphasis on the doctrinal authority of Theodore is rather linked to the critique offered by Hnana of Adiabene. Hnana was a highly respected and exceptional teacher in Nisibis who inspired many with his exegetical works, his humility, and his ascetic lifestyle. He had great influence on East Syriac monasticism, which since 486 and the abolition of celibacy had decreased in significance. However, in his writings Hnana deviated from the official

35

doctrinal consensus of the Church of the East and attacked the obligatory authority of Theodore of Mopsuestia. He favored instead the writings of John Chrysostom. Babai the Great († 628), of whom more will be said later, rejected him as an Origenist, Theopaschist, and Monophysite. During the controversy, Ishoyahb's synod (585) not only supported the doctrinal authority of Theodore but also affirmed that John Chrysostom himself had admired the bishop of Mopsuestia. Eventually the debate escalated to the school, and some three hundred students, among them Ishoyahb II of Gdala and Ishoyahb III of Adiabene, two later catholicoi, left Nisibis. The resolution of the synod of 585 remained ineffective not least because Metropolitan Simon of Nisibis did not take part in the synod and supported Hnana. In about 590, Hnana was even able to draw up new statutes for the school.

During the long Persian–East Roman war (572–91), repeated diplomatic efforts were made to bring hostilities to an end. One of these missions took place under the leadership of Ishoyahb I of Arzun. It was sent by Shah Hormizd IV (579–90) to Emperor Maurice in 586/7. Ishoyahb was received with honors by Emperor Maurice and in addition to the Persian–Roman peace negotiations was also asked about his faith. The catholicos presented a written creed, which Maurice handed over to the patriarchs John of Constantinople and Gregory of Antioch. These judged the creed to be orthodox and without error. This agreement on belief between the Byzantine church and the Church of the East found its expression – 156 years after the Council of Ephesus – in a shared eucharistic celebration.

After the violent death of Hormizd IV, Chosroes II (591–628) deposed the usurper Bahram Chobin in 591 and assumed power. Under his rule the Sassanian empire reached the height of its expansion. Ishoyahb I did not support Chosroes' seizure of power, and the relationship between patriarch and shah was correspondingly strained. Ishoyahb finally fled to the Christian Arab king Numan III in Hira and died in 596 during this hurried escape.

Chosroes II elevated to catholicos the ascetic bishop of Lashom, Sabrisho, as Ishoyahb's successor at the synod of 596. The Christian second wife of Chosroes, the Aramaic Shirin, had interpreted an aged monk she saw in a dream, who stood beside the Persian shah, as Sabrisho. For this reason, Chosroes held Sabrisho in high regard, and Sabrisho supported the shah in his dealings with the eastern Roman empire.

Even under Ishoyahb I, but especially under Sabrisho I (596–604), who had once been a hermit himself, monasticism was again fully integrated into the church. This was made easier by the renaissance of monasticism under Abraham of Kashkar, who was a student in Nisibis and who, following an eremitic sojourn in the Egyptian desert, renewed East Syriac monasticism on this model. The great monastery he founded on Mt Izla, on the southern edge of the Tur Abdin, became a spiritual center and theological wellspring for the Church of the East in the sixth and seventh centuries.

During Sabrisho's time the conflict over Hnana of Adiabene persisted. Because of the close relationship of Hnana's movement to monasticism, the conflict was addressed only in general terms at the synod of 596, which had ostensibly wanted to resolve the problem. Nevertheless, Theodore of Mopsuestia was again extolled and defended as commentator par excellence. Even under the next leader, Catholicos Gregory (605–8), the conflict with Hnana remained unsettled. The first synod of the seventh century (605) thus proclaimed Theodore of Mopsuestia the irrefutable standard of East Syriac orthodoxy. Anyone who opposed Theodore, whether in the past, present, or future, was expressly condemned.

From Babai the Great to the Arab conquest

In 602 Shah Chosroes II had the opportunity to expand the Persian empire to the west, an action which had not been possible militarily against Justinian, nor against Maurice. When Maurice was violently deposed by the usurper Phokas, an action Chosroes considered sufficient grounds for ordering the Persian army to march on the Roman empire. Jerusalem, Alexandria, Damascus, and Antioch were captured, and the Sassanians advanced as far as Chalcedon, at the threshold of Constantinople. The Arab kingdom of Hira was also annexed to the empire of the Sassanians. During the campaign of 604 Catholicos Sabrisho accompanied the Persian shah. However, the old man remained behind at Nisibis, where he died after a short time.

Chosroes II and the bishops considered the zealot Gregory of Kashkar a suitable successor. He had vehemently opposed Hnana. However, through the influence of Shirin and the court physician Gabriel of Sinjar, Shirin's moderate countryman Gregory of Phrat (605–8), by clever use of the similarity of names, was elevated as the new catholicos. Gabriel of Sinjar, who originally belonged to the Church of the East, had been excommunicated by Gregory of Kashkar on charges of bigamy, upon which Gabriel turned to the non-Chalcedonian Miaphysite (West Syriac, Syrian Orthodox) side, for political much more than theological reasons. The doctor had cured Shirin's barrenness and so was able to win her support for his plans to obstruct Gregory of Kashkar. Nor was Gregory of Phrat any great blessing for the church, as he was interested above all in his own personal gain. After his death, his property was confiscated by Chosroes II, and the shah forbade further occupation of the See of Seleucia-Ctesiphon. Consequently the office of catholicos-patriarch remained vacant from 608 to 628. During this period Babai the Great (551–628) and Archdeacon Aba of Seleucia led the East Syriac church.

Babai the Great was one of the most outstanding theological figures of the East Syriac church at the turn of the seventh century. He was born in Beth Zabdai and studied medicine and theology at Nisibis. He then turned to the monastic life in the great monastery at Izla, whose archimandrite he became in the year of Gregory's election as catholicos (604). During the years of the vacant patriarchal see, Babai was administrator of the catholicate and visitor of the monasteries. The literary legacy of this important thinker is enormous; in Abdisho bar Brika's catalogue of literature, it comprises eighty-three books.

In Babai's day two problems presented themselves most prominently: on the one hand, the conflict with Hnana remained unresolved, and on the other, the Miaphysites (anti-Chalcedonian, Syrian Orthodox) were gaining strength in the Persian empire. In the Roman empire the Miaphysites were deemed heretical on account of their opposition to the Council of Chalcedon (451). However, the Church of the East, which spoke of two natures, could also see only heterodoxy in "one nature (*mia physis*) of the Logos incarnate."

With the support of Empress Theodora, the exiled Alexandrian patriarch Theodosios (535–66) had ordained two bishops in 542: one was Theodore of Arabia, who concerned himself primarily with Arab Ghassanians in the Syriac desert and Transjordan region. The other was Jacob Baradaeus. While on adventurous journeys from Syria to Isauria, he ordained priests and bishops and thus laid the groundwork for a West Syriac anti-Chalcedonian church organization. Jacob became the symbolic figure of West Syriac Christianity, which is sometimes called "Jacobite" after him. In 558/9 Jacob Baradaeus succeeded in ordaining Ahudemmeh of Beth Arabaye as metropolitan of Takrit. With this event, the basis of a West Syriac (Miaphysite) hierarchy was established in Persia, although the East Syriac church with its catholicos-patriarch at Seleucia-Ctesiphon still represented the majority of Christians in the Sassanian empire. Besides Takrit, the monastery of Mar Mattai was a center of Syrian Orthodoxy in the Persian empire.

In 612, at the suggestion of the subversive physician Gabriel of Sinjar, Chosroes II arranged for a religious disputation between East and West Syriacs, that is, between representatives of the Diphysite Church of the East and the Miaphysite Syrian Orthodox, which had gained strength in the Persian empire during the sixth century. The significance and influence of the theology of Babai the Great may be measured by the fact that his Christological terminology was adopted by the Church of the East in the presentation of its faith at the disputation, though Babai himself did not participate.

The creed of the Church of the East of 612 speaks of the inseparable unity of the God-Logos and the human nature, recognized in Jesus Christ as one person (*prosopon*). It is further expressed in Babai's terminology that "Christ is two *kyane* (natures) and two *qnome*." In the past, the Syriac term *qnoma* had been equated with the Greek *hypostasis* or even translated as "person." Thus the misconception developed that the Church of the East believed in two natures and two persons in Christ. However, for neither Babai nor the creed of 612 did *qnoma* denote a self-existent hypostasis. *Kyana* refers to the general, abstract nature, that is, the human being and the God being, while *qnoma* describes the concretization and individualization of this nature. Babai thus usually employed the formulation "the two natures and their *qnome*" which are united from the moment of conception. Both Babai's most important treatment of the matter, the *Book of Union* and the document of 612 clearly express that each nature needs a *qnoma* in order to exist concretely. Were one to equate *qnoma* with *hypostasis*, one would reach a faulty understanding of the statement; a translation of "person" is incorrect. Because of this terminology, the East Syriacs were also unable to comprehend the definition of the Council of Chalcedon, which speaks of two natures in one person and hypostasis. This finds clear expression in the Christological letter of the future catholicos Ishoyahb II of Gdala, which was written in 620 and used Babai's terminology.

Babai's Christology, which was accused of being real Nestorianism, ought to be seen as an orthodox and specifically East Syriac approach to the mystery of Christ. Through the creed presented by Shah Chosroes II in 612, Babai's concepts attained significance for the entire Church of the East, and they remain valid today.

Following the high point of Sassanian power, the capture of

Palestine and Egypt under Chosroes II, the beginning of the seventh century was marked by the advance of the Byzantine emperor Heraclius (610–41). Since his rise to power, he had reorganized the Roman empire. Most important to him was strengthening the eastern provinces, which eventually led him to mount a noteworthy campaign against Persia (622–8). The military successes of Emperor Heraclius shook the Sassanian empire and resulted in a revolt against Chosroes II. In 628 he was murdered in a plot involving his son Shiruye (Shiroi). The efforts of the Sassanians to achieve political stability were doomed to failure by rapid changes in imperial leadership. In less than four years five shahs and two queens – Boran and Azarmdukht – followed one another in quick succession.

With the death of Chosroes II the vacancy of the See of Seleucia-Ctesiphon also came to an end. Babai the Great was chosen as the new catholicos. He refused the appointment, however, and died in the same year. The bishop of Balad, Ishoyahb II of Gdala (628–46) then became the new patriarch of the Church of the East. Like most East Syriac scholars of the sixth and seventh centuries, he had been educated at the school of Nisibis, though he was among those students who abandoned the school and the city under the influence of Hnana. In Balad, north-west of Mosul, he was retained by the local bishop as a teacher for the newly founded theological school. As early as the religious disputation of 612, he appeared as bishop of this city.

After his election as catholicos, Ishoyahb began reorganizing the Church of the East and placed special emphasis on theological education. Many schools were reopened or newly founded. In his opinion, besides an appropriate education, only an episcopacy with moral integrity could be persuasive, especially in the debate with the Miaphysites. In this regard, he tried to gain the favor of state authorities.

Queen Boran wanted to calm the situation in the Persian empire with a definitive peace treaty, and in 630 she sent an official diplomatic delegation to Emperor Heraclius with this goal. This delegation consisted of the highest dignitaries of the Church of the East under the leadership of Catholicos Ishoyahb II. Accompanied by the metropolitans of Nisibis, Beth Garmai, Adiabene, and Gustra, and the bishops of Mahoze, Damascus, and Nineveh (the future catholicos Ishoyahb III), the delegation met the Byzantine emperor in Aleppo. Beyond the peace treaty, the discussion again turned to religion, and the catholicos presented his faith. The debate resulted in Ishoyahb II's being permitted to celebrate the East Syriac liturgy in Aleppo. The Byzantine bishops present and the emperor himself received communion from the hand of the catholicos of the Church of the East.

The diplomatic mission was also crowned with political success and brought the region a few more years of temporary peace. At this time, the expansion of East Syriac Christianity reached China. As the 781 stele of Xian (Changan, Singan-fu), the capital of China under the Tang dynasty, recorded, a group of missionaries sent by Ishoyahb II reached China in 635. Additional metropolitanates were subsequently founded by Ishoyahb II at Hulwan (Iran), Herat (Afghanistan), Samarkand (Uzbekistan), China (with sees at Xian and Lo-yang), and eventually also in India, whose Christians had already been mentioned by Cosmas Indicopleustes and which had been under the influence of the Church of the East since at least the end of the third century.

In 632 the final Sassanian ruler, Yazdgird III, assumed the throne, while the Arabs were already advancing from the south and beginning to conquer the Near East. When they captured the Persian capital Seleucia-Ctesiphon in 632, Yazdgird fled to the area around Merv. With his violent death in 651 the Sassanian empire vanished from history.

In 637 Ishoyahb II moved his see to Karka de Beth Slokh and tried to find a *modus vivendi* with the new rulers. Arab Christian literature mentions a correspondence with the prophet Muhammad and the caliph Omar. Ishoyahb II is reputed to have received from each a letter of protection for Persian Christendom. However, these letters were produced much later, in order to show the Muslims who then opposed Christians the amicable relations between the first catholicos under Islamic rule and the prophet himself, as well as the caliph. In the seventh century an epochal change took place in the Near East. In 646 Ishoyahb II died, having been the last catholicos under the Sassanians and the first of the era of the Arabs.

2

THE AGE OF THE ARABS
650–1258

Wilhelm Baum

The period of Catholicos Ishoyahb III and the dawn of Islam

The relationship between Islam and the Church of the East varied according to the political situation. Muhammad is said to have had an East Syriac teacher named Sergius Bahira. While this may be merely legend, the Prophet of Islam was nonetheless influenced by the Christian missionaries with whom he became acquainted in Yemen and along the trade route to Iraq. Thus his view of resurrection, for example, may have been colored by the East Syrians he had known in his youth. The earliest suras of the Qur'an suggest apocalyptic influences. In the tenth century the Arab author Abu l-Farag al-Isbahani († 967) reported that Muhammad had heard the eschatological preaching of the East Syriac bishop (?) Quss b. Saida while in Ukaz, and this shaped his thinking. In any case, Muhammad had a positive impression of the Church of the East.

However, Christians soon had to pay a poll tax and wear distinctive clothing. It is nevertheless presumed that Muhammad concluded a treaty with Sayyid, king of Najran, and the East Syriac bishop Abu l-Harith of Nadjran, which guaranteed the Christians certain privileges for payment of the poll tax, and priests and monks were exempted from this payment. It is clear that a similar treaty was established under the second caliph, Umar. Treaties of this type were later also forged, in order to legitimate earlier treaties which had been lost. As previously noted, such a thing was reported by Patriarch Ishoyahb II of Gdala, who claimed he knew Muhammad and had received from him privileges for the Church of the East. Caliph Umar confirmed this, and Ali extended it because the Christians had fed his troops.

Even long after the Arab conquest, Christians outnumbered

Muslims in Egypt, Palestine, Syria, and Mesopotamia. Gunde-shapur, Nisibis, and Merv remained intellectual centers of the Church of the East, where writers, teachers, translators, and clerks were educated.

In the ensuing years, the Islamic rulers gained ever greater influence over the naming of the new catholicos, who was elected only by those metropolitans and bishops designated as delegates. East Syriac secretaries or physicians often had their candidates named by the caliph or his deputies. Between 650 and 1050 twelve of the total thirty catholicoi of the Church of the East were imposed by the Islamic rulers.

Ishoyahb III of Adiabene (650–8) – one of the most important catholicoi of the Arab era – was born in 580, became bishop of Nineveh-Mosul in 628, and was named metropolitan of Adiabene in Arbela around 637. In 630 he took part in the delegation the Persian queen Boran sent to Emperor Heraclius, and in 650 he was elected catholicos. The historian at-Tabari reported that Ishoyahb III mediated the return of the cross of Christ to Heraclius. As catholicos he occupied in the East the same universal position as the pope did in the Latin church of the West. In a letter to the metropolitan of Rewardashir (present-day Zaydun), he summarized his views regarding primacy in the East and mentioned congregations in India. Ishoyahb had to contend with efforts for independence in the Persian province of the church – his rival Simeon of Rewardashir produced a law book in the Persian language – and only through a personal visit to Rewardashir was the catholicos able to persuade the metropolitan to recognize the supremacy of Ctesiphon.

After the Arab conquest of Ctesiphon, Ishoyahb left the imperial capital and moved his residence to the monastery of Beth Abe farther north-west in Mesopotamia, where he also wanted to found a theological school. However, as the monks there expressed hostility toward his ascetic manner, he located the school in his birthplace in Adiabene.

Ishoyahb III authored a biography of the monk Ishosabhran, who died in 620 as the last martyr of the Sassanians, as well as theological tracts, sermons, and letters. His *Liber epistolarum* contains 106 letters, which have been edited by Ruben Duval on the basis of the manuscript Vat. Syr. 157, dating from the tenth century and taken to Rome in 1716 by Joseph Simon Assemari. His *Book of the Overturning of Opinions*, dedicated to the bishop of Beth Lapat (Gundeshapur), has not survived. During his term in office the catholicos, together with the learned monk Henanisho, compiled the hymnal *Hudra*. Consequently the church year was divided into eight series of weeks (Annunciation, Nativity, Epiphany, Lent, Resurrection, Apostle, Summer, Elias, Moses, and Consecration of the Church). The "responses" form the foundation of the work; the oldest fragments of the *Hudra* can be dated to the ninth or tenth century. The *Taksha*, a compilation of liturgical texts including the rites for the consecration of water, the consecration of the altar, and baptism, was also edited by Ishoyahb and made binding upon the whole church, including the Malabar coast. Manuscripts of the definitive edition of the *Taksha* go back as far as the fifteenth century. In addition, Ishoyahb III reformed the statutes of the school of Nisibis. Besides the theological disciplines of dogmatics, exegesis, canon law, and liturgy, philosophy, medicine, logic, and music were also taught. Additionally, the catholicos endeavored to prevent the Arab tribes of Oman and Bahrain from converting to Islam. When he died, Metropolitan Elias of Merv, author of a history of the Church, was with him.

In the early years of Islam, numerous new monasteries were founded, and many writings and anthologies about the lives and works of founders and monks were produced. Through the studies of Jean-Marie Fiey, the locations of some 150 East Syriac monasteries have been determined, of which eight lay in the outlying provinces and 142 in the central provinces, especially in the north. In the literature of the Apostolic Church of the East a phase of critical analysis of church-historical and juridical questions began; philosophy and medicine subsequently came under similar scrutiny.

From the hermitage of Abraham of Kashkar (491–588), the "Great Monastery" also called the Monastery of Mar Abraham developed on Mount Izla, a southern ridge of the mountainous high plateau north of Nisibis. Aged over ninety years, Abraham died here *c.*588 as a hermit. Later there were also married monks here, though they were expelled by Abbot Mar Babai the Great († 628/30). One of the monks who left the monastery was Jacob, who then founded the monastery of Beth Abe. We are well informed of his story by the *Book of the Abbots* written around 840 by Thomas of Marga, who was later himself abbot of the monastery. Today almost nothing remains of this famous monastery. At the death of its founder Jacob, the monastery had about eighty monks; the number later grew to over 300. Over the course of some 200 years the monastery produced several catholicoi, and under the eighteenth abbot, Kyriakos (*c.*800), David of Beth Sinaye traveled to China. That monks from Beth Abe were chosen as metropolitans in China and Yemen attests to the reputation of the monastery, which was called the "mother of patriarchs and bishops."

In the second half of the seventh century Beth Abe became a center of East Syriac academic life, where, in particular, biographies and sayings of Mesopotamian and Egyptian monastic fathers were collected. One member of this monastery was the aforementioned Henanisho, who not only reworked the *Hudra* with Ishoyahb III but also, at the request of Ishoyahb's successor Catholicos Giwargis I (George) assembled the legends and sayings of Egyptian monks under the title *Paradise of the Fathers*. In this extensive work many strands of tradition were brought together, including the *Historia monachorum* attributed to Jerome. A second edition of the volume includes in its 177 chapters accounts of Mesopotamian ascetics, as well. In 676 on the Bahraini island of Dirin, Giwargis held a synod whose canons were preserved together with a circular letter to a Persian priest. On the island of Kharg outside of Rewardashir, an East Syriac monastery dating from the fifth to eleventh centuries was discovered and gravestones with "Nestorian crosses" found.

Among the monasteries, that of the legendary apostle Mar Mari, lying about 90 kilometers south-east of Baghdad, played a special role as a pilgrimage site. The future patriarchal seat of Rabban Hormizd, north of Mosul, also belonged among the most famous foundations. Nine patriarchal graves and a library have survived there. Like most of the eight monasteries still functioning in Iraq today, it is now in the hands of the (Uniate) Chaldean Church.

Many manuscripts were produced in the monasteries, among them liturgical texts and legends. The sixth-century *Cave of Treasures* – in which the passion of Christ is interpreted with reference to the story of Adam – was translated into Arabic early on and formed the basis for the second and third parts of the Ethiopian *Book of Adam*.

One successor of Giwargis I was Henanisho I († 700). His legacy included a series of theological writings, letters, and a commentary on Aristotelian analysis, as well as a commentary on a few books of Aristotle's *Organon*. A *memra* (verse homily) on his teacher Ishoyahb III is preserved in an eighteenth-century manuscript. Under the Umayyads (661–750), Henanisho was banished in 692 by the governor of Iraq, who appointed John the Leper as his successor. Catholicos Henanisho fled to a monastery in Nineveh. No new election took place during his lifetime, so the seat remained vacant for fourteen years. The governor interfered repeatedly in the election of the catholicos, in addition to encouraging rivalries among the high clergy – conduct which was also seen in the period of the Abbasid caliphate. Following the death of Catholicos Saliba († 728), the electors were unable to choose a successor, but after another vacancy of three years, Caliph Hisham ordered that Pethion (731–40) be elected.

The China mission in the seventh and eighth centuries

The Syriac colonies, trading posts, and bartering places became areas of expansion for East Syriac Christianity. Although it is not entirely impossible that even before the period of the Tang dynasty isolated Christians made their way to China, reports such as those of the missionary activity of the apostle Thomas must be considered legendary. The *Hodoiporia*, a short Greek geographical text of the fourth century, reports that Christianity had spread as far as "the land of the Huns, Diaba (Sielediva = Ceylon), Greater India, Lesser India (Nubia), and Aksum." The "Nestorians" were the apostles to the Huns, the Turks, the Malabar coast, and the island of Sielediva-Taprobane (Pigulewskaja).

According to the account in the *Chronicle of Seert*, the Church of the East had already gained a foothold in Arab territory. Abdisho, an Arab from Mesene, had founded the first monastic community in Hira, and Bishop Abraham of Kashkar had begun to evangelize Arab nomads in Mesopotamia. Around 520, Catholicos Silas (503–23) supported his co-religionists in Yemen with the Jews against the "Monophysite" Ethiopians. In this case, he was indirectly serving the Persian shahs, who often employed representatives of the Church of the East as diplomats. During the persecution of non-Chalcedonians by the Byzantine emperor Justin I, Silas accepted refugee "Monophysite" monks into the Persian empire. The West Syriac bishop Simeon opposed East Syriac efforts in Hira, and John of Ephesus reported that Simeon had converted many "heretics" – by which he meant East Syrians. In response, the East Syrians called upon the Persian state authorities for help against the "Byzantines." The entire situation shows that a decision in favor of one of the competing expressions of Christianity among the East Syrians, as well as the Armenians, Ethiopians, and Copts, was always determined in part by political considerations.

As early as about 360, Merv, on the way to Central Asia in present-day Uzbekistan, may have been Christianized by Bishop Bar Shabba. This is mentioned in the *Chronicle of Seert* and also in fragments from the East Syriac monastery of Bulayiq in the Turfan oasis. In the seventh century, according to the report of an anonymous chronicle compiled around 680, Metropolitan Elias of Merv converted the khagan of the Turks, who apparently belonged to the Turkish tribes living in the south of Syr-Darja in the mid-seventh century. These could not, however, have been the first Christian Turks, since as early as 581 Turks with crosses on their foreheads had been placed in Byzantine prisons. Catholicos Timotheos I (780–832) also wrote in one of his letters of the conversion of the king of the Turks.

Even during the Sassanian era Christianity had advanced from Central Asia into the Far East, with missionary activity beginning during the reign of Emperor Tai-tsung of the Tang dynasty. It is known that in 552 two East Syriac monks smuggled silkworms to Byzanz, which was the beginning of a sericulture in the West. In 635 the monk Alopen arrived at the imperial court bearing pictures and books and was received by the emperor, who commissioned him to translate the books into Chinese. Alopen may have come from Sogdia, since the imperial courtiers were able to converse with him in his native tongue. The emperor subsequently issued an edict, in which he granted the "religion of enlightenment" freedom to preach and permission to found a monastery in the imperial capital, since Christianity emphasized goodness and benefited the people. In 638 in the I-ning quarter of the imperial capital, Xian, an East Syriac monastery was established, which was later occupied by twenty-one monks. Later Catholicos Saliba (714–28) named metropolitans for Herat, Samarkand, and China.

In Chinese texts Christianity is referred to as the "Persian religion." In 642 the translation of a Christian text into Chinese was completed, and under Emperor Kao-tsung (650–83) churches were built in all of China's provincial capitals. One gets the impression, however, that Christianity was spread primarily by foreigners, especially Persian merchants. Under the empress Wu (690–705) Christianity was regarded as competition for Buddhism and was persecuted. Not until 745 did Emperor Hsüan-tsung again legitimate Christianity and present the monasteries with tablets expressing this official recognition.

On the stele dedicated to Issu (Jesbuzid), a priest from Balch, which was erected in Xian in 781 and discovered in 1625, the entire early history of the East Syriac missionary endeavors is recorded, and Catholicos Henanisho is mentioned. The stele praises the imperial official Issu, who devoted himself to the study of Chinese culture. Two texts from the Cave of the Thousand Buddhas in Tun-huang may also be attributable to him. Because Christianity

Figure 2.1 Nestorian monument of Xian/Sianfu (781). Photo: courtesy of Kitab-Verlag, Klagenfurt.

emerged from the Far West, that is, East Rome (Chin. *Ta-Tsin*), the East Syriac monasteries were to be called "Ta-Tsin monasteries" in the future. A total of eighty seven priests and Bishop King-tsing (Adam), all of whom may have been foreigners, are named on the stele. In addition, there is talk of a second group of Syriac missionaries, who entered the country some fifty years after Alopen. The Chi-lieh named here is also mentioned in 714 in the Chinese sources. He was active in Canton, where he had difficulties with censorship, and is referred to as a member of a Persian delegation in 732. In the following years still more delegations came to China, perhaps some traveling by sea.

The writings from Tun-huang, the *Radiant Teaching from Ta-Tsin Sutra* and the *Mysterious Peace and Joy Sutra*, which were written between 717 and 720, are also among the Christian texts of the ninth and tenth centuries. Both texts were edited in 720. Ninth- and tenth-century Turkish letters from Christians, bearing the names David and Sergius, were also found at Tun-huang, as well as a silk painting depicting Christ as the Good Shepherd, discovered in 1943. A Tibetan book from Tun-huang, dating from the period from the eighth to the tenth centuries, is entitled *Jesus the Messiah*, and Syriac grave inscriptions have been found as far away as the harbor of Hang-tschou.

The powerful general and minister Kuo Tzu-i appears to have sympathized with the East Syriac church; he donated large amounts of money for the restoration and enlargement of the churches and for conferences of the hierarchy of the Church of the East. His companion Issu – the priest mentioned on the 781 stele – was vice-commander of the army in 756.

The early flowering of the East Syriac church in China, with Xian as its center, persisted until the middle of the ninth century. A Buddhist list of instructional texts from around 800 indicates that between 782 and 788 an Indian scholar named Pradschna came to Xian, where, with the help of the "Persian" monk King-tsing (Adam) of the Ta-Tsin monastery, he translated texts from Uighur. It is said that he translated numerous Christian texts into Chinese, and he was among the most striking personalities of the Church of the East in China. By the turn of the millennium, more than 500 writings, including the entire New Testament and a few books of the Old Testament, had been translated from Syriac into Chinese.

In the eighth century Kashgar was ruled by a Christian prince, and around 810 a Bishop David held office in "Beth Sinaye" (China). The further development of Christianity may also be observed in travel reports from China. In about 850 the Arab merchant Suleiman visited China; his report, conveyed by a fellow traveler, Ahmed Abu Said († 934), was used by the cosmographer al-Masudi († 956). He mentioned the revolt of Huang Chao, which was mounted against Charfu (Canton) in 874. Following this popular uprising, the Tang dynasty collapsed. Al-Masudi reported that the city, whose residents included Christians, Jews, Muslims, and Zoroastrians, was beseiged. Abu Said also learned from a man from Basra that in 872 he had had an audience with Emperor I-tsung, who had shown him a picture of Jesus. Clearly the Chinese emperor had access to Christian literature in his library. Al-Masudi also noted that the adherents of the Church of the East rejected the designation "Nestorian," which had originated with the Melkites; they preferred to call themselves "Ibad" (servants of God). In 942 Abu Dalaf, a poet at the court of the Samarids in Bukhara, accompanied a Chinese delegation on the return to their homeland and

Figure 2.2 Coins from Bukhara (eighth century). Photo: courtesy of Aleksander Naymark, Indiana, USA.

reported that in a number of cities he encountered Christians and visited their churches.

In the meantime, Christianity also made strides in the kingdom of Tibet. On the route from Kashgar to Lhasa, early ninth-century inscriptions relating to the Christianity of the Transoxus region were found south of the oasis of Chotan – where there were three Christian churches – in the vicinity of Drangtse (east of Leh on the upper Indus). In 841/2 the monk Nösh-farn was sent to the khan of Tibet. This expedition was documented by a Sogdian inscription in Tankse with "Nestorian crosses" (eighth century). In Kansu, in the "dead city" Kara Khoto of the Tangut kingdom, Persian manuscripts, two Syriac works, and a Christian Turkish text were found. One of the Syriac texts includes a prayer with a plea for rain, and the other is a hymn to the Resurrected One. In addition, an East Syriac metropolitan served among the Tanguts. Christianity was spread primarily by merchants, though it remained the faith of a small minority and, because of this, can be seen as the antithesis of the imperial Christianity of Byzantium and Rome.

There was soon a setback in the missionary movement, and the Christians lost the good will of the court. In 845, under Emperor Wu-tsung, persecution of Christians, who numbered about 260,000, began. Countless churches were destroyed, and 2,000 monks and nuns are believed to have been laicized. Catholicos Theodosius I (853–68) noted that China did not participate in his synod.

In his *Kitab al Fihrist* Ibn at-Nadim († 995) recounted the story of Muhammad, the son of Isaac, called Abu l-Faradj, who in 987 heard of the persecution of Christians and destruction of churches. In Baghdad he met an East Syriac monk who had been sent to China by Catholicos Abdisho I seven years earlier in order to ascertain the situation of Christians under the rule of the Sung Dynasty. The monk found the churches ruined and communities obliterated and had returned home because he had been assigned no further tasks. However, after the year 1000, the canonist Abdallah b. at-Taiyib still referred to Christian bishops in India and China. In the second half of the eleventh century, the metropolitan of Chorassan, who had been consecrated by Catholicos Sabrisho III, journeyed to China, where he remained for the rest of his life. There are nevertheless very few witnesses to the continued survival of East Syriac Christians in China after the middle of the eleventh century. Delegations from the West still arrived at the imperial court of the Sung, and merchants continued to travel via the sea route to the "Middle Empire," but only in the period of the Mongols did the Church of the East again begin unambiguously to grow, this time clearly less among the native Chinese than among immigrants from the north.

East Syriac Christianity in India

According to Indian tradition, in the year 52 the apostle Thomas landed on the Malabar coast, where he founded seven churches at Palayur, Cranganore, Parur, Kokkamangalam, Niramun, Chayal, and Quilon. Then he is said to have arrived on the Coromandel coast, at Mylapore near Madras, where he suffered martyrdom in AD 68. The earliest written verification of this legend dates from the sixteenth century. Eusebius and Socrates reported that Thomas had been a missionary in Parthia, while the church fathers of the fourth and fifth centuries traced Indian Christianity back to Bartholomew, a tradition which arose in the mid-second century. Christianity was perhaps transmitted along the trade route from Egypt to the Malabar coast. The Thomas tradition may have been accepted only after the breakdown of regular trade between Egypt and India in the third century.

According to the *Acts of Thomas*, which originated in Edessa in the early third century, the apostle came to a Parthian king, Gundophares, who has been historically verified by the discovery of coins from his time and who reigned during the first century in what is today Pakistan. Thomas was first described as Apostle to the

Indians in 378 by Ephrem the Syrian, then in 389 by Gregory of Nazianz, and again in 410 by Gaudentius, in 420 by Jerome, and in 431 by Paulinus of Nola. The Thomas tradition came to be rooted in Edessa, where the bones of Thomas – brought from India – were an early object of veneration. In the seventh century Pseudo-Sophronius referred to the grave of the apostle Thomas in "Calamina" in India, and Isidore of Seville adopted this in his etymology. The age of the shrine of St Thomas at Mylapore near Madras is unknown. Gregory of Tours reported that Thomas's corpse was transported from India to Edessa.

According to records from the Portuguese period, some 345 Syrians were believed to have come to Cranganore with seventy-two Jewish Christian families under the leadership of one Thomas of Cana. The doubtful nature of this tradition is made clear by the fact that in other reports the arrival of this Thomas of Cana is variously dated to 745, 774, or 795 (Gillman and Klimkeit). A tradition which first appeared in writing after the arrival of the Portuguese in India located this arrival from Persia in the fourth – though also in the eighth (*sic!*) – century. Their descendants have been called "Southerners" (in Malayalam, *Tekkumbhagar*) up to the present day, while the numerically larger group of earlier resident Christians are referred to as "Northerners" (in Malayalam, *Vatakkumbhagar*). Each group claims social superiority over the other. The Southerners maintain they are descended from the legitimate wife of Thomas of Cana, while the Northerners trace their lineage to an indigenous concubine or second wife, and both sides try to "prove" their positions with publications. The Northerners also draw on the tradition of the apostle and claim descent from Brahmans proselytized by Thomas. Their spiritual leader, whose seat was in Mylapore or Cranganore and later in Angamala, bore the title "Metropolitan-Bishop of the Seat of St Thomas and the whole Christian Church of India," and a hereditary archdeacon held jurisdiction over the clergy.

Another founding myth of the beginnings of Christianity in Kerala was first recorded by the Portuguese in the sixteenth century. In 1533 Miguel Ferreira asked an *abuna*, who was not referred to by name, about the East Syriac Christians in India. He consequently heard the story of the two saints Sapor and Prot, who were said to have come to India from Armenia in the eighth or ninth century. In 1730 a West Syriac priest, Mathew Kathanar, wrote a history of the church in south India, in which he also discussed the 823 arrival of the two priests Sapor and Prot in Quilon, where they apparently received from the king a parcel of land on which to build a church.

In the mid-twelfth century the Arab cosmographer Idrisi noted that the king of Ceylon had in his royal residence Aghna not only four Jewish, Muslim, and Ceylonese viziers, but also four Christian ones from the community of Thomas Christians. A "Nestorian cross," dating back perhaps as far as the early Middle Ages and discovered on a pillar in the ancient royal city of Mantota, the port of the capital Anunadhapura, preserves the memory of the former Church of the East in Sri Lanka. Other stone monuments include six surviving East Syriac crosses with a Pahlavi inscription – one on Mount Thomas in Mylapore near Madras, four in the vicinity of Kottayam, and one in Travancore in Kerala – which all bear the same Middle Persian inscription, including the appeal of Gabriel, son of Chahabokht, that the Messiah have mercy on the donor of the cross. The crosses may date from the period of the sixth to ninth centuries. Only recently, in 2001, another "Nestorian cross" was discovered in Goa.

The *Chronicle of Seert* reports that a Bishop David of Basra engaged in missionary activity in India around 295/300, and it seems that Joseph of Edessa was named bishop of India by the catholicos of the Church of the East in 345. From Byzantine sources it is known that sometime after 354 Emperor Constantius sent Theophilus, who is assumed to have come from the Maldives, as a missionary to India. According to the *Chronicle of Seert*, in 420 the catholicos sent his translation of Diodore of Tarsus to the "Lands of the Islands" and to India. Before the fifth century, the geographical treatise *Hodoiporia apo Eden* was written, in which it was stated that Christians had reached the territory of the Huns, "Diaba" (Ceylon), "Greater India" (Aksum), and as far as "Lesser India." According to the account of Ishodad on Merw, Mar Komai, with the help of an Indian priest named Daniel, translated the Letter to the Romans from Greek into Syriac around 425. The *Chronicle of Seert* reports that around 470 Metropolitan Mana of Rewardashir sent all the books he had translated from Greek into Syriac "to all the islands in the sea and to India," in order to ensure correct theological instruction of the clergy.

Catholicos Sabrisho (596–604) also expressed interest in the Indians, to whom Ishoyahb II (628–46) eventually sent additional bishops. The jurisdiction of the Church of the East over the Christians of the Indian Malabar coast was clearly established under Catholicos Ishoyahb III († 658) around 650. He addressed two letters to Mar Simeon of Rewardashir, who refused to consecrate a bishop for India. There one can read that the Church of the East extended to "qalah," which "lay 200,000 parasangs" from Persia. But here "qalah" does not mean Quilon, which did not exist at that time, but Qalang in Malacca. The community, ecclesiastically dependent on Rewardashir, paid taxes to the bishop and thus acknowledged the sovereignty of the church. Between 650 and 850 a separate metropolitanate of India was established, which was mentioned around 1350 by Amr b. Matta in his *Book of the Tower*.

However, the earliest detailed knowledge we have of Christians in this region comes from the Christian traveler Cosmas Indicopleustes, who evidently followed the usual route of East Syriac traders and around 547/50 reported that he had visited Christians in Ethiopia, India, and Ceylon. In addition to the caravan routes, port cities also became sites of Christian expansion. In his youth, Cosmas met Catholicos Mar Aba (540–52) and possibly belonged to the East Syriac church. He did not place the East Syriac church in the category of Christian "sects." Cosmas particularly emphasized that he did not know if there were still Christians in Ceylon, and he noted the presence of Christians in "Kalliana." Researchers have searched for this location in the vicinity of Bombay; historians such as Peter Kawerau identify it with Quilon. Cosmas also cited a Syriac church in "Male," by which he probably meant the Malabar coast of Kerala. He mentioned priests from Persia on the island of Socotra, as well. The testimony of Cosmas is the earliest evidence for the spread of Christianity from Persia to India.

Unfortunately, no Christian structures from the Middle Ages remain standing today. However, there are a few documents of local kings of Kerala inscribed on copper plates. The dating and interpretation of the plates, however, are ambiguous. It is unclear whether the Church of the East expanded here mainly among immigrant merchants or indigenous Indians. Over time, some copper tablets from the eighth century have been lost. However, a total of five plates from two series of ninth-century plates have been preserved. Dating from c.880, the period of King Stanu Ravi, are two deeds from Governor Ayyan Atikal Tiruvatikal of Venad for the Terisapalli church in "Kurakkeni Kollam" (Quilon), which had been built by a certain Maruvan Sabrisho, founder of the city of Quilon around 825. These older deeds of donation consist of three copper tablets; one tablet has been lost. Clearly the king bequeathed the city to the Christian merchant Sapir Iso (Sabrisho) – who is presumably to be identified with the church founder Eso da Tapir.

Figure 2.3 First copper plate (the reverse is blank) of the older series from the times of King Stanu Ravi (ninth century) with privileges for the Terispalli Church in Quilon. Kottayam, Kerala (India). Photo: courtesy of Christoph Baumer, Switzerland.

The older series includes two plates; the conclusion is missing. One side of the first plate is blank; a total of 27 lines of text in Old Tamil, written in Vatellatu script, remains, in which the founding of the city and the church is recounted and the privileges detailed. A number of families were given to the church as serfs. Three plates from the third series have been preserved, two in the Syrian Orthodox seminary of Kottayam and the third, which includes the signatures, in the Mar Thomas church in Tiruvalla. The beginning of the second privilege, which resembles the first and of which 89 lines remain (the beginning is missing), is perhaps a later copy of the privilege and may originate from the same period as the first privilege.

According to the plates, Christians were guaranteed privileges by Ayyan; for instance, they were permitted to sit on carpets and ride elephants – special rights to which only the aristocracy was entitled! In addition, Christians were granted a monopoly over weights and measures and administration of the king's seal, and a merchants' guild and a union of Jewish traders were placed under the protection of a Christian merchants' guild. The witnesses, Jews, Muslims, and Zoroastrians, signed in Pahlavi, Arabic (in Kufic script), and Hebrew. The copper plates were handed over by the Syriac bishop Mar Jacob to the Portuguese trading post in Cochin for safekeeping and were subsequently forgotten. In 1806 they were discovered by the Englishman Macaulay and given to the seminary in Kottayam.

The second set of the somewhat more recent plates is made up of four plates; the first of these has been lost. It includes the privileges for the *Manigraman*, the leaders of the Christians in Quilon. The most

Figure 2.4 Front and reverse of the third copper plate with Pahlavi, Kufic, and Hebrew signatures. Tiruvalla, Kerala (India). Photo: courtesy of Christoph Baumer, Switzerland.

recent plate, from *c.*1320, is a privilege of King Vira Raghava Chakravarti for a certain Iravi Korttan in Cranganore, from which it follows that at least some of the Christians in Kerala were prosperous.

Three plates may be seen today in the Malankara Orthodox Seminary in Kottayam and two in the episcopal palace of the Mar Thoma Christians in Tiruvalla. The East Syriac Christians had evidently formed a merchants' guild in Kerala. John of Marignola reported in 1348 that the Christians were owners of the public scales. These sources confirm the existence of the Church of the East in Kerala in the eighth century and permit the conclusion that the founding myths recorded in the sixteenth century contain a kernel of historical truth. As a rule, those church buildings which have survived in India date back to no earlier than the sixteenth century, but in the Church of Mary in Manarcad near Kottayam, gravestones from 910/20 with Malay and Tamil inscriptions have been found.

In a Syriac document of 874, the region of Quilon is called "qalimaya." The Muslim Suleiman reported in 841 that from Quilon,

Figure 2.5 Stone cross with Pahlavi inscription. Valiyapalli Church in Kottayam, Kerala (India). Photo: courtesy of Wilhelm Baum.

"bethuma" the grave of Thomas, could be reached in ten days. Ishoyahb of Nisibis referred to the grave of Thomas in India, as did his contemporary Salomon of Basra. Marco Polo was one of the first Europeans to visit it, followed around 1291 by John of Montecorvino. In 1340 Amr b. Matta mentioned Thomas's grave in India, and the Muslim Mufazzal b. Abil-Fazail reported in 1358 that the hand of the apostle was venerated at his burial site. It appears that the Hindu rulers of Viyajanagar also honored the grave. In 1547, on the great Mount Thomas near Mylapore, the Portuguese found an East Syriac stone cross from the sixth to the ninth century with Pahlavi inscription, which had clearly been copied many times. Additional stone crosses were discovered in the region around the city of Kottayam, which remains to this day the intellectual center of Kerala. From the chronicles of Amr b. Matta and Saliba b. Yuhanna (fourteenth century) it is known that India had a metropolitan in the Middle Ages. In the times of Yahballaha III (1281–1317) the metropolitan of India is listed in fifteenth place (alongside China, Tangut, Tabaristan, Turkestan, and Samarkand). However, it is not known where the see was.

Documents from the beginnings of Christianity in India agree with the oldest travel reports from Europe; King Alfred the Great of England (871–901) was devoted to the apostle Thomas and as early as 883 sent Bishop Sigelmus of Sherborne to India to venerate the apostle's grave. The ties between the Thomas Christians and the Church of the East remained in place throughout the Middle Ages.

Figure 2.6 Nestorian cross, found in Mantota, the port of the former capital of Sri Lanka, Anuradhapura (destroyed in the eleventh
century). Photo: courtesy of Wilhelm Baum.

Moreover, the Armenian Abu Salih (fourteenth century), in his
*Description of the Churches and Monasteries of Egypt and Neigh-
boring Lands* cited not only the shrine of Thomas in Mylapore and
the churches in Quilon but also "Fashur" in Sumatra as centers of
the East Syriac church. In modern historiography, this has been
taken as an indication that East Syriac Christianity had also spread
as far as beyond India and South-East Asia (Gillman and Klimkeit).

Timotheos I (780–823) and the Abbasid period (749–946)

The East Syriac church also expanded to the west and north and
soon reached Egypt. As early as the sixth century, Abraham the
Great of Kashkar traveled to Egypt, where he acquired ideas for his
future monastic reforms from the region's desert fathers. Mar Aba
(741–52) installed a local bishop for the faithful of the Church of
the East in Egypt, but the Coptic patriarch of Alexandria was not
pleased with the "sectarians" who had emigrated from Mesopota-

mia. In the ninth century an East Syrian, Gabriel Bochtisho, addressed the governor of Egypt with a letter from the caliph; he sought to transport the bones of Nestorius to the church of Kokhe in Ctesiphon. However, it was no longer known where Nestorius had been buried. The Copts were in conflict with the members of the Church of the East because the latter often served the Arab government. One Ibn Nestorius even rose to the office of vizier in the tenth century. South of Cairo there was an East Syriac monastery near Al-Adaweyah, whose great church stood until the thirteenth century and was later turned into a mosque. For the large East Syriac community in Cairo, Catholicos Abdisho I consecrated a separate bishop around 965. In the ninth century the Coptic patriarch condemned the "heterodoxy of the Nestorians." Around 1015 a metropolitan with jurisdiction over three suffragan bishops, forty-seven priests, and 7,300 families, was named for Cairo, and in Alexandria there was another metropolitan, who oversaw two suffragan bishops, twenty-three priests, and 4,025 families. Beginning in the twelfth century, however, the numbers of the Church of the East again declined.

After the fall of the Umayyad caliphs, the center of Islamic power shifted under the Abbasids to Mesopotamia, and the Church of the East gradually adapted itself to the new circumstances. Under the Abbasids, restrictions were again placed on Christians, and the government interfered with the selection of the catholicos. Caliph al-Mansur, founder of the new imperial capital Baghdad, either supported the catholicoi or took them prisoner, according to the political circumstances. Aba II lived for a time in his homeland Kashkar, though he then returned to his residence at the Kokhe church in Ctesiphon. He produced theological writings and wrote a commentary on Aristotle's *Organon*.

Catholicos Henanisho II (775–80) had a collection of earlier acts and synodical resolutions of the Church of the East edited. During his time in office, severe persecution of Christians occurred under Caliph al-Mahdi (775–85). As a result, many Christians migrated to the Byzantine empire and settled there, and those who remained behind were viewed with suspicion by the Muslims. Again under Caliph al-Mamun (813–33), who founded the "House of Sciences" in Baghdad, there was an exodus of Christians to such places as Sinope on the Black Sea.

The catholicos became the official representative of the Christians to the Abbasid caliphate. In the ninth and tenth centuries members of the Church of the East played a significant role at the court of the caliph, gaining respect in particular as personal physicians and court doctors, but also in the administration of Syria, Iraq, and Egypt. The monasteries educated an outstanding new generation of civil servants. High officials could rise to the post of vizier; however, as a rule, attainment of this position required them to convert to Islam.

Timotheos I (780–823) came to office through simony but developed into one of the most important ecclesiastical writers and most capable organizers of the Apostolic Church of the East, which by then extended into India and China. Timotheos was elected after an eight-month vacancy of the patriarchal seat; his ordination in May 780 followed a two-year schism with opposing synods. He had to acknowledge the metropolitan of Kashkar's right of convocation and the metropolitan of Elam's right of consecration after the election of the catholicos. Timotheos transferred the residence of the catholicos from Ctesiphon to the newly founded city of Baghdad and settled on the western bank of the Tigris in the "Deir Kalilisho" (in Arabic, *Dayr al-Jathaliq*, that is, "monastery of the catholicos"). However, the catholicos was still consecrated in the church of Kokhe in Ctesiphon.

As a result of the victories of the Byzantine emperor Leo IV, Caliph al-Mahdi had many churches destroyed. The Christians were accused by the caliph of praying day and night for the triumph of the Byzantines. The East Syriac physician Isa defended his fellow believers before al-Mahdi and explained that the Greeks hated the East Syrians even more than the Jews. The caliph questioned a Byzantine captive about this, and the prisoner replied that the "Nestorians" ought hardly to be considered Christians and stood nearer the Arabs than the Byzantines.

Because of his good relations with the court, Timotheos I succeeded in having several churches rebuilt. He was held in high regard by the caliphs al-Mahdi and Harun ar-Rashid; he worked under a total of five different caliphates and promoted missionary activity in India, China, Turkestan, Yemen, and around the Caspian Sea. Timotheos established six new ecclesiastical provinces, of which the Syriac and Armenian endured the longest, and he named a metropolitan for Tibet. He appointed a bishop in Yemen; under him, China received a metropolitan. In a letter, Timotheos referred to the ordination of a metropolitan in Turkestan. In another document, this one addressed to the monastery of Maron, he reported that the "khagan" (king) of the Turks had requested missionaries from him and that he had named a metropolitan. In the twelfth century, in his *Book of the Tower*, Mari b. Suleiman spoke of the conversion of the Keraits; Timotheos also brought the khagan of the Turks to the faith and sent him letters. He sent four monks to the peoples of Dailam and Gilan south-east of the Caspian Sea. In this regard, Timotheos wrote that the missionaries in the East traveled just as far as the traders and merchants, and he declared in one letter that professionally educated missionaries had journeyed to the lands of the barbarians, "to the ends of the East," where there was neither wheat nor barley, only rice and other kinds of "dry grain."

During the 43-year catholicate of Timotheos I, the Church of the East claimed tens of millions of adherents in 230 dioceses with twenty-seven metropolitans. In a letter to the monks of the monastery of Mar Maron, the patriarch affirmed the Church of the East's understanding of "orthodoxy": "For us the word of orthodoxy has remained correct and unchanged, and we would never have contradicted our creed by embellishing or diminishing the pearl of truth which the holy apostle preserved in this region of the East. Where you are, however, Christian heretics reign. Whether Christians or heretics, those who enjoyed the sympathies of the rulers of the time induced the priests and the faithful to conform. Because of this, there have been additions to and excisions from the creed in your area. That which Constantine the Great confirmed, his successors have cast off and rejected." Statements such as this make clear that the development of Christianity proceeded from more than one center and cannot be understood as a "top-down" movement of the "imperial church."

Several works of Timotheos, such as the *Treatise against the Council of Chalcedon*, have been lost. He saw in the Islamic rulers a purifying strength for Christianity. His disputation with Caliph al-Mahdi, translated from the original Syriac into Arabic and reproduced in several editions, offers insight into the Christology of the catholicos. The discussion between Timotheos and the caliph, who was well-disposed toward him, is said to have taken place at court over the course of two days; it is possible, however, that this is a literary fiction. The fifty-nine letters that have been preserved – Abdisho b. Brika mentions 200 – provide a glimpse into the extensive philosophical and theological knowledge of the catholicos, as well as his pastoral efforts. The high level of theological reflection is evident in his forty-seventh letter, which contains the earliest example of the use of the "Syro-Hexapla." The catholicos refers to the transmission of this work to him and to errors in the translation of Greek names.

From Aristotle he cited in particular the *Topics, Rhetoric, Poetics,* and *De generatione et corruptione.* The synods of 790/1 and 804, which addressed the preservation of East Syriac doctrine and the subordination of bishops to the catholicos, must also be numbered among the successful accomplishments of his term in office.

A collection of ninety-eight canons has been preserved under his name. Timotheos endeavored to provide the clergy with a foundational theological education and to make missionary activity easier through the study of other cultures. He also took Melkites (Orthodox) and Jacobites (Syrian Orthodox) into his service if there were manuscripts to be obtained from Byzantium or the library of the Jacobite monastery of Mar Mattai.

At the time of Timotheos I, the Thomas tradition was in evidence among Christians in India, and it was used to restrict the jurisdiction of the catholicos. The church historian Grigorius Abu l-Faraj (Barhebraeus) reported that Christians in the East declared to the patriarch that they were disciples of the apostle Thomas and wanted nothing to do with the seat of Mar Mari in Seleucia-Ctesiphon. This represents the earliest reliable evidence that the Indian Christians portrayed themselves as "Thomas Christians." The dependence of the so-called "Thomas Christians" on the church in Persia indicates that Indian Christianity was not of apostolic origin (de Vries). When Timotheos I was asked by a bishop for payment of travel expenses to a synod, the catholicos replied that monks journeyed to India and China with only a staff and a satchel – and without any monetary compensation. In his legal collection, the East Syriac theologian Ibn at-Taiyib preserved two letters of the catholicos which concern India. One letter to the Indian Christians includes instructions for the election of the metropolitan, which should be announced first to the king if the catholicos confirms it. In the second letter, to the archdeacon of India, Timotheos complained about abuses occurring in the election of bishops. Writings such as these clearly demonstrate the broad reach of the Church of the East, which at the time of Timotheos I was certainly wider than that of the pope in Rome. There was even an East Syriac community in Jerusalem, as we know from the mid-seventh-century correspondence of Ishoyahb III. However, Timotheos was the first to set up a bishopric in Jerusalem, which came under the jurisdiction of the metropolitan of Damascus. The first bishop was appointed by name in 893. The ruins of an East Syriac monastery with a mosaic inscription have been found between Jericho and the Jordan, and in 1165 John of Wurzburg referred to Jerusalem's "Nestorian" community, which in the mid-thirteenth century included four churches in the city. In the Church of the Holy Sepulcher, the Church of the East had its own altar to the left of the sacred tomb.

Beginning in the early ninth century, the move among East Syrians away from Syriac toward the Arabic language became more noticeable. Catholicos Timotheos first wrote his disputation in Syriac but held it in Arabic; discussions of the validity of Muhammad's ideas and the Qur'an were widely disseminated in the latter language. The secretary to the catholicos, Abu l-Fadl Ali b. Rabban an-Nasrani (the "Christian"), wrote a polemical work against Muhammad and the Qur'an. He also compiled the East Syriac synodical documents into the *Synodicon Orientale* and produced the *Rules for Resolutions of Canon Law and Inheritance* and a treatise on civil law. Around 840 Amar al-Basri authored an apology (*Book of Questions and Answers*) in Arabic. In his theology of the Trinity, he rejected the Islamic concept of the divine predicates, and the Arab side responded with a written refutation. Israel of Kashkar also defended the dogma of the Trinity against the Muslim group, the Mutalizites.

Among the most significant theologians of Timotheos's time was the exegete and apologist Theodore bar Konai, whose book of *Scholia* from 792 offered an apologetic presentation, similar to a catechism, of East Syriac Christianity. It contains a valuable overview of heretical doctrines and non-Christian religions such as Islam, with which Bar Konai sharply disagreed. His *Scholia* and his *Church History* are also of interest regarding the history of the catholicoi. His work provides fragments of the official position of the Church of the East toward Islam and set the standard for later works of its kind.

Catholicos Sabrisho II (831–5) wrote a report of his inspection of ecclesiastical schools and issued an order regarding their operation. When the caliphs transferred their residence to Samara, Abraham II (837–50), who had been elected by the laity, also moved there. The catholicos intended Metropolitan Ishodad of Merv, who had written commentaries on books of the Bible, to be his successor. However, Ishodad could not assume the office at the caliphal court on account of enmity between him and the physician Gabriel Bochtisho. The bishops elected an opposing candidate, who was also unable to assert himself against the doctors at court. Theodosius (853–8), who had been taken prisoner by the caliph, was finally, after a protracted conflict and with the protection of Bochtisho, able to act on his election. The catholicos subsequently ordered that metropolitan synods be held every four years. In 850

Caliph al-Mutawakkil instituted new measures against the Christians, who had gained access to public office in large numbers. The Muslims, however, could have no friends among the infidels.

Catholicos Sergius (860–72) was finally able to return to Baghdad in 865. With the election of Catholicos John IV bar Abgar (900–5) the people of Baghdad asserted their right to select the catholicos. His writings on ecclesiastical law are preserved in part in Syriac and in part in Arabic translation; twenty-eight canons regarding the ordination of priests were included in the compilation of Ibn at-Taiyib. In 913 Catholicos Abraham III (906–37) received a document assuring his priority over the Melkite and Jacobite patriarchs. In 1074 Catholicos Sabrisho III (1064–72) – who likewise had his precedence over the Jacobites (Syrian Orthodox) and Melkites (Orthodox) confirmed by the caliph – was entrusted with the enforcement of Islamic law. The relationship between Islam and the Church of the East was ambivalent and tense; it changed according to the political situation of the caliph.

East Syrians as cultural mediators

In the Islamic provinces of Assyria and Babylonia (Iraq), the East Syriac church used its position as the dominant Christian church against the other Christian groups. From the mid-eighth to the mid-eleventh century, East Syriac physicians exercised significant influence at the caliphal court.

As a rule, these doctors came from the medical school at Gundeshapur, where Syriac and Indian, as well as Greek, medicine was practiced. Prior to 376/7, a monastery was founded in Gundeshapur. The city's theological school, where Rabban Hormizd studied from 587 to 595, was first mentioned at the end of the sixth century, and at the end of the seventh century, the future catholicos John visited this school. The Bochtisho family also enjoyed great influence there. A letter from Patriarch Timotheos indicates that the theological and medical schools were two separate institutions, but both came under the leadership of the metropolitan. A letter from Metropolitan Ephrem of Elam to Gabriel Bochtisho, the future personal physician of the caliph, states that Gabriel had received exegetical, patristic, and philosophical instruction from Ephrem at Gundeshapur. The school also possessed an extensive library. In the ninth century, the significance of the school of Gundeshapur declined, and Baghdad assumed its position.

Also of great importance was the monastery of Deir Kunna in

Iraq and its school of Mar Mari. Among the scholars of the monastery was the logician and Aristotelian Abu Bishr Matta b. Yunus († 940), who was praised by the Arab philosopher al-Biruni. His translation of Aristotle's *Poetics* is the earliest textual source for this writing, and all other extant, reliable Arab, Syriac, and Hebrew translations since the tenth century, as well as the Latin revisions, may be traced back to this work.

The secular scientific and literary work of the "Nestorians" flourished during the first phase of the Abbassid period. There were entire dynasties of physicians who for generations held prominent positions at court. Most notable among them was the Bochtisho family, who over the course of three centuries produced physicians and professors of medicine and philosophy, as well as writers. In 765 George, the progenitor of the line, was summoned from Gundeshapur to the caliphal court by al-Mansur. He translated works from Greek into Arabic for his patron. George's son Bochtisho entered the service of Harun ar-Rashid in 787. In 807 Bochtisho's son Gabriel successfully eased the clothing restrictions on Christians, and he pushed through the elections of the two successors of Timotheos I. Bochtisho's son Gabriel worked with the young Hunain b. Ishaq († 873). In Paris there is a manuscript (BN, Ms. Ar. 2859) from Hunain's translation of Galen's "About the direction of medical schools for students" which has two comments regarding the ownership of the manuscript: "acquired from the Christian physician Gabriel ibn Bochtisho" and "acquired in the year 407 (1016/17) from Husayn ibn Abdallah ibn Sina" (= Avicenna). It was Gabriel who obtained a letter from the caliph to the governor of Egypt authorizing the transfer of the bones of Nestorius to the church of Kokhe; however, the location of Nestorius's grave had already been forgotten.

The East Syriac doctors and philosophers often translated from Greek into Syriac and only then into Arabic. Also of great importance were their accomplishments in the fields of grammar and lexicography. It is possible that an East Syriac physician traveled to Japan in 739 as a member of the entourage of a Japanese official and while there assisted with Emperor Shomu's († 748) plans for a hospital. However, nothing is known of the establishment of East Syriac Christian congregations in Japan.

The employment of Christian physicians at the court of the Abbasids often worked to the advantage of the church because, in the face of discriminatory measures, they could exploit their connections and often also their considerable wealth. In this way,

punishments and taxes were averted and approval for the foundation, that is, the rebuilding, of monasteries was obtained. However,
corruption and simony plagued these arrangements. Christians
were likewise influential in financial management and bureaucracy,
leading to the development of a new caste, which soon adopted the
Arabic language, causing Syriac to fall increasingly into disuse.
Occasionally, to further their careers, officials such as these converted to Islam. They then pursued an ambiguous religious politics
because their wives and other relatives often remained Christians.
Over the course of the ninth century, the school of Gundeshapur
lost its significance, and its eventual fate is unknown.

Hunain b. Ishaq, the most important of the East Syriac translators, did not come from the Iranian Gundeshapur. He was the son
of an apothecary from the Arab tribe of Ibad and a lecturer at the
medical academy in Baghdad. Hunain mastered Arabic, Persian,
Syriac, and Greek. This East Syriac Christian from an Arab tribe
had studied medicine and had come to know the cities of the eastern
Roman empire and Alexandria during his many travels. From these
trips, he brought with him back to Baghdad numerous manuscripts,
which served as the foundation of his further studies. He was a
physician, writer, and teacher in Baghdad during the reign of ten
caliphs. As personal physician of the caliph al-Mutawakkil and a
courtier, he had to endure conspiracies against him, as well as their
consequences: a two-year imprisonment in the residence of the
catholicos and excommunication by the catholicos. He was evidently also a deacon of the Apostolic Church of the East. He began
his extensive translation activity at the early age of seventeen; he
translated more than 260 works and wrote over 100. He, his son
Ishaq († 910/11), and his grandson were assigned translations of
Aristotle, Galen, Euclid, Archimedes, and Ptolemy. Hunain stated
in a letter about the writings of Galen that of the 400 works of the
Greek physician, 129 had been translated into Arabic or Syriac, 100
of those by Hunain himself. In writing about the translations of
Galen, he offered a glimpse into his methods:

> When I was a young man – twenty years old or a bit older –
> I translated from an error-ridden Greek manuscript for a
> doctor from Gundeshapur. Later, when I was about forty
> years old, I asked my student Hubais to correct the transla-
> tion. In the meantime, I had added a number of Greek
> manuscripts to my collection. I had compared these manu-
> scripts and in this way had assembled a single, correct copy.

Then I compared the Syriac text with this and corrected it.
This is how I usually proceed with all my translations. After
a few years, then, I have translated the Syriac text into
Arabic.

Hunain b. Ishaq also made great strides in healing diseases of the
eye, which was of particular importance in view of the prevalence of
such maladies. In addition, he wrote a *Book of Logic* and a history
of the world from Adam to his own time (661). Regrettably, his
translation of the Septuagint, which al-Masudi praised for its high
quality, has been lost. Hunain also authored an apology for Christianity and rejected the advice of an acquaintance that he convert to
Islam. In his treatise *The Way to Recognize Truth in Religion* he
argued against opportunism in religious questions and deficiencies
in education. As a scholar who was at home in both the Syriac and
Arabic languages, he also produced lexicographical and linguistic
works. Through the development of neologisms and the borrowing
of foreign words, he created an academic Arabic terminology and
transformed Arabic from the language of the Bedouins into an
instrument in which complicated scholarly problems could be
expressed. The medical historian Withington referred to Hunain as
the "Erasmus of the Islamic Renaissance."

A history of pharmacy and physicians originated with Ishaq b.
Hunain; he also translated a Neoplatonic work on the nature of the
human being. In 951 a Christian monk, a Spanish Jew, and Arab
doctors came together in Cordoba to revise Hunain's old translation of the pharmacological teachings of Dioscorides; thirty years
later the work was expanded by a Spanish-Arab physician.

Among the theologians of the Apostolic Church of the East, there
were trends which resisted the pressures of Islam. Besides Timotheos I and his secretary, these theologians of controversy included
above all Abd al-Masib b. Ishaq al-Kindi (ninth century). However,
his membership in the Church of the East is doubted by some
scholars, who see him as a Jacobite (Syrian Orthodox). In correspondence with a Muslim, al-Kindi sharply criticized Muhammad
and the inconsistency of Muslim ethics. This work, first made
known by al-Biruni, is an apology for Christianity, and nowhere
else was the dark side of Islam so clearly and unambiguously presented. Al-Kindi displayed his knowledge of Muhammad's biography and the Qur'an and criticized the superstition of the lower
classes and the indifference of the elite. Because of his historical
knowledge and familiarity with dialectic, it was not difficult for him

to drive his opponents into a corner. Al-Kindi's correspondence partner, who came from the Hashemite family, knew the canon of the Church of the East and the differences between it, the Jacobites, and the Melkites, and he also stated that he had already had religious discussions with Timotheos I. In addition, he mentioned that the Prophet Muhammad had looked favorably upon the Church of the East and had assured it protective privileges. He was familiar with the liturgy and the fasting regulations and referred to his conversations with bishops. The Trinity and the good news of the cross were, however, entirely mystifying to him. He tempted his opponent with the Islamic marriage regulations and visions of paradise and hell. However, his claim that Abraham was the first Muslim was rejected by al-Kindi, who characterized the wars of Islam as raids, like those of the Bedouins. Al-Kindi criticized Muhammad's murderous plans, vindictiveness, and polygamous marriages to fifteen wives. "Muhammad preached nothing that we did not already know and that our children learn in school." The military successes of the Muslims are divine punishment for sinful peoples. Muhammad's teachings were deliberately distorted by later leaders. In the area of ethics, al-Kindi compared the law of retaliation to the teachings of reason and the Christian doctrines of forgiveness and mercy. He maintained that the internal contradictions of the Qur'an may be explained by its varied transmission. The affected rhyming language of the Qur'an offers no proof of its divine origin. The promise of sensual pleasure reflects only the luxurious life which Muhammad had come to know at the Persian court. Circumcision as a religious act was rejected; the pilgrimage to Mecca was traced back to the ceremonies of sun worshipers. The demand for "holy war" was contrasted with the Christian law of love, the death in war of Muslims with the martyrdom of many Christians. Al-Kindi contemptuously rejected the plea to convert to Islam for the allure of sensual pleasures or the material advantages it offered. In conclusion, he put forth the good news of Jesus and invited his (discourse partner) to compare the two religions and then reach a judgment.

Around the year 1000, the Arab philosopher al-Biruni used this possibly fictitious correspondence in the *Chronology of Oriental Peoples*. Manuscripts of this work, which was published and translated several times, date back as early as the sixteenth century, and the work was known in Europe from the 1141 Latin translation of Peter of Toledo. Just as the later "Bahira legend" does, this apology demonstrates that despite the more or less peaceful coexistence of

Christians and Muslims and their influences upon one another, they remained fully conscious of their differences.

The Church of the East mediated the culture of antiquity to the Arab Bedouin religion and, despite the military and political successes of the Muslims, never abandoned its intellectual conflict with Islam. The position of the Christians grew weaker with each passing century. This is indicated, for instance, by the amount of the poll tax the Christians paid. At the beginning of the ninth century, approximately 130,000 dirham were collected, a century later, only some 16,000. According to Islamic law, the return of an apostate Christian to the Church was punished by death. Around 970 the Shiite Fatimids succeeded in conquering Egypt and established a second caliphate in Cairo. The Christians there also paid the poll tax and in return received the protection (*dhimma*) of the government. The invasion of the Seljuks eventually led to a strengthening of the Sunni branch of Islam. Christianity withstood the Islamic invasion, but divisions in the oriental churches of the Jacobites (Syrian Orthodox), Copts, and Melkites (Orthodox) weakened their opposition; in addition, more and more Christians converted to the religion of the conquerors. Greek gradually disappeared as a colloquial language; it lived on only in the liturgy of the Orthodox (Melkites). Because of Islamic language laws, Syriac also became a purely liturgical and literary language, as Arabic became the *lingua franca* of the Christians.

Church history and church law

It seems that the writing of church history played a less significant role in the Church of the East than among the Orthodox and Jacobites. The Syriac churches calculated time from the era of Alexander, which began on October 1, 312 BC; a few East Syriac writers, however, calculated time according to the ascension of Christ, which was fixed in the year 30. These standards were maintained by East Syrians up until the modern era.

The Syriac legend of Abgar was composed perhaps as early as the mid-third century; in the form of the surviving *Teaching of Addai*, however, it originated in the fifth century and included more legendary embellishments than Eusebius.

The *Chronicle of Arbela* is the subject of scholarly dispute. It purports to have been written by Meshiha-Zeka in the first half of the seventh century. The surviving section includes the period from 100 to 550. According to its account, Arbela was converted by

Addai in the first century. Peter Kawerau is persuaded of its authenticity. He produced a new edition of the chronicle, based on the Berlin manuscript Ms. Or. Fol. 3126, found by the Orientalist Alphonse Mingana in the village of Ergur, where around 1750 an East Syriac bishop's seat had been plundered. Julius Assfalg pointed out its linguistic inconsistencies, and Jean-Maurice Fiey believes it to be a forgery by Mingana.

The sixth-century *Chronicle of Edessa* cannot be unambiguously classified as "Nestorian." It recounts the history of the Edessan monarchy from its beginnings around 133 until AD 540.

In the first half of the ninth century Thomas of Marga, who was for a time secretary to Catholicos Mar Abraham II and eventually became metropolitan of Beth Garmai, wrote his *Book of the Abbots*, a history of the East Syriac monastery of Beth Abe.

The *Chronicle of Seert* – also called the *Nestorian Chronicle* – is an anonymous Arabic work which was composed on the basis of earlier Syriac sources shortly after 1036. Its name comes from the episcopal seat of Seert in Kurdistan, where the East Syriac archbishop and scholar Addai Scher († 1915) discovered a manuscript which had been written before the fourteenth century. The surviving sections of the *Chronicle of Seert* describe the Roman imperial period from 251 to 422 and from 484 to 650. They report the campaigns of the Sassanian Shapur I against the Roman emperor Valerian and the deportation of captured Christians to the East. The chronicle includes among others a report of the Christianization of Merv under Bar Shabba.

One source for the *Chronicle of Seert* is the church history of Daniel bar Maryam (seventh century), who was a contemporary of Ishoyahb III. He wrote an *Ecclesiastical History* (*Ekklesiastike*) in four volumes. Around the year 800, Catholicos Timotheos referred to Daniel's method of briefly reiterating the reports of the catholicoi. Daniel was familiar with the alleged correspondence between Jesus and King Abgar of Edessa and discussed the date of the death of Jesus.

In 1018 the theologian Elias bar Shinaya of Nisibis (975–1049) wrote a chronicle of the world in Syriac and Arabic, which is of great significance for cultural history. It is preserved in a single bilingual manuscript, which is in part an autograph (London, Brit. Mus. Add. 7197). The first section includes excerpts from earlier historical works and chronological tables. Elias relied on Eusebius and a series of Greek, Syriac, and Arabic authors. He was among the most prolific Syriac- and Arabic-writing authors of the Church of the East; his works encompass linguistics, history, church law, and theology. An apology for East Syriac Christianity, *The Conference* (al-Magalis), took the form of a letter concerning his discussions with the vizier Abu l-Qasim al-Hunain b. al-Magribi in July 1026 in Nisibis. Another work dealt with the *Evidence of the Truth of Faith*. Also presented in the form of a letter was the treatise *On the Merit of Abstinence*, in which he defended celibacy. Elias's *Book of the Removal of Care* cited a series of ancient authors but also the Arabic philosopher al-Kindi; the earliest manuscript of this book dates to 1357. His *Book on the Right of Inheritance* is preserved in an Arabic translation. Among his secular academic works, of greatest significance are an Arabic–Syriac glossary and a grammar of the Syriac language, published in Rome in 1636 under the title *Thesaurus Arabico-Syro-Latinus*. His brother, the physician Abu Said, authored a medical textbook for students and a work on the healing of diseases of the eye. Elias of Nisibis, who always specifies his sources, also uses a *Chronicle of the Catholicoi*, which is unfortunately lost. He quotes it in the context of the death of Catholicos Saliba Zhaka (+728). Elias is one of the first East Syriac historians and counts the years according to the Muslim calendar, i.e. after the Hedschra. But he adds also the dates of the Seleucid era. It is remarkable that he tries to synchronize the dates of the catholicoi with those of the caliphs. Although Elias gives an account of world history his chronicle offers *de facto* the oldest chronology of the catholicoi, because the list in the manuscript of the Vatican Library which follows the work of Elias Damascenus, who lived in the ninth century, was added in the thirteenth century (Cod. Arab. 157, Fol. 82r). Therefore the oldest lists are provided by Mari b. Sulaiman and Salomon of Basra, as well as by the work of Barhebraeus. All modern lists like E. Tisserant and J.-M. Fiey are dependent on Elias of Nisibis, the *Chronicle of Seert*, Mari b. Sulaiman, Salomon of Basra, and the anonymous list in the Vatican manuscript.

The student of Elias bar Shinaya, Ibn Butlan (called al-Muhtar Yuwanis), worked as a doctor and philosopher in Baghdad. After a trip to Egypt and Constantinople, he was a witness to the schism between the churches of Rome and Constantinople in 1054. Besides his satirical novel *Banquet of the Physicians*, the descriptions of his travels to the cities of Aleppo, Antioch, and Laodicea are of special significance. His almanac of health was translated into German as early as the sixteenth century.

Distantly related to the historical works is the historical part of the theological encyclopedia *Book of the Tower* (Kitab al-Majdal) of Mari b. Suleiman († *c*.1160), which contains the biographies of the catholicoi of the East up to Abdisho II. The work, which was based on lost chronicles from the seventh and eighth centuries and drew on the *Chronicle of Seert*, thus belongs among the most important sources for the history of the Church of the East and its relationship with shahs and caliphs. Around 1350, modeling his work on this example, Amr b. Matta wrote an encyclopedia of the same name, which was subsequently copied in large part by the only slightly younger Saliba b. Yuhanna. The work is preserved in an autograph copy (Cod. Vat. Ar. 110). This represents the most extensive presentation of the relationship between Islam and Christianity at this time.

The Church of the East also strove to assemble the sources of religious and secular law. The *Synodicon Orientale* (*Sunhados*) developed gradually out of the church orders and canons of the synods. As early as the fifth century, Catholicos Mar Aba I authored a book on the laws of inheritance. The *Canons of Rewardashir* (seventh century) were translated from Persian, and the legal code of Catholicos Timotheos I, written in 804/5, became well-known. Presumably, the *Synodicon Orientale* dates back to this catholicos, as well.

Among the most prolific of theologians and authors of the Church of the East in the eleventh century was Abdallah b. Taiyib († 1043). He was a philosopher, monk, priest, and jurist, who studied medicine in Baghdad and worked as secretary to the catholicoi John VI (1012–16) and Elias I (1028–49). Ibn at-Taiyib disagreed with the writings of Aristotle on logic and metaphysics and commented on the *Isagoge* of Porphyry. He also produced commentaries on the writings of Hippocrates and Galen on the natural sciences. He concerned himself with improving education for the people and the clergy and founded a few schools, in which he lectured on his works. A twelfth-century manuscript of his commentary on the entire Bible survives. According to the Syriac tradition of the "catholic letters," he wrote commentaries on only James, 1 Peter, and 1 John. His essay *Paradise of Christendom* is a commentary on all possible theological questions; a manuscript from Diyarbakir dates to 1332. For his commentary on the Psalms (*The Blossoming Garden*) he translated the Psalms from Syriac into Arabic. His *Commentary on the Four Gospels* was completed in 1018; the oldest manuscript comes from the eleventh century. The work itself is preserved in numerous manuscripts. He translated the famous *Diatesseron* of Tatian from Syriac into Arabic. In the

Treatise on the Trinity Ibn at-Taiyib defended Christian dogma. The collection *The Law of Christendom*, in which he systematically organized earlier sources, belongs among his most important canonical writings. The work includes a series of canons of various synods, beginning with the Council of Nicaea and the canons of Chalcedon and continuing up to the collections of Timotheos I and the catholicoi of his time. It presents a brief summary of the East Syriac synodicon with a special section on the *Regulations of the Fathers for Worldly Affairs*. East Syriac church law was systematically summarized in this compilation; it even served as an example for the Coptic church law collections. Separate chapters dealt with engagements and marriage, rights of inheritance, guardianship, debts, partnerships, taxes, and deeds, but also questions about hospitals and prisons.

Of the East Syriac authors of the thirteenth century, Salomon of Lake Van in Armenia, who became bishop of Basra in 1222, is particularly worthy of note. His *Book of the Bee* is one of the few East Syriac universal histories, from creation to the last things. In this work, the conveyance of the bones of the apostle Thomas to Edessa after his martyrdom is reported, while others assert that he was buried in "Mahluph" in India.

One of the most learned East Syriac writers of the time was John b. Zobi (late twelfth or early thirteenth century), a monk from the monastery at Beth Qoqa in Adiabene. Today only a few of his writings – commentaries on baptism and the eucharist and assorted grammatical and philosophical works – have been edited.

Missionary activity in Central Asia

Literary and archeological sources testify to the early expansion of the Church of the East into Central Asia. The 549 *vita* of Mar Aba mentions that he consecrated a bishop for Turkestan. In Djambulin (Kazakstan) a clay jar from the fifth or sixth century bearing a Syriac inscription was found. Around the mid-ninth century, Samarkand on the Silk Road was one of the "exterior metropolitanates." About 35 kilometers from Samarkand in the modern-day region of Urghut some 25 Syriac rock inscriptions were discovered. In Pendjikent (Tajikistan) a clay fragment with the first two psalms in the Peschitta version from the seventh or eighth century was found; orthographic errors indicate that the writer was Sogdian. In the tenth century the Arab historian Ibn Haukal referred to an East Syriac monastery in Sogdia. In Kirgistan an eleventh- or twelfth-century inscription on a tile was found, and in the village of Aq-Beshim an eighth-century Christian church was unearthed in 1954. Also noteworthy are coins minted by Christian rulers which bear the "Nestorian cross" and which are preserved today at the Hermitage in St Petersburg.

In the ninth century East Syriac Christianity reached the south of Lake Balkash. In the eleventh century, initially as a consequence of the religious persecutions in Iraq and Persia, the Apostolic Church of the East gradually expanded into Central Asia. In addition to Jewish and Zoroastrian groups, both West and East Syriac Christians traveled there. In 1897, in the vicinity of Perm a paten with a Syriac inscription, resembling the codex Rabbula of 586, was found. A silver bowl from the fifth or sixth century displayed in three scenes the crucifixion, burial, and resurrection of Jesus; beneath these can be seen Daniel in the lions' den and the denial of Peter. The Syriac inscriptions are written in Estrangelo.

With the shift farther east, competence in Syriac declined and the change to Turko-Tartaric began. In Bulayiq in the oasis of Turfan, where Christianity constituted a minority, an East Syriac monastery has been discovered. Some 350 fragments of a Sogdian *vita* of Bar Shabba, the first bishop of Merv, were found there. A Sogdian translation of the *Antirrheticus* of Evagrius Ponticus also belonged to the library of the church. Only a small sample of the monastery's 400 to 500 Syriac texts have been published to date. Bilingual Syriac–Sogdian texts, as well as about a dozen Turkish writings, have also been uncovered. The martyrdom of St George is patterned on earlier Syriac examples. The "Magi fragment" discusses the visit of the Magi to Bethlehem. A topic of the Bar Sabba fragments is the resurrection of the body. The Sogdian Christian and Turkish Christian texts are not original works but rather translations from Syriac, and in this way, the mother church remains present in the diaspora. Although Syriac continued to be the language of the church there, vernacular psalm fragments and lectionaries indicate that Sogdian was used in the liturgy. This corresponds to the politics of the catholicos, who desired maintenance of the vernacular. We know nothing, however, of a metropolitan entrusted with the care of the monastery. The church in Central Asia was loosely structured; for reasons of distance, regular participation in the synods of the Church of the East was not possible.

Beginning with the Uighurs in the eighth century, the oases, which had their center at Chotscho (Kao-chang), became progressively more Turkish. In this Uighur realm, East Syriac Christians, as

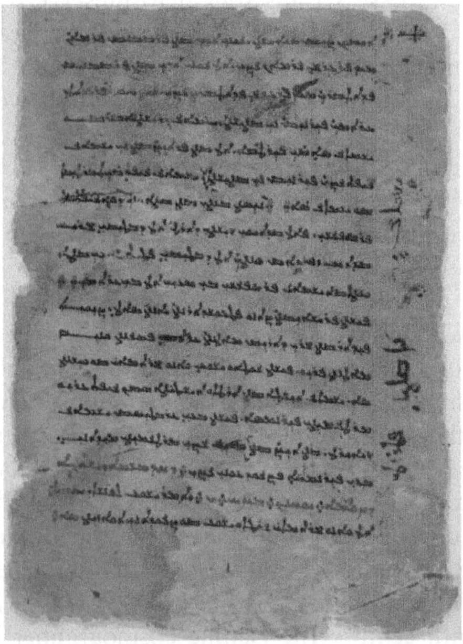

Figure 2.7 Front of a page from an East Syriac lectionary (Luke 16) from the Sogdian Turfan Psalter found in Bulayiq, north of the Turfan oasis (ninth/tenth century). Photo: courtesy of Berlin-Brandenburgische Akademie der Wissenschaften (Turfan-project).

well as Manichaeans and Buddhists, had established themselves. A church erected around 900 and decorated with frescos is found there. Portrayed in the fresco is a Sogdian priest with a chalice in one hand standing before two Turks and a Chinese woman. Likewise, Christian texts, among them a large number of apocryphal writings, reached Central Asia through Manichaeism. In the ninth and tenth centuries there was also an East Syriac monastery in Talas. In 1265 the metropolitan left the city of Hami (Komul) for the consecration of the catholicos Dinkha. Discoveries relating to Christianity there originated in the period from the ninth to fourteenth centuries and show that Christianity clearly was part of the Uighur kingdom of Chotscho. The literary remains are written in Sogdian and old Turkish.

The coexistence of different religions fostered syncretism; there are texts, for instance, in which Jesus is portrayed as Buddha; one fragment states that after his crucifixion, Jesus entered nirvana.

Nevertheless, the East Syrians sought to preserve the "purity" of their faith; for "world," they more often used the Greek loan word "cosmos" than the Indian "samsara" favored by the Manichees. In Turkish texts, Buddhist and Christian expressions were often used together.

From the victory of the Seljuks at the battle of Manzikert (1071) to the Mongol invasion, the political influence of the Christians in the Orient decreased in favor of that of Islam; this can be seen in the way use of the Syriac language among Syriac Christians was gradually reduced to only the liturgy and theological literature. As a minority, the Christians had to adapt to the will of the majority; this is reflected in oracular texts and a Turkish wedding blessing, which recall Buddhism and other neighboring religions. Nevertheless, the influence of other cultures on Christianity was less here than it was in China. The Muslim philosopher al-Biruni described the celebration of the "Rose Festival" among the Christians of Choresmia as a commemoration of Mary bringing a rose to the mother of John the Baptist. He further indicates that the majority of the people in Syria, Iraq, and Chorassan belong to *Nasturiyun* (Arab. "Nestorians"). In the thirteenth century the Islamic cosmographer Kaswini portrayed the Turkish people of Ghozz as Christian.

The Jacobite historian Grigorius Abu l-Faraj (Barhebraeus, ibn al-Ibri † 1286) reported in his *Church History* that East Syriac missionaries proselytized the Mongol tribe of the Keraits after one of their chiefs was rescued by an appearance of St Sergius and accepted Christianity. He requested that Abdisho, the East Syriac bishop of Merv, send him priests to baptize the people. Around 1012 the metropolitan wrote to Catholicos John VI that the khan of the Turkish Keraits had been surprised by a snowstorm and had feared for his life. He experienced a vision, in which he saw St Sergius, who promised he would be rescued if he allowed himself to be baptized. Two hundred thousand Turkish Keraits were baptized, and the bishop requested that the catholicos send priests and deacons. In questions of liturgy, the Church of the East proved willing to adapt to local usages. For example, it is known that the Mongols especially prized mare's milk. At the beginning of the eleventh century the first Christian prince of the Keraits provided his successors with an example by keeping a special mare, whose milk he placed before the cross and Gospel book, spoke prayers over, blessed with the cross, and then drank. Later the East Syriac priests were also present at the spring festival, when the Mongols brought the mares together, blessed them, and sprinkled the earth with the koumiss

Figure 2.8 Gravestone from Kirgistan (thirteenth/fourteenth century). Photo: courtesy of Ulrike Baum, Klagenfurt.

(mare's milk). Some khans of the Keraits adopted Christian names. In the fourteenth century the Persian historian Raschid ad-Din also referred to the spread of Christianity among the Keraits.

Christianity also gained acceptance among the Kitan in northern China, who moved west in the twelfth century to make way for the Kin people and founded the Karakitai kingdom, which was partially Christian. The Naiman, north of the Keraits, were also won for Christianity. The Turkish-Tartar peoples were the chief supporters of the second wave of missionary activity at the turn of the millennium.

Among the most significant memorials of Central Asian East Syriac Christianity are the surviving gravestones. In Kazakstan many of these, with Syriac and Turkish inscriptions, have been preserved. In 1886 in Semirjetschie (Semiryechensk), south of Lake Balkash near Pischpek and Tokmak in northern Kirgistan, two East Syriac cemeteries were found in the villages of Burana and Karadzigac with 568 gravestones from the mid-ninth to mid-fourteenth centuries, where over 3,000 people had been buried. Among them were also Indians and Chinese. Some of the corpses had been brought there from distant places, indicating the international contacts of the Turks. The Russian historian Daniel Chwolson published the inscriptions, which show that the Syriac language had been used there. In the vicinity of the village of Pokrovka on the south bank of the Issyk Kul Sea and in Amalyk (Mazar), the residence of the khan of Tschagatai, there were other East Syriac cemeteries. Amalyk and Navakat near Pischpek were the seats of East Syriac metropolitans. Only 15 percent of the inscriptions were in Turkish, the rest in Syriac, and they indicated that between 1337 and 1339 many Christians died of the plague. Relatives of the khans were also buried there. Near the town of Ak-Besim a church from the eighth or ninth century was found, which in the eleventh century was turned into a mosque.

Among the Onguts in Hoangho-Bogen in China the Christians used Turkish exclusively, though they wrote it with Syriac letters. This also makes clear that knowledge of Syriac declined the farther east one traveled; many gravestone inscriptions contain grammatical errors. In Olon-Süme, the center of Ongut territory, a church surrounded by a great number of such inscriptions from the Mongol period was found. Many amulets showing Christian motifs with Buddhist and shamanistic elements were discovered nearby.

In southern China gravestones inscribed with the Syriac and Uighur scripts were found. While it had been believed in the nineteenth century that Uighur writing had developed out of the East Syriac script, today it is known that it was further developed out of the Sogdian. However, East Syriac vertical script influenced the writing customs of the Manchurians. Syriac was carried to China as an ecclesiastical language and left its mark on Uighur. Out of the Uighur alphabet the Mongol was subsequently developed. In Zayton the East Syriac cemetery lay to the north of the city. Other Christians, such as Armenians, were also buried in the cemeteries.

Catholicos Elias III (1176–90) founded the metropolitan seat of Kashkar near the Gur-Khanen on the Silk Road, where there had already been a bishop since the eighth century. In the ninth century there was also a Christian church east of Kashkar on the southern route of the Silk Road in Khotan. In addition, East Syriac crosses with Sogdian inscriptions were found in Ladakh.

Besides the Keraits and Onguts the people of Merkiten on Lake Baikal also converted to Christianity. Likewise finds from the tenth to thirteenth centuries prove that the Tunguzic Kitan or Kitai in Manchuria converted in part to the Church of the East. Over time, they spread as far as Mongolia. Burial crosses were also found in the region of Liaoyang. In the mid-twelfth century in the oasis of Khotan on the southern fork of the Silk Road a Christian king governed. In the thirteenth century the Christian prince Najan (Naiyen), who was mentioned by Marco Polo, reigned, then rebelled against Kublai and was defeated and murdered in 1287. The Kitai had ruled in Peking until 1125, then migrated west, where the Karakitai founded a new kingdom following the collapse of their kingdom in China. In 1141 their Gur-Khan (ruler of the people), Khan Yeh-lü Ta-shih († 1142), defeated the Muslims of Choresmien under the leadership of their sultan Sanjar at a great battle on the Aral Sea. The Gur-Khan may have been Buddhist, but East Syriac Christians fought in his army.

The severe defeat of the Muslims in 1141 was known even in Europe. Around 1144/5 the European historian Otto of Freising heard in Italy of a Syriac bishop, the "priest-king John" who had conquered the Muslims in Asia and was ready to advance to the Holy Land. The rumors of the existence of Christian khans among the Mongols and the victory over the Seljuk sultan Sanjar may have grown into the myth of the Christian king behind Islam, which for many centuries inspired ever renewed hope in Europe that alliance with Christian rulers in Asia would enable the warding off of the Islamic threat. In the first place, European knowledge in this area remained very vague; around 1220 they identified the Mongols under Genghis Khan with the priest-king. Only with increased knowledge did they understand that the great khan was not prepared to accede to the wishes of European Christians for a coalition and that the Mongols were not themselves Christian, though the Church of the East was, as a rule, tolerated in their realm. When Marco Polo found the Christian Onguts, he saw in their king the priest-king John (Prester John).

The number of metropolitan seats increased from nineteen in 820 to twenty-five in the fourteenth century; the number of bishoprics fell from 105 in 820 to 96 in the year 1000, then increased to about 200 by the fourteenth century. A survey of the extent of the Apostolic Church around 1054 shows that the Church in the West was weakened by the split between the patriarchates of Rome and Constantinople, while the Church of the East, despite its minority status, expanded. The seat of the catholicos was as before in Baghdad. There were twenty metropolitan sees of the Church of the East:

1 Ctesiphon (Iraq)
2 Gondeshapur (Iran)
3 Nisibis (Iraq)
4 Teredon (Iraq)
5 Mosul (Iraq)

6 Adiabene (Arbela, Iraq)
7 Grarmai
8 Halwan (Iran)
9 Rewardashir in Fars (Iran)
10 Merv in Chorassan (Turkmenistan)
11 Tabriz in Atropatene (Iran)
12 Herat in Segestan (Afghanistan)
13 Haran (Iraq)
14 Ray (Iran)
15 Dailam (Iran)
16 India
17 Xian/Changan (China)
18 Samarkand in Turkestan (Uzbekistan)
19 Damascus
20 Jerusalem

There were bishoprics in Cyprus, Mopsuestia, Melitene, Manbij, Otrar (Kzyl-Orda) on Syr-Darja, Xian, Kalah (Malakka), Mylapore near Madras, Cranganore, Kottayam, Quilon, and on the island of Kuria Muria south of Arabia. The Tangut, Ongut, Naiman, Kerait, and Makrit peoples converted to the Church of the East. "Persian" Christians lived in large sections of China and Manchuria. The church certainly lost many bishoprics in Mesopotamia, Syria, and Iran through the Arab conquest. In 1142 the catholicos Abdisho III and the Jacobite (Syrian Orthodox) Maphrian Dionysius reached a reconciliation of Syriac Christians, which lessened the internal discord of the Church of the East. In Arabia and Yemen Christianity was largely extinguished, but the island of Sokotra continued to have East Syriac bishops until 1280 and eventually belonged to the church on the Malabar coast. The missionary activity among the Mongols opened new perspectives for the church. It encountered "a constellation, which has never been repeated: with the conversion of the Mongols to Roman Christianity and a union with the Nestorians – which, for political reasons, many were prepared to accept – it could have become the universal religion of Asia" (von den Brincken).

Among the peoples of the Central Asian steppes, Christianity became the dominant culture with far-reaching consequences. In Europe knowledge of these events was as good as nothing since there were hardly any relations between Rome and Byzantium on the one side and between Rome and the Oriental churches on the other. Only occasionally, while on pilgrimage to Jerusalem, did Westerners encounter members of the Church of the East.

The image of the Apostolic Church of the East in thirteenth-century Europe

In Europe the East Syrians were first mentioned in 1110 by Petrus Alphonsi in his dialogue between a Jew and a Christian, in which Muhammad and his alleged contact with an East Syriac monk were discussed. However, his name was not given until 1141 when Peter of Cluny, in a letter to Bernard of Clairvaux about Muhammad and his "Nestorian" teacher, mentioned Sergius Bahira. Thus the Bahira legend was known in Europe as well. Bahira, who was expelled from the church, was sent by Satan to Arabia, where, as Muhammad's teacher, he became in a way responsible for the advent of Islam.

At the beginning of the crusades, hardly any East Syriac Christians were known to the crusaders; they dealt primarily with Melkites (Orthodox), Maronites, Jacobites (Syrian Orthodox), and Copts. In the crusader states there were few East Syriac Christians. In Jerusalem there were a few East Syriac merchants and perhaps also a bishop; there was a congregation in Edessa. An East Syriac monastery in the vicinity of Jericho was established in the fifth century but was abandoned in the early ninth century. Until the conquest of Jerusalem by Saladin (1187), the Church of the East was hardly ever mentioned by European authors, although beginning in 1098 there must have been contact between East Syriac Christians and crusaders, especially in the region around Antioch. The relationship of the crusaders to the "Nestorians" was thus marked above all by ignorance and misunderstanding.

In 1055 the Seljuk leader Togoril Bey seized power in Baghdad; in 1071 the Seljuks defeated the Byzantines in the battle of Manzikert. They conquered Damascus and occupied inner Asia Minor. During a conflict of Catholicos Abraham III with the Orthodox patriarch of Alexandria, the head of the Church of the East wrote to the grand vizier that "we Nestorians are the friends of the Arabs and pray for their victory. Far be it from you to view the Nestorians, who have no other king than that of the Arabs, in the same light as the Greeks, whose king refuses to cease making war against the Arabs." He won the debate not only through his arguments, however, but also through the payment of 2,000 gold pieces.

The Abbasid caliphate stood until the conquest of Baghdad by the Mongols (1258), but since the tenth century, the Buyids and Seljuks had been the de facto rulers. During this phase, relations between Christianity and Islam deteriorated. The Persian Shiite

Buyid dynasty – like the Fatimids in Egypt – adopted a more tolerant attitude toward the Christians than the Sunni Seljuks. In 1055
the transfer of power from the Buyids to the Seljuks resulted in the
first destruction of Christian churches and monasteries. However,
the expansion of Seljuk rule created new missionary opportunities
for the Church of the East. In 1122 a purported Indian archbishop,
John, attracted attention in Rome when he appeared before Pope
Calixtus II and claimed that he lived in Hulna in India, the burial
site of the apostle Thomas, whose corpse on his death day was
sat upon a throne and distributed communion. The pope did not
believe him. Around 1126 the French abbot Odo of Rheims
noted that the Indian archbishop had also been in Byzantium. To
this day it remains unclear if the alleged archbishop was truly a
representative of the Church of the East. All the same, the archbishop is always associated with the grave of the apostle Thomas.
This report may also have been a reason for the adoption of the
legend of the priest-king John. Around 1145 Otto of Freising portrayed the priest-king as a "Nestorian" and possible redeemer, who
eventually became the great hope of Christendom threatened by
Islam.

Gradually people seem to have come to believe that Prester John
was a real person, as Pope Alexander III wrote him a letter in 1177
stating that he had heard the priest-king wished to be instructed in
Catholic doctrine; to this end, he sent his personal physician to
John. However, he had to recognize the supremacy of the pope. We
do not know if a letter from the Church of the East preceded the
pope's letter, nor is anything known of a reply to the letter. It is also
assumed that it was possibly addressed to the Christian ruler of
Ethiopia, of whom Europeans likewise had heard.

The chronicler Richard of San Germano reported in 1223 that a
"Nestorian" king, popularly called Prester John, had set out from
India carrying with him the relics of the apostle Thomas. He was
robbed and murdered in Russia. In this case, the Thomas myth is
clearly linked to the Church of the East.

In 1217 during the campaign of the crusaders against Damiette,
Jacques de Vitry († 1240), the bishop of Akko, arrived at the mouth
of the Nile together with East Syriac Christians who had no bishop
of their own. In his letter of 1217 he portrayed the inhabitants of
the kingdom of the priest-king John as "Nestorian," though they
were, in fact, Jacobites. At that time he had no knowledge of East
Syriac ("Nestorian") rulers in the East. During his stay in Damiette,
Jacques de Vitry had the opportunity to improve his understanding.

In 1220/1 outside of Damiette he wrote in his *Historia Orientalis* that the "Nestorians" were named after the arch-heretic Nestorius, who had infected the lands of the priest John between the Saracens and India with his teachings. Combined with the Jacobites, their numbers would have exceeded the Latin and Orthodox Christians. Although they defended themselves against Islam, they denied that Mary was the Mother of God and claimed that Christ existed in two persons. They consecrated leavened bread and used the "Chaldean" (Syriac) language. He sensed for the first time how great the influence of the East Syriac church must have been.

In his seventh letter, Jacques de Vitry wrote to the pope in 1221 and reported on the *Relatio de Davide rege*, translated from Arabic, which recounted the myth of David, the great-grandson of the priest-king John. Jacques identified the Christians under King David with the adherents of the Church of the East. David invaded Choresmien, captured Kashkar, Samarkand, and Bukhara, and demanded the submission of the caliph. He stood just five days' march from Baghdad. The caliph requested mediation from the catholicos "Iaphelech" (Jaffeleth) and the "Patriarch of the Indians." Jacques clearly had some vague knowledge of the advance of the Mongols under Genghis Khan, who in 1221 had conquered the Muslim rulers in Central Asia and the Caucasus. His contemporary Oliver of Cologne visited the East Syriac church in Antioch and expressed his views thereof cautiously, for only God knew whether their doctrine was truly heretical. His judgment contrasted with that of most Latin Christians. Cardinal Pelagius reported the matter to Pope Honorius III, who authored an encyclical which brought these concerns to the attention of the whole of Europe. At the same time, Oliver of Cologne brought word of a prophecy popular in East Syriac circles that the Christian king of the Nubians would destroy Mecca. In the years 1217 to 1220, through the reports of Jacques de Vitry and Oliver of Cologne, the West was made familiar with the East Syriac church, of which they had previously had almost no knowledge. It was thus linked with the advances of the Mongols toward the West.

3

THE AGE OF THE MONGOLS

Thirteenth and fourteenth centuries

Wilhelm Baum

The Church of the East and the Mongols

The Mongol empire was founded at the end of the twelfth century by Genghis Khan. He first allied himself with the Christian prince of the Keraits, Togoril, who did not lead a particularly Christian life but who very probably became the original model for the priest-king John. Togoril first had to prove himself against his uncle Gur-Khan; with help from the Kin people of Peking he defeated the Tartars and as a reward received the title "Wang-Khan" or "Ong-Khan" from the Chinese court; with this title, he entered history. Genghis Khan's father, Jesügei, also helped Togoril achieve victory over his uncle. However, disagreement later developed between Genghis Khan and Togoril, and Togoril was murdered in 1203 while trying to escape. Over several generations, the family of the great Mongol khan intermarried with the family of the "Gur-khans." From the Persian historians Juvaini and Raschid ad-Din, we have precise information about these genealogical connections. Genghis Khan wed Togoril's daughter Ibaqa-Beki, his eldest son Jochi her sister Bek-Tumish, and his son Tolui († 1231) her sister Sorqaqtani-Beki. The latter became mother of the great khans Mongke and Kublai, as well as the Il-Khan Hulagu, who were fond of the Church of the East because of their mother, though they did not themselves convert to christendom.

After Genghis Khan, first his son Ogdai († 1241) came to power, followed by Ogdai's son Kuyuk († 1248), of whom it was said he was a Christian. After the death of her husband, Sorqaqtani-Beki became the head of the line of the house of Tolui, and in 1250 she obtained for her son Mongke the position of great khan; eighty years after her death, East Syrians still venerated her picture in the church at Kanchow. The great khan Mongke appointed the East

84

Syriac Keraiten Christian Bolghai as chancellor. Already at the beginning of the thirteenth century the Christian Chinkai – a Kerait or Ongut – had served as Mongolian chancellor and governor of the colony in the Altai mountains; in northern China, for all practical purposes, he controlled the government. Following the conquest of the Keraits, the Christian Qadaq became commander of the army and under Kuyuk eventually even "Atabek" (administrator of the empire).

After seizing power the great khan Mongke sent his brother Hulagu on a campaign against the Muslims in Mesopotamia. In 1258 Hulagu captured Baghdad and became founder of the empire of the Il-Khans in Persia. In accordance with Mongol custom, he married Doquz-Khatun, one of his father's wives, who was a daughter of Itiko, the younger son of Togoril. Doquz-Khatun became a special patron of East Syriac Christianity and even had her children baptized. The Persian historian Rashid ad-Din reported that Hulagu undertook nothing without first asking her advice, and her piety was particularly emphasized by Armenian historians. Her confidant was the Armenian monk Vartan, whom she told that she hoped Christianity would increase with each passing day. East Syriac Christians, who had for centuries been members of a minority, were now pushed to the center of political power. Makika II (1257–65) maintained the caliphal palace in Baghdad as his residence. As Kirakos of Ganzag reported, East Syrians, Jacobites, and Armenians saw the Mongols as avengers of oppressed Christianity; they were pleased by the fall of the capital of Islam.

Acting on the counsel of Doquz-Khatun, Hulagu directed a campaign against Syria and conquered Nisibis, Harran, and Edessa, and among the advancing Mongol troops were many adherents of the Church of the East. During the capture of Aleppo, he was greeted by the historian Grigorius Abu l-Faraj (Barhebraeus). In March 1260 Kitbuqa, a Naiman who belonged to the Church of the East and who had earlier taken part in the seizure of Baghdad, marched on Damascus. The Arab historian Maqrizi noted that the Christians celebrated the conquest of the city as the victory of the cross over Islam. However, on September 3, 1260 the Mongol troops were defeated by the Egyptian Mamluks at Ain-Galut. With this the expansion of the Mongols in the Orient came to an end. After the reconquest of Syria by the Mamluks, the Christians had to pay a high price for their alliance with the Mongols. For their part, the Mongols abandoned their plans for a worldwide empire. The khans of the Golden Horde favored Islam and Orthodoxy, while the

Il-Khans had striven for decades to enter an alliance with the pope and Western Christianity against Islam. These political arrangements also influenced the relationship of the Church of the East to the Church of the West. A delegation of the Il-Khan Abaqa appeared at the Second Council of Lyon in 1274, indicating the good relations of the khan family with the Christians.

In the meantime, in China Kublai Khan (1260–94) made Taitu (Khanbaliq, Peking), established instead of Karakorum, the new residence of the great khans. After the death of Mongke († 1259), he assumed power – in a not entirely legal fashion – as great khan. Presumably his brother, Khan Arikboge, who had converted to Christianity and was supported by the Christian chancellor Bolghai, opposed Kublai's seizure of power. Beginning in 1262, more and more East Syriac Christians appear in Chinese documents. In 1248 Peking became an East Syriac bishopric.

The Christian Ongut people, whom the Chinese called the "white Tartars" (*Pai-Tata*) inhabited present-day Sui-yuan in northern China, north of the Yellow River on the passes from Mongolia to China. Emperor Tai-Tsung (1123–36) authorized their settlement there. Through their participation in Genghis Khan's battles against the Naiman, the Onguts became allies of the Mongols. The royal dynasty in Kosang (Olon-sume, north of the modern city of Kuei-hua) cultivated contact with the family of the great khan. The Christian Ongut king Gorguz (George, † 1298) married a granddaughter of Kublai. In the middle of the year 1260 Gorguz also became acquainted with the merchants Nicolo and Marco Polo, whom the great khan eventually sent to the pope with the request to send scholars to China. In southern China, in Hang-chou and Yang-chou, East Syriac churches were also built. At the Vatican there is a 1298 Gospel from Diyarbakir (Cod. Vat. Syr. 662), which according to Kolophon was created for Sara-Araol (Chin. Ye-li-wan), sister of the Ongut prince Gorguz. Evidently the princess was able to read the Gospel in Syriac. John (Chin. Chu-an, † c.1314), Gorguz's son, converted to the Church of the East.

Also among the East Syriac Christians who pursued their careers at the court of the great khan Kublai was the physician Isa (Ai-hsieh, Ishohua, † 1308), whom Rashid ad-Din called "Isa Tarsa Kelemechi," Isa the Christian and translator. Kublai appointed him head of the office of astronomy and medicine in 1263, and in 1284 sent him to Il-Khan Argun in Baghdad, which he reached in 1285. Following a visit to Rome – he was perhaps the first Chinese to make such a visit – he returned to his homeland. In 1291 he became commissioner of the office of Christian affairs, which had been established in 1289, and his contributions were described in the *Yuan-Shih* (chapter 134). It was said that he understood all the languages of the West. Isa died highly regarded as the "Prince of Fulin" and left behind five sons. A tombstone inscription was preserved in the work "Hsueh lou chi." After his death his son Yeh-li-ya (Elias) took over the position of commissioner for Christian affairs.

The Church of the East could operate freely throughout China. Around 1275 an East Syriac archdiocese was set up in Peking, over which the metropolitan Mar George presided. Kublai also sent envoys, Marco Polo's father and uncle, to the pope in order to obtain scholars and relics from Palestine for Peking. The Church of the East enjoyed freedom from taxes and a variety of other privileges. Through the office of the commissioner for Christian affairs, even lists of functionaries' salaries were preserved. In the fourteenth century, however, the khans withdrew their favor from the Church of the East. In 1311 the Mongol Yuan Emperor Buyantu (1311–20) issued a decree ordering that certain newly founded Christian monasteries be turned into Buddhist shrines. In the substantial literature of Chinese government officials, some may be recognized by their Christian names as members of the "Yeh-li-ko-wen," as Christians were called in China.

For some forty years the East Syriac Christians in Mesopotamia lived under Mongol rule. The Armenians also succeeded in establishing good contacts with the Mongols. In late 1247 the Armenian general Sempad traveled to see the great khan and offer him submission in the name of King Hethums I. At first the Europeans found it difficult to categorize the "Mongol storm" politically. On the one hand, in 1220 the Mongols destroyed Samarkand and Bukhara with particular ferocity; churches and Christian congregations were annihilated; during the destruction of the Christian metropolitan seat of Merw in 1221 over a million people are thought to have been killed. However, on the other hand, as undisputed conquerors, the Mongols tolerated Christianity in their newly won territories. Additionally, the undisturbed traffic over the Silk Road during the period of Mongol rule made contact between the catholicos of the Church of the East and the missionary regions of Central Asia easier. Merchants and missionaries disseminated Christianity. A series of East Syriac metropolitanates stood along the Silk Road. There is talk of metropolitans in Sin (China), Katai, and Khanbaliq (Peking); however, the jurisdictional relationships between them was not clear.

At first there were six ecclesiastical provinces in the Church of the East. According to the synodical resolutions of the fifth and sixth centuries, the metropolitans were obligated to appear at synods called by the catholicos every two and later every four years. Only the "metropolitans of the outer lands" were explicitly excused from this duty, for which was substituted a requirement that they submit a written report to the catholicos every six years. In the second half of the seventh century there were two metropolitans in East Asia with over twenty bishops each. A 1315 edict mentioned seventy-two dioceses in the Yuan empire of the Mongols in China! The Far Eastern metropolitan seats were – especially among the nomads – no longer tied to specific cities, such as Amalyk, Samarkand, Kashkar, Navekath, Xian, and Khanbaliq. We hear of metropolitans in "Turkestan," among the "Onguts," or in the region of "Tangut." At the death of a metropolitan, due to the tenuous connection with the catholicate, a diocese often had to be jointly administered with a neighboring one, as for instance Samarkand by Turkestan, Kashkar by Navekath, Amalyk by Khanbaliq, or Sin by Tangut. Because of political relationships along the Silk Road, the approval of the catholicos was often difficult to obtain; the catholicos did not feel himself obligated to grant dispensations. Thus the requirement that at least three bishops take part in the consecration of another bishop was not always obeyed. In many cases, a Gospel book, representing Christ himself, was laid in the place of the missing third bishop.

The Church of the East sought to adapt itself to the circumstances in Asia and had greater success than the later missions of the Catholic Church, which always tried to maintain Roman centrality and the Latin liturgy. This "inculturation" of the East Syriac church also led to a corresponding influence of such religions as the shamanism of the Mongols. The prohibition of mixed marriages – particularly among the clergy – which had been decreed as early as the synods of 554 and 585, was no longer strictly enforced, especially among the princely families. The clergy no longer recognized any obligation of celibacy. There were also deacons who had taken minor orders, exorcists, and sacristans. Archdeacons served as vicars general and liturgists. Despite all this, however, the Church of the East – apart from the almost entirely Christianized Turkish peoples – was viewed as a church of foreigners and as a minority. Contributing to this image were above all the facts that, on the one hand, Syriac was maintained as the liturgical language – although knowledge of it decreased the farther east one traveled – and, on the other, that the higher clergy came mostly from the regions of Syria and Persia.

The relationship between the Church of the East and other Christians – Armenians, Georgians, Russians, and scattered Melkites – was good. This is demonstrated, for example, by the fact that they sometimes shared cemeteries. This "ecumenical cooperation" was first disrupted at the end of the thirteenth century, when Latin missionaries attempted to conduct their activities in the territories of the Church of the East and among its members.

The Church of the West discovers the Church of the East

East Syriac Christians fought in the armies of the Mongols. The myth of the Christian priest-king John beyond the lands of Islam was therefore projected to the Mongols. The closer the Mongols came to Europe, however, the more it became apparent they would not enter into an alliance against the Muslims.

Matthew of Paris repeatedly opposed the Mongols; he handed on the 1237 letter of the Dominican prior Philipp: an East Syriac archbishop, Jafelinus (Jaffeleth), under whose jurisdiction India and the realm of the priest John stood, expressed his intention to convert to the Roman church. At the end of July 1237 Pope Gregory IX authorized a delegation to the "archbishop of the Nestorians in the Orient," but the results of this undertaking are unknown. Before 1251 the Frenchman Alberic of Troisfontaines wrote his world chronicle, which ended with the year 1241. He portrayed the Tartars as a hostile power who had killed the priest-king John. He described the Europeans' limited knowledge prior to their first contact with the Mongols and no longer placed any special hope in the Church of the East.

After the first Mongol invasion of Europe, Pope Innocent IV, who had been elected in 1243, energetically supported a clash with them. In 1244 Jerusalem was conquered for a second time by the Muslims. At the First Council of Lyons – to which the Church of the East was also invited – the pope recommended measures against the Mongols and sent the Franciscan John of Piano Carpine to the great khan Kuyuk in Mongolia. Under the influence of his Christian advisors, Chancellor Chinkai and army commander Qadaq, Kuyuk pursued policies friendly to the Christians.

The report of John of Piano Carpine included the first account of East Syriac Christians in Europe. The "Nestorians" were numbered among the peoples subjugated by the Mongols. Thus Carpine described the Uighurs as adherents of the "sect of the Nestorians" (*de secta Nestorianorum*), although the greater part of this people, from whom the Mongols adopted their writing, were Buddhists. Carpine wrote that in front of the tent of the great khan – who, according to courtiers, wanted to convert to Christianity – stood a portable chapel, in which the Christians conducted their worship services. Carpine also observed the Christians at the great khan's court and became acquainted with the chancellor Chinkai, although he neither pursued theological disputations nor showed any particular interest in the members of the Church of the East.

At the same time, Andreas of Longjumeau established contact with the Tartars; however, he first had to return to the Orient and reached the great khan only in 1251. In 1246 the East Syriac Christians in the crusader states received a letter of protection from Pope Innocent IV, in which a bishop of Jerusalem was also mentioned. This represents the first official contact between the Roman papacy and the Church of the East.

Also during this period, Vincent of Beauvais produced his historical encyclopedia. Through the Dominican Simon of St Quentin he was familiar with the remarks of the East Syriac monk Simeon Rabbanata (Chin. Li-pien-a-tai), whom Andreas of Longjumeau had met in Tabriz at the end of 1246. He was the first East Syriac to have contact with European intellectuals. Around 1247 he presented himself to the pope as vicar of the Orient of the East Syriac church. Innocent IV finally permitted Rabbanata through Andreas of Longjumeau to request union with Rome. The bishop of Nisibis sent a creed of the Church of the East to Rome to verify its orthodoxy. The Dominican Andreas learned Rabbanata's life history. He reported that in his youth, following Togoril's murder, he had taken Togoril's niece to the court of Genghis Khan because he was her father confessor. Between 1233 and 1241 the great khan Ogdai had sent him to Azerbaijan as commissioner for Christian affairs. The Armenian historian Kirakos of Ganzag referred to Rabbanata in his historical works, as did Grigorius Abu l-Faraj (Barhebraeus). The West, however, failed to understand this representative of the Church of the East. The Dominicans disparaged him as a magician, a trader, a usurer, and an anti-Catholic heretic who was doomed to hell. In this matter, the fact that Rabbanata considered Frederick II guardian of the Holy Sepulcher probably played a role, as well; Matthew of Paris also knew of his commitment to the emperor. In 1259 Rabbanata died at a great age in Persia.

Establishment of additional direct Western contact with representatives of the Church of the East occurred in 1248 when King Louis
IX of France landed in Cyprus on the way to Palestine. There he
received a legation from the Tartar general Eljigidei, which offered
to cooperate with the Christians. The letter, written in Persian, was
handed over by David and Markos, Christian envoys from Mosul.
After centuries without any such relations, between 1245 and 1255
direct contact between the churches enabled each to increase its
knowledge of the other's world.

The first detailed report of the life and doctrines of the Church of
the East in Central Asia was contained in the travelogue of the
Franciscan William of Rubruk, who, under orders from King Louis
IX of France, journeyed to the great khan. On the Tartar steppe in
present-day southern Russia, William first encountered Sartaq, the
representative of Batu, the lord of the khans of the Golden Horde,
who also recommended him to the great khan. He learned that
contrary to all rumors, Sartaq was not a Christian. Nevertheless, in
1254 Pope Innocent IV congratulated him on his "conversion."
Although the chroniclers Juvaini and Barhebraeus also mentioned
that Sartaq was a Christian, it appears that he was only well dis-
posed toward Christianity. While among the Christian Naiman,
William learned that they were familiar with the myth of Prester
John, who was portrayed as a member of their tribe. Besides
adherents of the Church of the East, however, no-one else knew of
this matter. At the court of the great khan, William became
acquainted with the East Syrians, who worshiped the cross without
the corpus. They were educated, could almost all read, and had a
bishop in the city of Segin (Siking in Shansi). They continued to use
Syriac in the liturgy, though some no longer understood it. Since
bishops only rarely visited the region, often mere children were
ordained priests. On the steppe they had adapted to the Mongol
way of life. Rubruk described the priests, some of whom had mul-
tiple wives, as drunkards and simoniacs. According to his report,
the new great khan, Mongke, had a Christian wife, who had borne
him a daughter. Besides Chancellor Bolghai, an Armenian monk
was another Christian at court. Mongke attended church and also
read the Bible. The representative of Christianity remained united,
although William was repelled by the drinking customs of the East
Syrians. In 1254 he celebrated Easter with the other Christians at
court. In the process, the East Syrians implied they were prepared to
recognize the pope. Except marriage and anointing of the sick, they
accepted all the sacraments. They permitted the remarriage of

priests. At the Mass, they used a horse blanket blessed by the catholicos instead of a consecrated altar. A few priests of the church were in the process of writing a chronicle of world history. On the Sunday before Pentecost, a religious discussion was held at the court of the great khan. Nevertheless, the contact with the hierarchy and theology of the Apostolic Church of the East seems to have been merely superficial. The primary point of conflict between the Catholic Church and the Church of the East, the doctrine of Christ, was never discussed during the trip. According to Rubruk, out of the family of the great khan, Arikboge, Mongke's brother, was particularly inclined toward Christianity.

William's works also contain many misunderstandings, which can be found repeated by Western Christians. For instance, concerning the display of the cross without the corpus: as Timotheos I had written in his apology for the caliph, the empty cross symbolized hope and immortality. It had nothing to do with the prohibition of human images in Islamic art. Frescos with religious scenes could certainly be found in monasteries along the Silk Road. A marble cross discovered in Fang-shan, some 60 kilometers south-west of Peking, bears the inscription: "Look at the cross (Sliba), at the crucified and risen Lord, and hope on him." In 1255 while in Paris during his journey home, William met Roger Bacon, who borrowed Rubruk's descriptions for his "Geography," William's often harsh judgments against the "Nestorians" stem in many cases from ignorance. Nonetheless, his work is one of the chief sources for information about the Church of the East in Central Asia in the thirteenth century.

Marco Polo lived in China from 1271 to 1293, and his report includes some information about the Church of the East. In Mosul Marco Polo referred to the "Nestorians" and the "Jacobites." Like the pope in Rome, the "Jatolic" (catholicos) also sent his intellectuals to India, China, and Baghdad. From Baghdad Marco Polo reported conflicts between Christians and Muslims. He recounted that Chaghatai, the founder of the Central Asian khanate (1227–42), had converted to Christianity, and he mentioned the construction of the Church of John in Samarkand, though only a tenth of its inhabitants belonged to the Church of the East. In the province of Tangut in northern China, especially in the cities of Su-chou and Kann-chou, he encountered Turks who had converted to Christianity. Marco Polo also told the story of Prester John, whose daughter had married Genghis Khan. He referred to the Christian king George – the Ongut prince Gorguz – in the Tenduc province; here it was claimed that the East Syriac Christians were Turks. In addition, he found Christians of the Church of the East in Kashkar, Urumchi (Chichintalas), and on the border with Korea, as well as in Manchuria. In Chen-chiang (Zhenjiang) on the Yangtze Kiang Marco Polo made note of two churches built by Mar Sarkis, the governor of the great khan, in 1278. In this same regard, the *Chronicle of Chenchiang* also reported about the Christians that in 1281 a Mar Sergis (Sarkis) built a monastery as well as six churches. His grandfather had been a doctor in Samarkand and had cured a son of Genghis Khan. In the chronicle, 196 Christian family members and 109 other Christians were mentioned. A 1295 request has been preserved, in which Mar Sarkis sought a tax reduction for the monastery he had endowed, where candles were manufactured. In 1311 the Christian frescos in the monastery church were painted over with Buddhist motifs. In Zaitun (Quanzhou) East Syriac gravestones with bilingual inscriptions in Turkish and Chinese (in Syriac script) were found. In Yangzhou (Yang-chau-fu) on the Great Canal, where Odorico of Pordenone discovered three East Syriac

Figure 3.1 Tombstone of Elizabeth, the wife of the Christian government official Xindu, in Yangzhou (1317). From *Ural-Altaische Jahrbücher* 14 (1976): 172a.

churches, a church was founded in 1317 by a wealthy merchant named Abraham. In 1981 there was found a tombstone inscribed in Chinese and Turkish (the latter in Syriac script), commemorating a woman called Elizabeth, who was the wife of Xindu, a government official known from Chinese literature.

On his return trip through India, Marco Polo came into contact with the Thomas cult on the Malabar coast (Coromandel coast). He visited the alleged grave of Thomas in Mylapore near Madras, which was also venerated by the Muslims. Clearly the church of the apostle's grave was also visited by non-Christians. Marco Polo mentioned peacocks at the hermitage of the apostle, to which the name "Mylapore" (city of peacocks) can apparently be attributed. In Quilon ("Coilum") he encountered Christians as well as Hindus and Jews. As he continued his travels towards Arabia, he visited the island of Socrata, where a Christian archbishop resided. This archbishop did not stand under the jurisdiction of the pope but rather the archbishop in "Baudac" (Baghdad), that is, the catholicos of the Church of the East.

The era of Catholicos Yahballaha III (1281–1317)

Two representatives of the Church of the East in China achieved great renown: Rabban Bar Sauma († 1294) of Khanbaliq (Peking) and Marcus (1245–1317), an Ongut from the present-day city of Toqto (Tung-shen) on the border of Sui-yuan and Shansi. They probably lived at first in the "Monastery of the Cross" in the Fangshan district of western Peking. Their biography, written in Syriac and based on an earlier Persian edition, has been preserved and provides a contrast to Marco Polo's travelogue.

Around 1275/6 the Christians Bar Sauma and Marcus decided to make a pilgrimage to Jerusalem. They traveled first through the land of the Tangut, in the modern province of Kansu, where many East Syriac Christians lived, and eventually through the Gobi Desert to Kashkar, the trading center in far western China. Kashkar was a bishop's seat, but the city had been devastated by a civil war within the family of the khan. Since the direct route to Persia was blocked, they journeyed north to Talas on the Issyk-Kul Sea, where the Ogedai khan Qaidu welcomed them. He sent them on to the empire of the il-khan, where Hulagu's son Abaqa then reigned. In Maragha they met Catholicos Dinkha I (1265–81), who had been elected at Abaqa's request after the death of Makika. They traveled past Arbela to Mosul (Nineveh), visited Nisibis, and viewed the East Syriac monasteries along the Tigris, including the shrine of Mar

Mari in Badreia. In Ctesiphon they stopped at the patriarchal basilica of Kokhe. Since 1268 the catholicos of the East had no longer lived in Baghdad but rather in Oshnou (Azerbaijan) and later in Urmia and Maragha.

Bar Sauma and Marcus were unable to travel to Jerusalem because the city was under the control of the Mamluk sultan Baibar I († 1277). The catholicos had recommended them to the il-khan, who had also given them a letter of introduction, but the war of the khans of the "Golden Horde" and the Mamluks with the il-khan prevented the pilgrimage. The two visitors from China first tried to travel through Armenia and Georgia and reach Palestine by sea, but the catholicos ordered them to return, as he planned to transfer leadership of the Church of the East in China to them. He consecrated Marcus, then some 35 years old, as bishop of Cathay (northern China). As such, he adopted the name Yahballaha. Bar Sauma was named vicar general. The wars in Central Asia made an immediate return impossible, so they passed two years in a

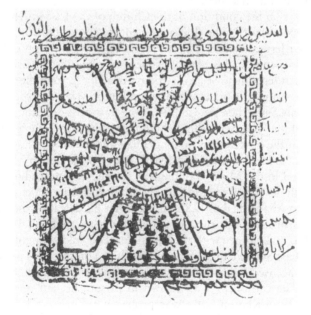

Figure 3.2 Imprint of the seal which the great khan Mongke had given to the Catholicos of the Church of the East (1302/4). From I. Gillman and H.-J. Klimkeit, *Christians in Asia before 1500*, Ann Arbor, MI, 1999, pl. 8.

monastery near Mosul. When Dinkha I died in 1281, the East Syriac bishops elected Yahballaha as the new catholicos of the East because of his understanding of relations with the Mongols. It was a political election, as the new catholicos had little command of Syriac and knew no Arabic at all. In the presence of the metropolitans of Mosul, Arbela, Azerbaijan, Jerusalem, Samarkand, and Tangut, he was consecrated Catholicos Yahballaha III in the Kokhe church on November 21, 1281. He received a seal, which his predecessor had been given by the great khan Mongke. Bishops, priests, and other notables were not to approach the great khan without a letter bearing this seal. It can be seen on a 1302 letter to Pope Boniface VII, as well as one to Benedict XI dated 1304.

From the Chinese imperial annals (Yuan-Shih), under the heading "Barbarian Lands," we learn of the situation of the Church of the East in India and read that in 1282 a delegation from the Christian king of Quilon (Chu-lan) traveled to Peking. The Christian ruler sent gifts, which were interpreted by the Chinese as tribute. One can assume that the Church of the East in Kerala had at the time an established church structure.

A report on the condition of the Church of the East in Jerusalem in the second half of the thirteenth century shows that the metropolitan of Jerusalem had four suffragan bishops, in Aleppo, Persia, Diyarbakir, and Nisibis. At that time, there were four East Syriac churches in Jerusalem: St Jacob (today Armenian), John the Baptist, Transfiguration of Christ, and Assumption of Mary. In the Church of the Holy Sepulcher, the Church of the East possessed the altar to the left of the Holy Sepulcher behind the column. In 1516 a pilgrim noted that the East Syrians no longer had a monastery in Jerusalem. However, a 1546 illuminated Syriac codex with Sunday lessons, now found in the Museo Borgiano in Rome, was, according to its subscription, written for the East Syriac church in Jerusalem.

Il-Khan Abaqa died in 1282, shortly after his defeat by the Mamluks. His brother and successor Taqudar converted to Islam and offered to make peace with the Mamluks. The "old Mongol" party in Iran (East Syriac Christians and Buddhists) opposed his position. Taqudar accused Yahballaha III and Bar Sauma of intervening with Kublai. The catholicos was thrown in prison; he had the khan's mother Qutui-Khatun, who was probably a Christian Keirat, to thank for his survival. In 1284 Taqudar's brother Argun (1284–91) succeeded him as il-khan. He was married to a niece of Doquz-Khatun, who in 1289, to honor Pope Nicholas IV, had one of her sons, the future Il-Khan Oljaitu, baptized with his name. The church of Maragha, which had been destroyed by Argun's predecessor, was rebuilt.

In 1287 Argun wrote to Pope Honorius IV that the great khan Kublai had commissioned him to liberate the "land of the Christians." Argun appointed the Uighur Bar Sauma to make the mission to Europe. Bar Sauma traveled through Constantinople, where he visited Emperor Andronicus II, and in June 1287 he reached Naples. He reported how many Mongols, Turks, and Chinese were Christians and that the children of several rulers had been baptized. Bar Sauma established an alliance between the Europeans and Argun, which sought the liberation of Jerusalem from the Muslims. In Rome the cardinals asked him which apostles had conducted missionary work in his regions, and Bar Sauma answered that Mar Thomas, Mar Addai, and Mar Mari had been there. From Rome he traveled on to Paris, where Philip the Fair received him. In Bordeaux he met King Edward I of England. Then he journeyed back to Rome where, in the meantime, Nicholas IV had been elected pope. The pope allowed him to participate in all the religious ceremonies of Holy Week and personally offered him communion. The sought-after alliance, however, never came to be. In the summer of 1288 he returned to Persia. The il-khan named him court chaplain and sent additional delegations to Europe.

Under Argun's successor Gaichatu (1291–5) relations between the Mongols and the Church of the East remained good. However, Il-Khan Ghazan, Argun's son, helped the Muslims in Iran win a decisive victory over the Christians, whose churches he then had destroyed. Thereafter Christians and Jews had to wear distinctive clothing. Despite his age, Catholicos Yahballaha was imprisoned, hung upside-down, and would certainly have been killed if the Armenian king Hethum II had not rescued him. During the year 1296 Yahballaha was returned to office, although just one year later the patriarchal residence in Maragha was plundered and destroyed by the Muslims. Arbela in Kurdistan became the new center of the Church of the East in Mesopotamia. The Persian historian Rashid ad-Din became minister at the court of Ghazan, who had moved the seat of the government to Tabriz. The il-khan ceased the persecution of the Church of the East and in 1303 visited the rebuilt monastery in Maragha, where the catholicos now lived.

In 1289 the Dominican Ricoldo of Montecroce traveled to the Orient, where he remained for ten years. In his *Liber peregrinationis* (before 1291) and the *Libellus ad nationes orientales* he described his experiences with the East Syriac church. The king of

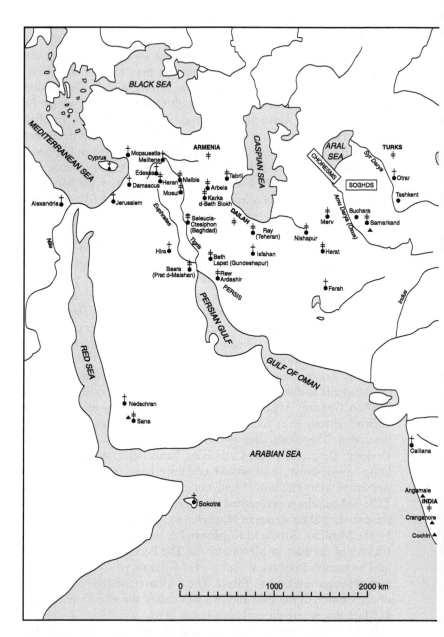

Figure 3.3 Map of the general view of the Church of the East in the Middle Ages.

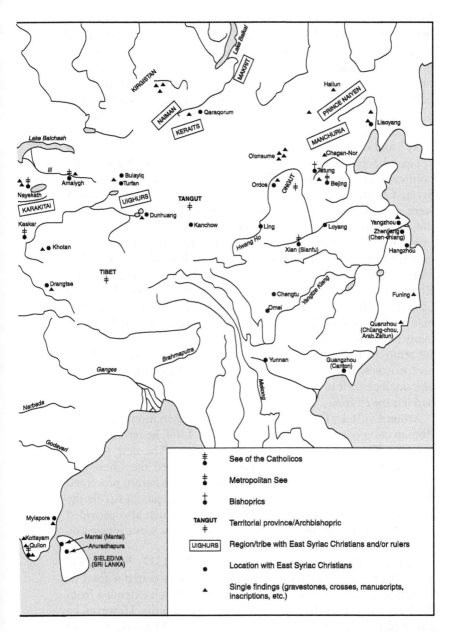

Map: D. W. Winkler.

Mosul was a "Nestorian," for whom ritual played a greater role than dogma. The liberal marriage rules with the possibility of divorce and remarriage did not please him. They also occasionally practiced circumcision – even of women! – as he himself had observed. They accepted the eucharist, which they received under both kinds, in their hands, and they did not recognize the anointing of the sick. They practiced abstinence and rejected the consumption of meat. Catholicos Yahballaha III had renounced their "hetero-doxy" and in 1290 permitted him to preach in Baghdad. The elite appeared prepared to accept union with Rome, though mostly for political reasons. In the *Libellus* Ricoldo emphasized that the East Syriac Christians did not want to be called "Nestorians," as they were not such and did not emulate Nestorius. They referred to themselves as "Nazantarei" or "Nazareni."

Around 1300 the Armenian Hethum reported that in Chaldea and Syria there were, in addition to the Muslims who used Arabic, many "Nestorians," who favored the Chaldean language. Doquz-Khatun came from the line of the holy three kings and became a Christian. He recorded that the apostle Thomas had converted many Christians in India; in the intervening centuries, however, many had fallen away from the church because the country was too far removed from other Christian territories. Personally, he knew no Christians from India. Hethum also stated that there was only one small city left in India which was inhabited by Christians; most had left the church.

Around 1302 Yahballaha undertook negotiations with the Roman curia regarding union. On May 18, 1304, he wrote to Pope Benedict XI, enclosing a creed with the letter. The new Il-Khan, Oljaitu (1304–16), although baptized, persecuted the Christians. The Kerait prince Irandjin, a nephew of Doquz-Khatun, prevented the conversion of the church of Tabriz into a mosque. In Arbela the Church of the East had a mountain fortress, which also provided military security, but on July 1, 1310, the fortress was captured by the Mongols, who massacred all its inhabitants.

Mar Yahballaha III died on November 13, 1317. He was the most significant catholicos of his time and consecrated a total of seventy-five bishops and metropolitans. His church extended from the Near East, across Central Asia to China and India. However, he also had to suffer the decline of his church in Mesopotamia and Persia. The period of Mongol sympathy for the Church of the East sending Christians to Europe to work out an alliance with the pap-acy had passed – a passing certainly not hindered by Oljaitu. Under

Oljaitu's son Abu Said (1316–35), the empire of the Il-Khans collapsed completely as it annihilated itself in civil wars.

The period of Catholicos Timotheos II (1318–32)

After the death of Yahballaha III, Timotheos II, onetime bishop of Arbela, was elected catholicos. His extensive work on the Christian mysteries, the *Book of the Seven Foundations of the Mysteries of the Church*, has been preserved in manuscript form. In it he considered as mysteries (Syr. *raze*; Lat. *sacramenta*) priestly ordination (the laying on of hands), the consecration of the altar, baptism, eucharist, the taking of monastic vows, burial, betrothal, and marriage. In addition, thirteen canons of Timotheos from his first synod (1318) have been preserved and were edited and translated in 1838.

During this time, the papacy sought to gain a foothold in the Orient. As early as 1291 Nicholas IV sent the Franciscan John of Montecorvino to Peking; Clement V appointed him archbishop. In 1305 John reported that he had spent thirteen months at the Church of the Apostle Thomas in Mylapore before traveling on to China, where his work was hindered by the "Nestorians." The Ongut king Gorguz, a member of the Church of the East, had converted to Catholicism and died in the meantime. Gradually conflicts intensified between the East Syriac Christians and the Latin missionaries as the latter attempted to convert adherents of the Church of the East to the Roman church.

In 1318 Pope John XXII established a new province of the church for Asia with its center at the Persian capital of Sultaniya. In connection with the 1321 martyrdom of the Franciscans of Tana near Bombay, we learn that there were also Christian communities in this region of north-western India. Whether these can be traced back to the community of "Kalliana" mentioned by Cosmas Indicopleustes is not known. At the same time, the China missionary Odorico of Pordenone and the Dominican Jordanus Catalanus were also staying in Tana, where fifteen houses were inhabited by "Nestorians." In Mylapore Odorico also found fifteen houses of East Syrians, whom he described as "useless heretics."

Around 1330 in his *Book of the Great Khan*, John de Cori wrote of the more than 30,000 "Nestorians" in Peking, who fiercely opposed the mission of the Franciscans. They received special privileges from the great khan, who nevertheless also supported the other Christians. If a union with the "Nestorians" in China were achieved, the entire land, along with the khan, could easily be won for Catholicism.

When Pope John XXII named Jordanus Catalanus bishop of Quilon in April 1329, he also informed him about the "Nestorians of Quilon" in a letter written in Latin. It is doubtful that the Pope had access to detailed knowledge of the situation or was in contact with Catholicos Timotheos II. His point was rather that if they sent two or three hundred missionaries to India, they could easily win over 10,000 of the schismatics. We know little more of the fate of the East Syriac Christians in India; only shortly before the arrival of the Portuguese do we hear of them again. In the end the Latin church's understanding of and conflict with the East Syriac church in the Middle Ages remained superficial. Jacob of Verona encountered "Nestorians" in Famagusta on Cyprus, and Nicolo da Poggibonsi, a traveler to Jerusalem, mentioned East Syrians in the Church of the Holy Sepulcher. In the fourteenth century there was also a monastery of the Church of the East in Damiette on the mouth of the Nile. In the popular anonymous travelogue *Niederrheinische Orientbericht* (*Orient Report of the Lower Rhine*), Prester John, who ruled over forty kingdoms, was portrayed as belonging to the Church of the East. King Balthasar came from his realm to Bethlehem, and St Helena exchanged his corpse with that of the apostle Thomas. Ludolf of Sudheim confused the East Syrians with the West Syrians. In his legend of the three kings, John of Hildesheim reported that the apostle Thomas had preached the gospel to the holy three kings in India; Prester John and the patriarch Thomas had also lived there. Hatred of the East Syrians reached its zenith in John of Sultaniya; Muhammad was the son of Christian parents and had been led astray by the "Nestorians." The accounts of the fourteenth century offer no new information.

John of Marignola, who traveled to China in the fourteenth century, was the last of the Latin missionaries. He journeyed to China via the land route, through the realm of the "Golden Horde." On the way, he reorganized the Christians in Almaliq in the khanate of Chagatai. In 1347, on his return trip to Europe from Peking, he found there was no longer a bishop in Quilon, but he noted that the Christians there controlled the pepper trade. He observed the East Syriac Christians' prohibition of the figurative representation of Jesus on the crucifix, though they permitted icons.

During the term of Catholicos Timotheos II, the theologian Abdisho (Ebedjesus) bar Brika († 1318) was also active. He was the last of the great East Syriac authors and the most important literary historian of the Church of the East. In 1285, as bishop of Siggar, he completed a Syriac Gospel. His catalogue of writers, which he wrote in 1315 as metropolitan of Nisibis and Armenia, is an invaluable source; it is preserved in a fourteenth-century manuscript. Abdisho also arranged the Gospel readings for Sundays and holidays. In addition to literature, he also wrote works on church law, an essay on the measurement of time and making of calendars, and a description of East Syriac doctrine (the *Book of the Pearl*). Abdisho also compiled the laws of the Church of the East in a two-volume work, completed no later than 1290. A manuscript from this year has been preserved in Trichur (Kerala, India). Abdisho's work was the last great medieval law collection of the Church of the East and was approved at a synod of Timotheos II.

The *Book of the Pearl*, written in 1297/8, treated in five chapters God, Creation, the Christian economy of salvation, the sacraments, and the Last Things. In the preface Abdisho explained that he wrote the work in an easily readable style to fulfil Catholicos Yahballaha III's desire to use it for instruction. In the first section, he began with the conception of God, favoring the approach of negative theology: "If we then say, 'not visible' and 'not composite' and 'not passible' and 'not changeable,' these words do not describe what He is, but rather, what He is not." In the second section, the Jewish age of the Old Testament was discussed as a preliminary stage of Christianity. He analyzed salvation history in the third section. In his view, Christianity is an agreement of theory and practice. "The sum total of theory is truth, and the sum total of practice is virtue." All Christians agree with the doctrine of the Trinity in the dogma of Nicaea. Neither the prophets nor the apostles had called Mary "mother of God"; the term "mother of Christ," however, is correct. The name "Nestorian" is incorrect, as Nestorius neither spoke the language of the Church of the East, nor was he its patriarch. It did not follow Nestorius, rather he followed it, which maintained as its immutable foundation the faith transmitted by the apostles. Abdisho portrayed the Church of the East in the spirit of Dionysius the Areopagite. In the fourth chapter he discussed the seven *raze* (mysteries, sacraments): the priesthood, baptism, anointing oil (from pure olive oil; only the Indian members of the church used coconut or sesame oil), the eucharist, the forgiveness of sins, holy sour leaven (*fermentum*), and the sign of the life-giving cross. This list remains valid in the Church of the East today. According to Abdisho, the apostles of the East, Thomas and Bartholomew, as well as Addai and Mari, gave the Church of the East the holy leaven, that it might be used for the eucharist. The fact that the West did not share this tradition proved that the faith had been altered there. The fifth chapter treats the Second Coming of Christ, the liturgy, fasting, prayer and alms, the resurrection, and the last judgment. When at prayer, Christians should put on a belt and face east, where the lost paradise lay. Faith is awaiting the return to life of all living things through Christ.

Also among the important writings of this time is the anonymous biography of Catholicos Mar Yahballaha III. The *Book of the Tower* by Amr b. Matta (*c.*1350) – bearing the same title as the work by Mari b. Suleiman of *c.*1150 – is significant as well and has been preserved in an autograph copy. Amr recounts the history of the patriarchs through Timotheos II, quoting many lost works and providing a biography of Yahballaha III, and emphasizes the advantageous position of the Church of the East. Saliba b. Yuhanna of Mosul produced an apparently plagiarized excerpt from this work, which also included a list of those bishops who had participated in his consecration. Among them were the metropolitans of Almaliq and of Tangut. In his conclusion, Saliba referred to the apostolic origins of the Church of the East and the apostles Thomas and Addai, as well as to Mari, the apostle of Mesopotamia, whose memory was celebrated in the famous monastery of Deir Mar Mari, named in his honor.

The dark centuries of the Church of the East

In the East Syriac cemetery in Pischpek in Kirgistan, the most recently dated tombstones come from the year 1345. The most recent Turkish tombstones from Amaliq date from 1368, and the most recent Syriac gravestones from the same location on the modern border between China and Kirgistan are from 1371/2. As early as the fourteenth century, the Church of the East had died out in large parts of Central Asia, China, and Persia. Because of the cutting off of China from the West beginning in 1368 under the Ming emperors, Christianity no longer received support there, and the Christians of the East in the Orient relocated to the mountains of Kurdistan. Thus began the "dark centuries," from which we have hardly any reports of the church. The seat of the catholicos moved from one location to another, depending upon where he believed he was most secure. Dinkha II (1332–64) resided in Karamles, his successor Shimun II in Mosul. His successor was Shimun III, followed by Elias IV († 1437). We do not know the precise length of time any head of the church spent in office, whether living in Maragha, Urmia, or Mosul. Around 1400 John of Sultiniya made reference to the "Suriani" in Kurdistan and Mosul, where the catholicos ("cathalech") also wielded secular authority.

Beginning around 1370 the empire of Timur Lenk (Tamerlane) arose in Central Asia with Samarkand as its center. During his campaigns, thousands of Christians were slaughtered, bringing about the de facto destruction of the Church of the East in Central Asia, which lived on only in the mountains of Kurdistan and in India. Tamerlane's campaign of conquest had the character of a "holy war." In 1393 he laid waste to Iran and continued on to Kurdistan and Diyarbakir. In 1400 he invaded Syria and had erected the infamous pyramids of skulls, which stood as reminders of his horrific military tactics. In 1402 he defeated the Ottomans in the battle of Ankara, and in 1403 he destroyed Christian churches in Georgia. He even established contact with Christian Europe and threatened to cross into Europe. The Spaniard Clavijo visited the ruler of Asia in Samarkand in 1404. In light of the unimaginable atrocities, it is difficult to believe that there are a handful of monasteries and churches in Iraq and Kurdistan which survived Tamerlane's era. The Church of the East never recovered from this disastrous period. There were no major scholarly and spiritual institutions any more. The Gospel book (*Evangeliar*) of Tell Ziqufa near Mosul, produced by one Elias of Mosul and containing numerous miniatures, indicates that even the "dark ages" were not without great cultural achievements (the book is found today in the British Library, Add. 7174).

Around the mid-fifteenth century the catholicate became hereditary and passed in most cases from uncle to nephew. Under the influence of mothers and older sisters, the honor of the catholicate was also bestowed upon children. As his predecessors had, Shimun IV Basidi (1437–97) resided in Mosul. In 1450 he is thought to have issued a decree firmly establishing the hereditary succession of the Bar Mama family; written sources supporting this, however, have not been found.

Some individual bishops' seats endured still longer. In 1430 one Timotheos was named metropolitan of Nisibis, followed by Abdisho in 1458 and Elias in 1483. The bishopric of Tarsus lasted until the middle of the fifteenth century. In Mardin (Tur Abdin) – seat of the West Syriac (Syrian Orthodox) patriarchate from 1293 to 1915 – a Gospel book contains a list of bishops including East Syriac bishops up to 1512; evidence of Chaldean bishops has been

Figure 3.4 Ruins of the former East Syriac monastery Mar Augin (Tur
Abdin), founded in the early fourth century. Photo: courtesy of
Hans Hollerweger, Austria.

preserved from 1553 on. In Arbela, Ishoyahb bar Mqaddam, also
known as a writer, held office from 1443 until 1452.

The information about India is somewhat better. The manuscript
Syr. 204 in the Vatican Library offers a glimpse into the situation of
the Church of the East before the arrival of the Portuguese in India.
At the time of Catholicos Shimun IV, who had lived since 1491 in
the Mar Aba monastery near Gazarta (Cizre) in modern south-east
Turkey, Christians in India had had no bishop for several generations; evidently the connection with the catholicate in Kurdistan
had been broken off. In 1490 Shimun sent a metropolitan to southern China, which at this time formed a single diocese with India. In
1491 the archdeacon, who stood at the head of the Christians of the
Malabar coast, sent three envoys to Mesopotamia – to the catholicos and to the West Syriac and Coptic patriarchs – to request that a
new bishop be consecrated for India. On the journey to Baghdad,
one of the delegates died. In Gazarta they met with the catholicos,
who instructed them to go to the monastery of Mar Augen and
select monks for the office of bishop. The monks Mar Thoma and
Mar Yuhanon were chosen and consecrated bishops. They traveled
to India with the two envoys and were enthusiastically welcomed
there. Thus ties to the catholicate were reestablished. The bishops

ordained priests, consecrated churches, and rebuilt the hierarchical structure. After some time, Bishop Mar Thoma returned to Mesopotamia to report to the catholicos. The new patriarch, Elias V (1502–3), consecrated three additional monks – Rabban David (Mar Yahballaha), Rabban George (Mar Dinkha), and Rabban Masud (Mar Jakob) – as bishops for India, Java, and China. In 1504 the bishops journeyed to India, where they continued their work of rebuilding the church. The monk Abraham of Karka de Beth Slokh (Kirkuk) produced a report on the relations of the Church of the East with the Malabar coast of India in the years 1489 to 1503; he preserved the impressive writings of the three Indian bishops Thoma, Yahballaha, and Dinkha about the earliest arrival of the Portuguese in India and the intrigues of the Muslims against the Europeans. The report of the monk Abraham is preserved in Cod. Syr. 59 in the state library of Berlin. In the letter, he writes of 30,000 Christian families in India; Cranganore, Palor, and Quilon were the most important Christian towns. A series of churches were built, such as the one in Mylapore, which lay a 25-day journey from the Malabar coast and preserved the grave of the apostle Thomas. The letter gives the impression that the Thomas Christians were doing well at that time.

That the East Syriac Christians in India were known in Europe even before the voyage of Vasco da Gama is demonstrated not only by the travelogue of Nicolo de Conti (c.1447), in which he stated that there were some 1,000 "Nestorites" at the Basilica of Thomas in Mylapore and that they were scattered across the whole of India like the Jews in Europe, but also in the travel report of Girolamo of San Stefano from around 1492. He wrote that there were Christian churches in Quilon which had frescos and crucifixes and about 1,000 worshipers – but no longer any priests of their own. In 1498, during his first trip to India, Vasco da Gama encountered Christians in Mombasa, who had emigrated from Ethiopia, Mesopotamia, and Egypt. The Portuguese also came into contact with Christians during the voyage of Pedro Alvarez Cabral in 1500 and the second journey of Vasco da Gama in 1502. An appendix to Vasco da Gama's first travel report notes that there were approximately 25,000 Christians in Quilon who paid the poll tax and some 300 churches, named in honor of apostles.

Vasco da Gama seems not to have come into contact with any Christians during his first journey to India; the conquistadors mistook the Hindus for Christians! In July 1499 Girolamo Sernigi reported to a Florentine friend that people around Calcutta had heard of Prester John. On August 26, 1499, King Manuel I of Portugal informed Emperor Maximilian I that there were Christians in India who had been cut off from the rest of the Christian world by the Muslims and whom he now wanted to support with monks and religious implements. In his letter of March 1, 1500, to the samorin of Calicut, King Manuel wrote that he had heard there were Christians in his region; in that regard, he referred to the preaching of the apostles Thomas and Bartholomew in India. In 1500 Pedro Alvarez Cabral encountered members of the Church of the East in Cranganore and Quilon, and Christians in Cranganore were mentioned in an anonymous travelogue. The Portuguese noted, however, that the king of Calicut was not, as Vasco da Gama had believed, a Christian.

On the return trip to Europe Cabral's fleet encountered at Cape Verde a ship in which the Italian Amerigo Vespucci was traveling. On July 4, 1501, Vespucci wrote to Lorenzo de Medici that he had heard from the Portuguese that the city of Enparlicat lay in India, and there the body of the apostle Mark was buried! There were also many Christians there. The Venetian ambassador to Portugal reported even before Cabral's arrival that he had found the island in India with the grave of the apostle Thomas. The Florentine ambassador reported the same. In July 1501 Manuel I offered the Catholic king of Spain an account of Cabral's experiences in Cochin: "In each kingdom one finds many true Christians, who were converted by St Thomas; and their priests rigorously follow the apostolic life, calling nothing their own save that which they receive as alms. And they live in complete chastity and have churches in which they celebrate Mass and consecrate unleavened bread and wine, which they prepare out of dried grapes and water, as they know no other way. In the churches they display no images besides the cross, and all Christians wear apostolic garments and never cut their beards or hair. There he obtained reliable information regarding the location where the body of St Thomas was buried, namely 150 leagues away, on the seacoast in a city called Maliapor, which is only sparsely inhabited. . . . And he also received a reliable report of great Christian peoples living beyond this kingdom who made pilgrimages to the so-called house of St Thomas."

The Indian Christian Joseph of Cranganore, who had in 1490 participated in the journey of Thomas Christians to the catholicos in Gazarta-Beth Zadbai between Mosul and Diyarbakir, traveled with his brother Mathias to Europe in late June 1501; they both wanted to make a pilgrimage to Jerusalem and Rome. Mathias died shortly after their arrival in Lisbon, but Joseph remained in Lisbon for six months and spoke there, as well as in Venice and Rome in 1502, about the situation in India. He was received by Pope Alexander VI, whom he informed that there were many Christians in Cranganore. He referred to the bishop of Cranganore and stated that the catholicos in Mesopotamia ("Armenia") also ordained bishops for China and India. He had patriarchs, archbishops, and bishops under him. He wore his hair shaved into the form of a cross. He also reported to the pope that the inhabitants of Cathay were white Christians. In Malabar, they were only familiar with Rome, Venice, and France. In 1507 his report was published in Vicenza with additional documents from Francesco da Montalboddo under the title *Paese novamente retrovati.* Joseph's account tempered the Europeans' exaggerated notions about the Thomas Christians, and his report of religion in India is among the earliest such reports in Europe.

On November 19, 1502, during Vasco da Gama's second voyage to India, another encounter of the Thomas Christians with the Portuguese occurred in Cochin, as reported by Thomé Lopes. The delegates presented gifts and expressed their pleasure at the arrival of the Portuguese. The rajah of Cochin wanted to enter into an alliance with them. They offered the Portuguese a base of operations and spoke of their liturgy and their six bishops. In Cranganore there were more than 30,000 Christians, who came under the jurisdiction of the catholicos of "Armenia." In the port cities one could still find mementos of the apostle Thomas. They expected above all protection from their Muslim neighbors and gave Vasco da Gama a staff which may have been a scepter of an earlier Christian rajah. Among Christian communities, Cranganore and Quilon received by far the most attention, although there were also Christians in such other places as Mylapore.

Around 1500 the Christians in India belonged primarily to the upper class; they enjoyed certain privileges relating to clothing, the use of carpets, etc. The archdeacon represented the communities to non-Christians. In a letter to the catholicos from the four above-mentioned bishops, Mar Yahballaha, Mar Dinkha, Mar Jacob, and Mar Thomas, the landing of the "Frankish brothers" is mentioned. Among them was Mar Jacob of Cranganore (1503–50), who received gifts of money from the Portuguese king. In 1503 Alfonso de Albuquerque traveled to India, and the Thomas Christians presented him with a gold cross for King Manuel. The Christians enjoyed a kind of autonomy, of which the Portuguese wanted to take advantage. For their part, the Christians sought the Europeans' help in regaining former privileges. Giovanni de Empoli, a companion of Albuquerque, described this early harmony in Quilon.

Between 1505 and 1507 Ludovico de Varthema from Bologna was in India. The grave of St Thomas was only eleven miles away from his place of residence. He produced an account of his travels, published as early as 1510, in which he told of Christian merchants in "Caicolon" (Kayankulam), 40 kilometers from Quilon, and noted that a priest came from "Babylon" every three years to baptize them. "These Christians observe Lent and celebrate Easter as we do and also have the same holidays and saints' days as we have, but they celebrate mass like the Greeks and venerate four more saints than all others: Sts John, Jacob, Mathias, and Thomas." He mentioned a non-Christian king in Quilon. Varthema also encountered Thomas Christians on the Coromandel coast, where they were persecuted and massacred. Peculiarly, Varthema seems also to have met Christians in Siam. Apparently there were also East Syriac Christians, who must have come from China, in the Siamese capital Ayutthaya. However, it is doubted that Varthema was himself in South-East Asia. Admittedly, if the city Catholicos Ishoyahb III (seventh century) called "Kalah" – which al-Masudi described lying in South-East Asia "halfway between Arabia and China" – is identified with the port in Malaya, and the "Fashur" of Abu Salih (fourth century) is found on Sumatra, the existence of Christians in South-East Asia appears not entirely ruled out. Perhaps about 1,500 and certainly more than 1,000 Christians lived in Pegu and Burma, where Varthema claimed to have seen them. As they had along the Silk Road, Christian merchants may have settled here along the "Silk Road of the sea" as well.

In 1514 Duarte Barbosa († 1521) referred to the existence of a Christian community in Mylapore. He mentioned the church of Quilon, allegedly built by the apostle Thomas, where the local king maintained the receipts from the pepper trade. He also noted the contact with the catholicos, who had sent a bishop and priests.

A 1509 document written on palm leaves discusses an archdeacon of the Thomas Christians, the head of his caste. Evidently both religious and political leadership lay in his hands. Since the archdeacon also commanded a Christian army of the rajah of Cochin, he was portrayed as the "Indian prototype of Prester John" (Athapilly).

Latin missionaries soon began to baptize Syriac Christians, but they had no understanding of the Oriental rite. Portuguese scholars tried to Latinize the Christians, an effort the Thomas Christians bitterly opposed. Mar Jakob of Cranganore complained about this in a letter to the king of Portugal. In 1517 the Portuguese, who two years earlier had established the "Estado da India," arrived in Mylapore, where they built a church near the legendary grave of St Thomas. The Portuguese soon consulted one of the four bishops who had come to the country in 1504. The bishop, who had come from Mesopotamia, explained that he had been living in Mylapore for fifteen years already, and he recounted the tradition of St Thomas, reinforcing his testimony by swearing an oath. At this time the East Syriac Christians used the East Syriac breviary (*Hudra*) revised in the seventh century, which on July 3 recalled the story of the missionary journey of St Thomas.

The papacy gradually established a Latin hierarchy in India. In 1533 the bishopric of Goa was founded and Joao de Albuquerque elevated as its first Latin bishop. King Manuel of Portugal had already informed the pope that there were Christians on the Malabar coast, in whose church only a cross was found, and that the apostle Thomas was buried in India. Portugal continued its expansion into India and captured Goa and Malakka. As early as 1542 the Jesuit Francis Xavier was in India and tried to subject the East Syriac Christians in Quilon to the papacy and make them into Latin Uniates. In 1545 he came into contact with Mar Jacob at the Franciscan monastery in Cochin, and he recounted his experiences with the Indian Christians to Ignatius Loyola in 1549. The Franciscans established a seminary in Cochin, but the East Syriac Christians refused to accept priests who neither knew nor understood their traditional liturgy. The Latinization measures of the Jesuits led in the following period to a split among East Syriac Christians, who wanted to preserve the authenticity of their traditions.

4

THE AGE OF THE OTTOMANS

Fifteenth to nineteenth centuries

Wilhelm Baum

Chaldean and Indian unions

The first union of the Church of the East with Rome was concluded at the Council of Florence. The Mediterranean island Cyprus was home to a group of East Syriac Christians who had since the thirteenth century repeatedly been the object of papal missionary endeavors. On August 7, 1445, following the acceptance of the creed before Archbishop Andreas Chrysoberges of Rhodes by Archbishop Timotheos of Tarsus (*Archiepiscopus Chaldaeorum, qui in Cypro sunt*), union was established between the Apostolic Church of the East and Rome. Timotheos petitioned the Lateran to allow him to take part in the Council of Florence, and his request was granted by a bull. As early as 1450 some of the converted left the Church of Rome. Since then the term "Chaldean," used by the pope, has referred to those East Syrians in union with Rome, though the efforts at Latinization and the problem of two hierarchies finally led to a collapse of this union in Cyprus.

At the beginning of the modern period the Church of the East had been reduced, outside of India, to a regional church in Kurdistan. In 1516 the Ottoman Turks conquered Kurdistan. According to the terms of a treaty with the Persians, the Nestorian regions were divided between the Ottoman empire and Persia. The Turks utilized the millet system, which permitted individual religious and ethnic groups broad rights of self-governance under the guidance of the ecclesiastical leader, who was required to collect taxes and enforce the laws. Under this system the catholicos of the East Syrians was the highest authority in the Christian region of Kurdistan. However, the Church of the East was first recognized as a "millet" in the Ottoman empire only in the year 1844!

In 1562 there were five bishops' seats in the vicinity of Urmiyah.

The catholicoi Shimun VI (1504–38) and Shimun VII bar Mama (1538–51) resided in the monastery of Rabban Hormizd in Alqosh near Mosul in Mesopotamia. Shimun VI designated his brother as hereditary successor; his brother, Mar Shimun VII, named in turn his nephew. When, upon the death of Shimun VII, the catholicate passed to the nephew, Mar Shimun VIII Dinkha (1551–8), the bishops of Arbela, Urmiyah, and Salmas voiced their opposition to this method of succession, and in 1552 elected John Sulaqa, the abbot of the monastery of Rabban Hormizd, as anti-patriarch; he adopted the name John VIII. John Sulaqa established contact with the Franciscans and took a step unprecedented in the East Syriac church: he traveled through Jerusalem to Rome, accepted the Catholic creed in the presence of Pope Julius III, was consecrated patriarch in 1553, and received the pallium. The pope sent him back to the Orient with two Dominicans, who were to instruct the Christians in the Roman faith. Evidently Sulaqa had given the pope the impression that Shimun VIII had died. Shimun had, however, declared his opponent's election illegitimate, and only the faithful of Mardin and Diyarbakir recognized Sulaqa, who returned in November 1553, as patriarch. On orders from Shimun VIII, he was arrested by the Turks and murdered in 1555. Abdisho IV was subsequently elected (anti-)patriarch; the first schism in the Church of the East had occurred. Sulaqa's successor Abdisho IV (1555–70) could not immediately travel to Rome; he received recognition from Pope Pius IV first in 1562. His successor fared similarly. In 1556 Abdisho IV sent the Chaldean bishops Mar Joseph and Mar Elias, accompanied by the two Dominicans, to Rome. Since then a disagreement had arisen over the question of whether the Thomas Christians stood under the patronage of the Portuguese crown or of the Chaldean patriarch (united with Rome). Beginning in 1553 the Thomas Christians in India were placed under the authority of the line of the Chaldean patriarch Sulaqa until Rome transferred their jurisdiction to the Latin Portuguese church in 1599. The Chaldean bishop for India, Mar Joseph, eventually had to answer to the king of Portugal in Lisbon, but he made such a good impression that he was sent back to India in 1565. Two years later he was again accused of heresy because he supported the doctrine of the Chaldean church. When he died in 1569 in Rome, the rumor arose that the pope had wanted to elevate him to cardinal.

In the following period it mattered to the popes only that the patriarch subscribed to the creed. Rome showed little concern for the realization of the union in practical terms. A copy of the creed written in Syriac in Abdisho's own hand is preserved at the Vatican. The pope asked the Catholic bishop of Nachitjewan to support the work of Patriarch Abdisho, who lived in Seert. He was to introduce the resolutions of the Council of Trent into the Orient, though nothing came of this. The people did not want Rome to control the life of their church, and they cared little whether the catholicos was recognized by the pope or not. In 1565 the pope granted the Chaldeans the retention of their traditional rites and customs. After the death of Abdisho IV and following an extended period of confusion, the bishop of Jezireh was elected as his successor; he took the name Yahballaha IV (1577–80). His successor Shimun IX Dinkha revived the system of a hereditary partiarchate for the Uniate Chaldean Church, and in 1581 he received his confirmation from Rome. To escape the oppressive measures of the Turks, he moved the seat of his rule to Salmas on Lake Urmiyah (Persia). Consequently, the Christians in the Ottoman empire no longer had contact with him, leading to the establishment of another patriarchate in Ottoman territory in Diyarbikar. Patriarch Shimun XIII Dinkha moved the patriarchal seat to Kotchannes and dissolved the union. The first union of the Chaldeans with Rome lasted from 1551 until 1672.

When in 1503 Catholicos Elias V consecrated three bishops for Christians in India, he conferred upon Mar Yahballaha the title "Metropolitan of India and China." The initially good relationship of the East Syriac Christians to the Portuguese had gradually deteriorated, and the Portuguese sought to hinder the arrival of the new bishops from Mesopotamia. Bishop Mar Dinkha had to flee inland in 1534. In 1558 the Latin diocese of Goa was elevated to an archdiocese. At this time, basing his claim on a papal bull, John (Yuhannan) Sulaqa extended his jurisdiction over India. The East Syriac catholicos Shimun VIII Dinkha finally opposed this action, consecrated Mar Abraham bishop in 1557, and sent him to India. The influence of the catholicos was still in force, though there were in India at this time East Syrian, Chaldean, and Latin hierarchies operating in parallel. Since the colonial power Portugal had sponsored first the Latin and then the Chaldean church, the direction of development during this time was clear. After the Chaldean bishop Mar Joseph was handed over to the Inquisition, Patriarch Abdisho IV named a new metropolitan, who tried to come to an arrangement with Rome. He was, however, recalled by the pope. Regarding this matter, the archbishop of Goa declared that in the future the Thomas Christians would come under the authority not of the patriarch of the "Chaldeans" but rather of the king of Portugal. It is difficult to say whether this political decree took effect at the grass-roots. A prayer book written in 1562 in Angamaly – the seat of an East Syriac archdiocese – indicates that the East Syriac liturgy was still in use there. In 1585/6 the Jesuit F. Roz, who knew Malayalam and Syriac, examined several liturgical books and determined that the "heterodoxies" of Nestorius, Diodore of Tarsus, and Theodore of Mopsuestia could be found within. A 1585 synod tried to cut off the Thomas Christians' contact with the Chaldeans.

In 1599, in order to avoid a schism, the so-called Synod of Djamper was held under the leadership of Archbishop Menezes of Goa. There the decrees of the Council of Trent were declared binding, the Roman calendar introduced, and the liturgy revised on the Roman model. Nestorius was condemned as a heretic, and allegedly Hindu customs were forbidden. Under duress, 150 priests and 660 laymen signed decrees stating that the Church of the East in India should be entirely subjected to Roman central authority. The Portuguese gathered the manuscripts of the Thomas Christians and systematic-ally burned them. Thus the Syriac medieval Christian literature of India was almost completely lost. A notable exception is MS 64 from the library of the metropolitan of Trichur in Kerala, which contains the Nomocanon of Abdisho bar Brika from 1290, that is, from within the lifetime of its writer. This is therefore the earliest known East Syriac manuscript from India.

The Thomas Christians became a filial church of the Latin church, and their connection to the catholicos was severed. 1599 is portrayed as the darkest year of Indian church history. It is never-theless typical that the Jesuit F. Roz, who eventually became the Latin hierarch of the Thomas Christians from 1599 to 1624, reached the conclusion: "These Christians are certainly the earliest in this part of the Orient. . . . Although they have lived under hea-thens, Jews, and Muhammadans, they have remained steadfast in their faith to this day."

After some fifty years of forced union, the priest Thomas Pala-komatta took action against the union. He turned first to the East Syriac catholicos, then also to the Coptic and Jacobite (Syrian Orthodox) patriarchs, to obtain a bishop independent of Rome. The East Syriac catholicos sent a Mar Ahatallah as bishop to India, but he fell into the hands of the Portuguese, was handed over to the Inquisition, and ended up on a pyre in Goa. Subsequently there developed in Cochin in 1653 the "oath on the Coonan Cross" against Roman jurisdiction in India. The Thomas Christians split: twelve priests elected Thomas Palakomatta metropolitan. Out of about 200,000 Thomas Christians, a mere 400 remained with Rome. The majority established contact with the West Syriac church in Antioch and the Syriac Orthodox patriarch in Mardin. The conquest of Cochin and Quilon by the Dutch (1661) made the break from Portugal and Rome easier. In 1665 the West Syriac bishop Mar Gregorius traveled to India and consecrated the leader of the uprising Mar Thomas I († 1670) as head of the Thomas Christians who had revolted against the Portuguese, thus establishing the jurisdictional connection to Antioch.

One segment of the opposition also turned to the catholicos of the East. In 1720 one Mar Thomas tried to established contact with the Church of the East, which was finally achieved with Dutch support in 1730. However, reestablishment of the Church of the East in India did not occur until the end of the nineteenth century. In 1874 the catholicos sent Bishop Mar Elias Mellos to India to assert his jurisdiction in India. Mar Elias remained there from 1874 until 1882. Under the leadership of Antonius Thondanatta a group of about fifty families in Trichur rebelled against the authority of Rome. They represented the kernel of the "new" Church of the East, which developed in the modern state of Kerala. Antonius was consecrated bishop by the East Syriac patriarch and took the name Mar Abdisho; his successor was Bishop Mar Timotheos from Kurdistan.

The "Mountain Nestorian" Catholicate and further unions with Rome

Little is known of the catholicoi of the Church of the East from the sixteenth to the eighteenth centuries. Of those recorded in the lists of names, not even the dates in office are known for some. Following Elias V was Shimun VI (1504–38), who lived and was buried in Rabban Hormizd. His successors were Shimun VII Ishuyau bar Mama (1538–51), Shimun VIII Dinkha (1551–8), Elias VI bar Giwargis (1558–91), and Elias VII (1591–1617). Cardinal Tisserant and Jean-Maurice Fiey postulate that there were two catholicoi of the same name in the time of Elias VI. Nevertheless, as the most recent research of Helene Murre-van den Berg demonstrates, the grave inscriptions preserved in Rabban Hormizd clearly show that Elias, who died on May 26, 1591, had governed for thirty-two years. On the whole, however, these are rough dates.

Around 1551 the East Syriac community in Tabriz disappeared, as Baghdad's did in 1553, and even that of its early center Nisibis in

1556. In Jerusalem, where there had been an East Syriac bishop since 1065, the office remained occupied until 1616. In the six-teenth century, possession of the monastery of Mar Augen in Tur Abdin was transferred to the West Syriac church. The Church of the East dwindled to a region bounded by Lake Van, Lake Urmiyah, and Mosul. For centuries the East Syrians led secluded lives among the Kurds, Persians, and Turks. During this time the Church of the East also lost the theological competence it had possessed for cen-turies, and the catholicos became a tribal prince, who exercised secular as well as spiritual jurisdiction. Often appointed while still a child, he stood under the influence of his mother and sisters, and decisions regarding the naming of bishops were also made in famil-ial clans. However, during this period the first modern Syriac folk literature developed. In the early seventeenth century, the priest Jausip († 1666) composed a poem in 112 stanzas about the Last Judgment, remorse, repentance, the life of Christ, etc. One Israel of Alqos († 1632) and Bishop Mar John of Mawana (c.1662) belong among the earliest representatives of the modern Assyrian literature, which has continued to exist into the present day.

While the Chaldean patriarchs no longer sent their creeds to the pope after 1670 and paid little attention in practice to the union with Rome, the catholicoi of the East grew closer to the pope. The catholicos of the East himself now took up the idea of union. In 1606 two messengers of Catholicos Elias VII appeared in Rome to prepare for union. In 1607 Catholicos Elias VII sent the pope a profession of faith, which was accepted. With this the formal church union was concluded between the catholicos of the East and the papacy for the first time. The "old" line of catholicoi became the "uniate" church, while the uniate line of Sulaqa in Urmiyah fell away from Rome.

In September 1610 the archimandrite Rabban Adam traveled to Rome to present Pope Paul V with a statement of faith. The pope gave this to his secretary, who, with the Holy Office, spent three years examining the theological views of the Church of the East. In the spring of 1614 the pope gave Rabban Adam a letter and gifts for Catholicos Elias VII to take with him; two Jesuits were to prepare for the conclusion of the union. The catholicos assembled his bishops for a synod in March 1616, and the pope was given an official document on the establishment of union. However, the East Syriac prelates protested against the oppressive measures of the Por-tuguese in India and turned to the pope for assistance. The two Jesuits returned to Rome and declared the statements of the synod insufficient. On June 29, 1617, the pope then asked the Church of the East to adopt a creed. When the papal envoy arrived at Rabban Hormizd in 1617, Catholicos Elias VII had already died. The uniate patriarch Shimun X, who resided in the monastery of Mar Yuhannan in Salmas near Kotchannes, also participated in the synod of union. The 1629 travelogue of the Minorites Francesco Quaresmino and Tommaso of Milan noted with regard to these events that the new catholicos, Elias VIII (1617–60), distanced himself from the politics of his predecessor and returned to "Nestorianism." He was in contact with Rome in 1619, 1629, 1638, and 1653, yet established no union. He, too, was buried in Rabban Hormizd.

The Chaldean patriarch of the Sulaqa line, Shimun XIII Dinkha (1662–1700), who had been united with Rome, dissolved that union in 1672 and founded a new "mountain Nestorian" patriarchate at the monastery of Kotchannes, which lay west of Lake Urmiyah in the region of Hakkari in Kurdistan. Thus while the former "Chaldean" patriarchate ceased to exist in Mosul, it lived on in the "mountain Nestorian" patriarchate in Kurdistan. Shimun XIII Dinkha lived first in Khosrowa and beginning in 1672 in Kotchannes. After his move, he had no further contact with Rome. The East Syriac catholicate of today is the legal successor of the initially uniate patriarchate of the Sulaqa line! There are accord-

Figure 4.1 Monastery Rabban Hormizd near Mosul (Iraq). Photo: courtesy of Initiative Christian Orient, Austria.

ingly two East Syriac patriarchates: one at Alqosh, that is, Rabban Hormizd, and the formerly Chaldean in Kotchannes.

Rome succeeded, nevertheless, in winning back a part of the "Chaldeans." New negotiations for union soon took place between Rome and the catholicos. After the death of Elias VIII of Rabban Hormizd, his nephew Yuhannan Maraugin succeeded him; as catholicos he took the name Elias IX (1660–1700). In 1668 he established contact with Rome, and on November 22, 1669, he wrote to Pope Clement IX expressing his desire to set up a school for priests in Rome. Despite much negotiation, however, union was never established. The successors of Elias IX in Rabban Hormizd were Elias X Maraugin (1700–22) and Elias XI Dinkha (1722–78). After the monastery of Rabban Hormizd was destroyed by the troops of the Nadir shah in 1743 – it was not rebuilt until 1808 – Elias XI Dinkha resided in Alqosh.

In the seventeenth century a third hierarchy was established. In 1667/8 Metropolitan Joseph of Diyarbakir renounced "Nestorianism" before two Capuchins and pledged union with Rome. At the end of 1673 he traveled to Rome and then returned to Diyarbakir; he received the pallium from the pope in 1681. In this way a second Chaldean patriarchate was founded in Diyarbakir in 1681 (1681–1828). Besides this, there were the two (non-uniate) patriarchates of Alqosh and Kotchannes. Before 1655, 40,000 Persian East Syriac families had become Catholic. The first patriarch was Joseph I (1681–96), who was appointed by Pope Innocent XI. His successor, Joseph II Sliba Beth Marcuf (1696–1712), also stands out as an author in both Syriac and Arabic, and he translated several Catholic writings into these languages.

As a rule, the Chaldean patriarchs of Diyarbakir took the name Joseph, while the "mountain Nestorian" patriarchs of Kotchannes favored the name Shimun (Simon), to emphasize their succession to Peter, who had written his first letter (1 Peter) from Babylon.

In 1711 the Chaldean patriarch Joseph II announced to the Vatican the success of his efforts and was praised by the pope. Pope Clement XI lauded Patriarch Joseph III for his steadfastness in the face of persecution. He and his successor Pope Innocent XIII (1721–4) directed the scholar Augustin Scandar to bring to Rome East Syriac manuscripts from the region around Mosul. Among the manuscripts acquired by Scandar was Cod. Vat. Syr. 204 with texts from India dating from the time of the Portuguese arrival. The Maronite Orientalist Joseph Simon Assemani (1687–1768) became one of the most important patrons of Syriac literature in Rome; the third volume of his great work *Bibliotheca Orientalis* (Rome 1728) included the first systematic presentation of East Syriac literature. In the first section of the third volume the invaluable book catalog of Abdisho bar Brika was reproduced in full, offering an impression of the richness of East Syriac literature.

At the end of the eighteenth century, beside the catholicate of Alqosh stood the "mountain Nestorian" patriarchate of Kotchannes under Shimun XVI Yuhannan (1780–1820) and the "Chaldean" patriarchate of Diyarbakir under the administrator Joseph V (1781–1828). Patriarch Shimun appealed, because of the persecutions, to the king of East Georgia, Irakli II (1762–98). Since that time many East Syriac Christians came to the land in the Caucasus. In the years 1925 to 1938 the Syrian journal *Kokva d-Madinkha* (*Star of the East*) was published there, and even Assyrian schools existed in Georgia. Today there are about 9,000 Assyrians (East Syrians) living in the country.

Elias XI Dinkha of Alqosh (Rabban Hormizd) reestablished contact with Rome in 1751 and in 1772 began negotiations regarding a new union, as the "mountain Nestorian" patriarch Shimun XV Michael Muktes (1740–80) of Kotchannes had before him. Thus, in 1772 the catholicate and the two patriarchates – the "mountain Nestorian" and that of Diyarbakir – stood together in union with Rome! The union with the "mountain Nestorians" rapidly disintegrated after a few years. Catholicos Elias XI of Alqosh died in 1778 in the monastery of Rabban Hormizd. Following his death, his nephews John Hormez and Ishoyahb – who had with his uncle concluded the union with Rome – battled for the catholicate. On April 30, 1778, John Hormez submitted himself to the pope. The pope, however, recognized his cousin Ishoyahb, who governed as Elias XII (1778–1804). Like his predecessors, he presented a profession of faith to Rome; in the end, however, union was not established. John Hormez was acknowledged by the pope as archbishop of Mosul; five bishops and the greater part of the East Syrians of Mosul followed him. The approval of Rome became an asset in questions of succession; it had no theological significance.

In May 1779, soon after he was recognized by the pope, Catholicos Elias XII of Alqosh dissolved the ties to Rome and reestablished the catholicate of the Church of the East in Alqosh, though it came to an end with his death in 1804. Also in 1781, the (uniate) Chaldean patriarch Joseph IV of Diyarbakir, to whom Clement XIII had sent the pallium in 1760, abdicated. He died in 1791. Now Rome had a free hand to set up a single uniate patriarch opposed to the

Figure 4.2 Former church of the Catholicos in Kotchannes in the mountains of Hakkari. Photos: courtesy of Helga Anschütz, Germany.

catholicate of the East. However, two candidates portrayed themselves as the new "Chaldean" patriarch: in Diyarbakir the nephew of the last patriarch, Augustin Hindi, as Joseph V (1781–1828), and in Mosul John VIII Hormez, nephew of Elias XI of Alqosh. Now there were two uniate and two non-uniate patriarchates! In 1818 Pius VII relieved John Hormez of his title as archbishop of Mosul and administrator of the patriarchate. Joseph V of Diyarbakir, the administrator of the patriarchate, was appointed by the pope apostolic delegate for the entire "Chaldean patriarchate of Babylon." The venerable monastery of Rabban Hormizd was revitalized by Gabriel Dqanbo; the monks recognized the Chaldean patriarch Joseph V as their head.

In 1830 Rome succeeded in normalizing relations with the (uniate) Chaldeans. After thorough investigation, John VIII Hormez (1830–8) was acknowledged by Rome as "Babylonian patriarch of the Chaldeans" with his seat in Baghdad. He wrote an autobiography in Syriac, which was published by the Anglican missionary George Percy Badger in 1853. John VIII had to follow the pope's order that he not consecrate any relatives as bishops. This was part of an effort to impede in any way possible the hereditary transmission of the patriarchate. In 1838, before the death of John VIII, Rome named an administrator: Joseph VI Audo (1848–78), who was confirmed by Pius IX. From then on, Baghdad stood as the Chaldean patriarch united with Rome, while the patriarchate of Diyarbakir was abolished and ceased to exist in 1804. Now only two leaders remained: the "Nestorian" catholicos of Kotchannes and the uniate Chaldean patriarch of Baghdad.

In 1869 the pope decided that in the future the Chaldean bishops' synods should elect the patriarch. However, the nephew of John VIII Hormez, Elias, had declared himself opposed to the abolition of the system of hereditary succession to the patriarch and terminated the union with Rome in mid-1831 in order to have himself consecrated metropolitan of Urmiyah by the "mountain Nestorian" patriarch Shimun XVII Abraham of Kotchannes (1820–1860). A synod of East Syriac bishops elected Elias (XIV) catholicos of the East in 1831, and he established his seat in Alqosh. He attempted to obtain the recognition of the "Nestorians" on Lake Urmiyah, though with little significant success; most Persian Christians remained loyal to the "mountain Nestorian" patriarch of Kotchannes.

At the beginning of the nineteenth century the majority of "mountain Nestorians" lived in the Hakkari region at an elevation

Figure 4.3 Catholicos Shimun XVII Abraham (1820–60), lithograph (1852). From George Percy Badger, *The Nestorians and their Rituals*, vol. II, London, 1987.

of some 4,000 meters in the region of today's borders of Turkey, Iran, and Iraq. Under the jurisdiction of the catholicos were about twenty bishops in the Ottoman empire and Persia, of whom three or four had the status of metropolitan. In Persia the Syriac Christians lived under the rule of the Muslim Kurdish aga. Initially Kurds and "mountain Nestorians" (Assyrians), who divided themselves in the villages into tribes under the leadership of a "malik" (head of the tribe), lived together in relative peace. However, the exertion of European influence in favor of the Christians and against the Muslims destroyed this equilibrium.

Russian and Western missionary activity in the nineteenth century

The start of the eighteenth century brought the renewed discovery of the "Nestorians" in the West. In his 1684 historical account of the peoples of the Orient, the French biblical critic Richard Simon discussed the "Chaldeans," whom he designated "Nestorians." In the eighteenth century, the rediscovery of the "Nestorians" in the West began with the aforementioned *Bibliotheca Orientalis* of Assemani. In 1776/7 August Friedrich Pfeiffer published excerpts from this work in German. In the fourth section of his *Thoughts on the Philosophy of the History of Mankind* (*Ideen zur Philosophie der Geschichte der Menschheit*, 1791), the German philosopher Johann Gottfried Herder wrote of the Nestorians, with reference to Pfeiffer, and noted, "A separate history of the Christian Orient, particularly of Nestorianism in its context, remains but a wish." He also mentioned Prester John and the translation of Christian literature into Persian. Nevertheless, he found in the Christian Syriac literature "no spark of that poetic gift which blazes from the soul and warms the heart; it is a wretched affectation. Their poetry consists in writing in verse form lists of names, sermons, and chronicles. They brought the riches of invention to none of the sciences they pursued."

In 1820, following a visit to Mosul, Claude James Rich, an employee of the East India Company, made Britons and Americans aware of the fate of Syriac-speaking Christians. Their use of the "language of Jesus" inspired great sympathy in the West. In 1825 the priest Joseph Wolf brought back to England and had published the manuscript of a Syriac Bible from Kurdistan. He, too, informed the general public about the situation of the Syriac Christians. Two thousand copies of the Gospel in the East Syriac language were printed in 1829. It is unclear if a copy ever reached the Church of the East.

The Austrian Anna Hafner Forneris, a native of Carinthia who traveled from Tifliz to Tabriz in 1830 and visited Urmiyah in 1840, has provided us in her 1849 account of her journeys with an impressive portrait of the life of the so-called "Nestorians," who had lost their scholarly institutions centuries earlier:

Regarding another sect: among the Nestorians, baptism is administered only twice a year, and if a child dies without having been baptized, they believe that if the father and mother are Christian, this quality was passed on to the child. They receive communion in both kinds, and this communion is in fact remarkable. The priest has a pile of thin wafers in the corner of a large cloth, which is draped over his head and covers his upper body. The communicants press forward anxiously, for each wants to be the first to receive. One calls out, "I must go out to the fields," another, "I to the mountains," the third, "I have workmen in the house," and so on. After receiving his share, each goes to a tub filled with wine and, using the ladle hanging there, takes from this a generous sip. Once all have had their fill, the priest, along with the elder of the village, turns his attention to the wine remaining in the tub, and they imbibe so much, until both shepherd and flock are entirely besotted, that they tumble from their seats and usually sleep off their inebriation in pleasant harmony on the church floor.

The Austrian also described the baking of the hosts and a curious custom which followed the death of a Christian, in which the priest, with regard to the Son, takes over the role of judge of the world. Accounts such as this make clear the situation of the "mountain Nestorians" before the advent of the Anglo-American mission.

In 1831 the Americans Eli Smith and H. G. O. Dwight entered the region of the Persian Christians in Azerbaijan; in 1833 they published their researches in Boston. They reported that none of the Christians possessed a Bible in classical Syriac. In 1834 Justin Perkins – the first American missionary to the Church of the East – arrived in Urmiyah as leader of a missionary outpost and remained there for thirty-six years; his book, *A Residence of Eight Years in Persia, Among the Nestorians with Notices of the Muhammedans*, appeared in New York in 1843. Through the missionary efforts of Perkins, there gradually developed an "Assyrian Evangelical Church with certain Nestorian characteristics" (Latourette). In 1835 Dr Asahel Grant traveled to Urmiyah. Six years later he published the book *The Assyrians or The Lost Tribes* in New York, in which he asserted the romantic thesis that the Assyrians were the descendants of the ten lost tribes of Israel, a thesis which caused a sensation among his contemporaries.

Around this time, the Kurds began to persecute the Christians, actions against which the European consuls protested at the High Gate. The protests of the Europeans led in 1830 to the Turks' requesting that Governor Rashid Pascha work to restore peace, which he accomplished in 1834.

The next great Christian power to show interest in the East Syrians was the empire of the tsars, which sought to extend its influence in the region of Lake Urmiyah. The "mountain Nestorians" waited in vain for the mighty tsar who was to liberate them. In 1827 groups of East Syriac Christians moved over the border into Russia because they anticipated support from the tsar against the Muslims, and in 1828 the Russians occupied Urmiyah and a part of Azerbaijan. With the peace treaty, the Russians withdrew from Urmiyah, and the border between Iran and Azerbaijan (then Russia) was established in its present location. Some of the Assyrians recognized the Russian church as their head; as further aid failed to materialize, they returned to the faith of their fathers.

The Anglican and Presbyterian Smith and Davies, who traveled to Urmiyah in 1830, were impressed by the aversion to the pope, the cross without corpus, and the unadorned churches of the Assyrians, whose veneration of the Virgin Mary reminded them of their own. In the Romantic era, they saw in the "mountain Nestorians" the authentic "ancient" Protestants. They were not particularly concerned with the splitting up of the church, nor with proselytism; they sought to help them by building schools and social facilities. In 1836 American Protestants succeeded in persuading the East Syriac Christians to write not only in the ancient classical Syriac script but also in the "Modern Syriac" dialect. In 1840 the first printing press was put into operation and used to print a Syriac edition of the Psalter. Following the first published work in Modern Syriac, an edition of the New Testament appeared in 1846 and of the Old Testament in 1852. In 1849 the monthly magazine *Zahire d-Bahra* (*Rays of Light*) began publication, which continued until 1915. In these ways a Modern Assyrian literature was successfully created.

The systematic study of the situation of the Church of the East began in the second quarter of the nineteenth century. After 1825 the Basel missionary Karl Gottlieb Pfander worked in Mesopotamia; he gave the catholicos books in Syriac and Persian. German Protestants also showed an interest in the Church of the East. In 1875 the northern German Protestant institute opened a missionary post in Urmiyah, which operated until 1939. In 1840 the English geologist William Ainsworth traveled with the Chaldean Christian Isa Rassam by order of the British Geographical Society and the Society for Christian Knowledge to the Hakkari region, where Catholicos Shimun explained his fears about the Roman missionary efforts. In 1842 he published his book *Travels and Researches in Asia Minor, Mesopotamia, Chaldea and Armeni* in London with the support of the Society for Promoting Christian Knowledge.

American Presbyterians began missionary work in the region of Lake Urmiyah around 1830. George Percy Badger, an Anglican theologian and printer, lived in Beirut in 1835/6 and, with the support of the archbishop of Canterbury and the bishop of London, began to work on behalf of East Syriac Christians at the end of 1842. In March 1843 he asked the English ambassador to the High Gate to work to persuade the rulers to recognize the catholicos as head of the civil government in Hakkari. Shortly thereafter, in July 1843, massacres instigated by the Kurdish leader Bedr Khan began, resulting in many thousands of East Syriac casualties. Bedr Khan used the tensions between Egypt and Turkey since 1840 to establish a free Kurdish state. The Kurds opposed the Ottoman central authority and sought to subjugate the Christians, in order to establish a national state. Only in 1847, upon the deposition of Badr Khan, did the situation settle down. In 1847 the catholicos, accompanied by Rassam and Badger, fled to Mosul and sought refuge in the English consulate, and afterwards to Urmia in Persia. The British and Russians then began to interfere with the internal relations of the Ottoman empire. The number of members of the Church of the East at this time is thought to have been between 100,000 and 150,000. In 1892, in *La Turquie d'Asie*, the French scholar Cuinet estimated there were 10,000 in Persia and 90,000 in Turkey; of these, 40,000 lived in cities and 50,000 among the tribes of the mountains.

In his two-volume work *The Nestorians and their Rituals* (1852), Badger noted that at the time of his visit, the East Syrians possessed hardly any manuscripts besides those of their religious rituals. In 1832 the Kurds under Muhammad Pascha had reduced the monastery of Rabban Hormizd to ashes. The church was ruined, the monks massacred, and every book they could find destroyed. By Badger's time the Chaldeans possessed only manuscripts, and the patriarchate in Mosul had about fifty. Badger heard that the Chaldean bishop of Seert still had a few books; there were also thought to be small collections in Baghdad and Mardin. He himself was able to obtain for the Society of Christian Knowledge over one hundred manuscripts, among them a New Testament from the tenth century. Badger made it clear to the catholicos that the Anglican Church was not interested in missionary activity but rather in offering help.

The involvement of the English government at the High Gate brought the massacres to an end. So in 1847/9 Catholicos Shimun XVII Abraham stayed in Urmiyah, where the French had been involved in missionary work since 1838. In 1845 the English and Russians succeeded in appointing a "sarparast" in Persia, who was to look after the interests of the Christians. However, political instructions from the capital often came to naught in the countryside, where feudal lords paid them no heed. In 1863 the British secretary of state Lord Russell cautioned Teheran against the consequences of a policy of oppression. Shah Nasruddin contributed toward the construction of a church in 1865. Christians did not enjoy legal equality in Persia; the witness of a Christian against a Muslim was not accepted by the courts. In 1881 the British ambassador to Teheran brought about a change in policy. In future, Christians would be permitted to stay anywhere in the region of Urmiyah; disputes with Muslims would in future be handled in the civil courts. In the same year the British consul in Tabriz reported to London that Christians in Azerbaijan had in the meantime received schooling and were learning English. Nevertheless, the complaints did not cease; many Christians longed for a Russian protectorate. Beginning in 1883 the American ambassador to Persia also supported the cause of the Christians. An evangelical Nestorian church also emerged in Persia and received a civilian spokesman in 1880.

In 1856, during the Crimean War, the British learned that in the so-called "Hatt-i Humayun Decree" the old Ottoman millet system had been reestablished. In 1863 the Syriac Christians for the first time turned directly to Queen Victoria of England for help; in 1868 they appealed to the archbishop of Canterbury. In this impressive document, signed by fifty-three bishops, priests, and maleks, the East Syrians protested their 700-year imprisonment, during which the Christians of the West had forgotten them. Rome was portrayed with the papacy as the "Muhammad of the West"; as for what they could expect from America, one should look to the fact that after thirty-five years of missionary activity, not one of the "converted" was in a position to read the biblical writings and offer commentary. Although the catholicos had turned to the brother of the tsar for assistance on April 14, 1868, the leaders of the Assyrians placed their greatest hopes on England. The consequence was the founding of the Assyrian Christian Aid Fund. In England the term "Nestorian" was from then on replaced by "Assyrian."

In this fashion a new self-consciousness gradually emerged in the Church of the East, whose members believed themselves to be the oldest autochthonous community in the region. The English church determined to support the Assyrians against their oppressors and to enable the publication of religious writings and the education of clergy. In 1876 an English commission led by Edward L. Cutts traveled to Kotchannes and afterwards to the Persian Urmiyah, where the situation of the Assyrians appeared to be even worse than in Turkey. Cutts published his impressions in the book *Christians under the Crescent in Asia*. The archbishop of Canterbury also sent Rudolf Wahl, an Austrian converted from Judaism, as a missionary to the Assyrians. The English ambassador Henry Layard, however, warned against too great an involvement, as this would only lead to further persecutions. Prime Minister Lord Salisbury wrote personally to the catholicos and warned him of cooperating too closely with the English church. In 1878, at the time of the Berlin congress, England entered into a treaty with Turkey to establish a protectorate governing Cyprus. As a consequence, England considered itself the guardian of the Christians in Kurdistan. The new archbishop, Edward White Benson, continued the Anglican Church's support of the Assyrians. Arthur John Maclean and William Henry Browne journeyed to Kotchannes in 1886 and met with Catholicos Shimun XVIII Ruben (1861–1903). Although the local authorities mounted opposition in Persia, the delegation was able to carry out its activities in Urmiyah, as well. Subsequently an education system was established among the Assyrians. Despite several diplomatic interventions by England, the Persian authorities sought to thwart this development. For twenty-three years Browne remained at the side of the catholicos in Kotchannes. Conflicts also developed with Catholic missionaries. Catholicos Shimun XVIII had greater sympathy for the Catholics than had his uncle and predecessor. In 1865 the Dominican prior Lion of Mosul visited him in Kotchannes. In 1869 Shimun XVIII, like the non-uniate Oriental patriarch, was invited by the Dominican Vincent Lemée to attend the Vatican Council as an observer. However, the catholicos did not go to Rome.

In 1884 in the journal *Année dominicaine*, the Dominican Bonvoisin reported that sentiment among the East Syrians in favor of union with Rome was increasing. This was, however, mostly wishful thinking. In 1886 Bonvoisin visited the patriarch in Kotchannes. Catholics and Anglicans each tried to win the catholicos over to their side. In 1891 he turned to the pope, through the Dominicans, with the request for help in building schools and seminaries. Thus the rumor emerged in 1892 that the catholicos was negotiating with the Chaldean patriarch Elias XIII Abolyonan regarding recognition of the pope. *Figaro* reported that the catholicos had arranged with the pope that after his death no successor would be elected, rather the office would be given to Elias. The English theologian F. G. Coan tried to persuade the catholicos to hold fast to those doctrines the Church of the East had preserved during the persecutions. The catholicos rejected the accusation of defection to the side of the pope. In 1894 the new Chaldean patriarch Abdisho V Khayyat sent the catholicos a papal document of November 30, 1894, in which the pope allowed the Oriental churches use of the non-Roman liturgy and attacked the Protestants. In Persia, Catholic Vincentian Fathers continued their labors in Salmas and Khosrowa, which was also called the "Persian Rome."

Interest in Syriac Christians was also stirring in Germany. The Orientalist Eduard Sachau visited Syria in 1879/80; he journeyed through Edessa and Mosul to Jezireh, Mardin, and Diyarbakir. He carried 250 manuscripts and 50 publications of the missionaries from Urmiyah back to Berlin; the Sachau Collection in the Berlin library was constantly expanded and included manuscripts from the sixth century on. In contained one of the oldest Syriac biblical manuscripts but also chronicles and literary works of the East Syrians (e.g. poems of Narsai). Sachau also encouraged the East Syrians to write in their vernacular, Fellihi. In the second half of the nineteenth century, Protestant missionary societies also worked among the "Nestorians." Interest in the East Syriac church has remained especially strong among the Protestant Christians of Germany since this time. The East Syriac priest John Pera, born in Urmiyah in 1850, studied at Hermannsburg from 1875 to 1880; he became the "father of Lutheran Nestorians." His son Luther Pera likewise studied at Hermannsburg, then worked until 1915 in Urmiyah and later in Germany. The catholicos sent Bishop Abimelek Timothy, who went to India in 1908, to Urmiyah to counteract the missionary efforts of the Protestants. In March 1913, Nadolny, counsel to the German legation, who had been sent to Urmiyah, intervened on behalf of the interests of the "Lutheran Nestorians" and the German Empire.

Interest in the "Nestorians" in Germany was also reflected in the popular novels of Karl May. Particularly in the book *Durch das wilde Kurdistan* (*Through Wild Kurdistan*), which even included the letter of Prester John, the author offers a kind of standard characterization of the Church of the East, which shaped the image of the church for the general public:

> In the valleys, which lie between them, live the last of those Christian sectarians, to whom this Tartar king belonged. At his time, they were powerful and influential; the seats of their metropolitans lay scattered across the whole Asian continent, from the coast of the Caspian Sea to the Chinese

seas and from the farthest northern boundary of Scythia to the southern tip of the Indian peninsula. They were counselors to Muhammad and his successors. The Christian echoes in the Qur'an were taken mostly from their doctrines and books. But with the fall of the caliphs, their power, too, came to an end, and with great speed; for their inner spiritual constitution lacked that divine purity which provides the strength for unconquerable resistance. Already under the rule of Ghazan, a son of Argun and a grandson of the renowned conqueror of Baghdad Hulagu Khan, the persecutions against them had begun. Then the great Tamerlane descended mercilessly upon them. With insatiable fury he persecuted them, destroyed their churches, and murdered with the sword all those who failed to escape to the remote mountains of Kurdistan. The great-grandchildren of these refugees live today in towns resembling fortresses. They, the remnants of the once so powerful Assyrian people, see the sword of the Turks and the dagger of the Kurds hanging forever over them and have endured in more recent times atrocities which would make your hair stand on end. A great part of the guilt for this belongs to those overseas missionaries, who gave their schools and temples the appearance of fortifications, thus arousing the mistrust of the powerful. Through these and other thoughtless actions they harmed their cause as well as their supporters.

Karl May used reports he had read in a number of different newspapers. He also stated that the Nestorians "were made to suffer great oppression . . . such that after a short time resentment began to fester and it seemed they might arise and exact revenge." In this regard, the Kurds boasted that the "Giaurs" were happy as long as they were left in peace. Through the novels of Karl May many people, especially in German-speaking regions, learned the fate of the "Nestorians," of whom they were previously unaware. The hero had to pray the Lord's Prayer in order to be recognized as a Christian. The creed was also quoted. He had a woman describe the massacre by the Kurd Bedr Khan:

They descended on us from all sides, these Kurdish monsters. They destroyed our homes, burned our gardens, ruined our harvest, desecrated our churches, murdered our men, young and old, tore to pieces our boys and girls, and hounded our women until they fell down dead, menaced by the monsters even as they breathed their last. The water of the Zab ran red with the blood of the innocent victims, and the peaks and valleys of the land were lit by the fires which consumed our towns and villages. A single, terrible cry sounded through the whole land. It was the death cry of many thousands of Christians. The pasha of Mosul heard this cry but sent no help, for he wanted to share the spoils with the thieves.

Karl May offered a picture similar to that of Franz Werfel in his novel of the Armenian massacre, *Die vierzig Tage des Musa Dagh* (*The Forty Days of the Musa Dagh*). The crime on a bridge was concretely portrayed:

Our young women were dragged over this bridge, to be carried off to Tkohma and Baz; they chose, however, to jump into the water, preferring death to this fate. Not one remained. Do you see the mountain to the right, with the stone wall? The people of Lizan escaped to that mountain, believing they could not be captured from below. But they had only a little food and water. To avoid starvation, they had to surrender to Beder Khan Bey. He promised them with his holiest oath their freedom and their lives; they had only to hand over their weapons. This they did; but he broke his promise and had them murdered with sabres and knives. And when the arms of the Kurds began to ache from this bloody work, they made it simpler; they threw the Christians over the nine-hundred-foot-high stone wall: old men, young men, women, and children. Out of more than a thousand Chaldani [i.e. Chaldeans/East Syrians] only one lived to tell what had happened up there.

Through the novels of the popular writer May, generations of young people learned for the first time of the Turkish-Kurdish genocide carried out on the members of the Church of the East.

Toward the end of the nineteenth century, the Church of the East got caught in the whirlpool of political interests held by the great powers Russia, England, and France, who all sought influence over the "sick man on the Bosporus," as the Ottoman empire was then called. The new sultan, Abdulhamit II, allied himself more closely with Germany and distanced himself from England, which had occupied Egypt in 1882. The Kurds were then given by the sultan a free hand against the Christians.

The Russians pursued their plans for expansion at the end of the nineteenth century only in the direction of Persia, though without regard for the Ottoman empire. Nor did they abandon their interest in the East Syrians. As early as 1851 Bishop Mar Yosip of Ada had sent an ambassador to Erevan and Tiflis. In 1861 one Michael of Urmiyah traveled to St Petersburg and requested that Sophoniah, a member of the holy synod of the Orthodox Church, come to the Caucasus to study the situation of the Christians. Sophoniah is thought to have made the trip in 1863, taking with him a petition for union with Orthodoxy, signed by numerous bishops. In 1882 the Russian general consul in Tabriz reported that several Syrians and Armenians sought to submit themselves to the Russian government. In 1884 Mar Gabriel in Tiflis negotiated the project of union. However, the Russian church did not consider the Syrians trustworthy; they were submitting themselves only to obtain money. At first they still feared the political complications of engagement with the Church of the East. The situation changed when the British lost the tobacco concession in Persia in 1892. Consequently Russian influence in Persia increased. In accordance with the requests of Mar Yonan and the exarch of Georgia, the holy synod now began to examine the situation of the Syriac Christians.

Envoys of the Georgian exarch traveled to Tabriz and Urmiyah, where they were received by Mar Yonan and some eight to ten thousand people. Of these, however, only three hundred were prepared to enter into a union with Russian Orthodoxy. It was clear that the realization of union would only be possible if political and economic aid were to follow. Nevertheless, the Anglicans sought to preserve the Church of the East. Browne feared the extinction of the church in a union with Moscow or Rome. The excommunication of Nestorius and the problem of the Council of Ephesus also appeared insoluble. The British worked to prevent at least the Christians of the Ottoman empire and the catholicos from entering a union with Russia.

In 1898 Mar Yonan traveled with four priests to St Petersburg and declared himself ready to conclude a union with the Russian Orthodox Church, in order to obtain the support of the tsar. In the monastery of Alexander Nevsky Lavra, he was accepted into the Orthodox Church. At the ceremony, a telegram of greeting from the tsar was read. Some 20,000 East Syrians converted to the Russian

Orthodox Church. Village by village, churches were absorbed into the Orthodox Church and solemnly "absolved" of their "heresy." Anyone whose name did not appear in the Russian calendar of saints had to adopt a new name. Nestorius was condemned as a heretic, and all were required to recognize the first seven councils. Bishop Mar Dinkha of Terwaga was among the prelates who did not participate in this union. He now served as bishop of Urmiyah, as well, supported by Mar Abimelek Timothy, one of the most important theologians of the Church of the East.

Mar Abimelek compelled the schools in Urmiyah to replace Luther's catechism with Abdisho's *Book of the Pearl.* A conflict developed with the Protestants, who were in part excommunicated and emphasized their connection to Hermannsburg. With the invasion of the Turks into Urmiyah in 1915, the work of the Lutherans came to an end for the time being.

The Russians declared they would limit their efforts to Persia and extended their best wishes to the British for their activities in the Ottoman empire. The Austrian historian C. F. Lehmann-Haupt explored the Persian district of Urmiyah in the year 1898. He estimated the number of "Nestorians" there at about 25,000 and those living in the Ottoman empire at 125,000. While Russia believed itself to be the protector of the Orthodox in the Ottoman empire, France saw itself as guardian of the Catholics, and England supported in particular the Oriental churches. The European colonial powers France and England, as well as tsarist Russia, used Syriac Christianity as an instrument in their *machtpolitik* in the Orient. The fate of the Church of the East would be decided by this new form of colonialism. By the beginning of the twentieth century, the East Syriac Christians had become a plaything in the politics of the great European powers and their churches.

5

THE TWENTIETH CENTURY

Dietmar W. Winkler

At the beginning of the twentieth century, the area settled by the Apostolic Church of the East had been reduced essentially to the rough, mountainous land of Hakkari along the present-day border between Turkey and Iraq. Besides this mountain region, Urmiyah and Van were the only areas with significant numbers of East Syriac Christians. The church which had once embraced all of East Syriac Christianity had, through the unions with Rome and the missions of the Anglicans, Lutherans, Presbyterians, and Russian Orthodox, as well as the attacks of the Kurds, become a tribal church, its members numbering about 150,000 at the beginning of the century. The church was made up of more than a dozen Christian tribes, of which the largest were the Baz, Djilu, Tiari, Tjuma, Diz, and Barwar. Western travelers, scholars, and missionaries gave them the name "Mountain Nestorians," while they simply called themselves "Christians" (*mshihaye*). In the second half of the nineteenth century the missionaries of the Anglican archbishop of Canterbury introduced the term "Assyrian," which they eventually adopted to describe themselves.

The patriarchate, conforming to the social structure of the mountain tribes, had become hereditary and was passed within a family from uncle to nephew. The offices of bishop and metropolitan were likewise hereditary and were taken over, in part, by the tribal rulers, the maliks (kings). Because of this hereditary succession, the episcopacy, priesthood, and patriarchate each remained in a closed group of families. At the start of the twentieth century, the Assyrian Church had one patriarch, one metropolitan, and seven to ten bishops.

Since about 1826 the seat of the patriarch had been in Kotchannes, on the right bank of the upper Great Zab. The patriarch was both ecclesiastical head and secular leader. After the death of Mar Ruben Shimun XVIII (1860–1903), his 17-year-old nephew Benjamin Shimun XIX (1903–18) succeeded to the patriarchal throne. The young ruler, who was still a minor, was supported by the respected metropolitan Isaac Khnanisho, who had his seat in Nuri.

In 1913 some 100,000 faithful were numbered among those East Syriac Christians who had established union with Rome and were called "Chaldeans." Almost entirely limited to the region of modern Iraq, they were largely spared the fate of most Assyrians in the twentieth century. The East Syriac Christians in India – the uniate Syro-Malabars and the metropolitanate of Trichur, which returned from these to the Assyrian Church of the East in 1876 – were also generally undisturbed by the consequences of European politics in the Middle East in the first half of the twentieth century. Nonetheless, events during and after World War I brought the Apostolic Church of the East to the verge of ruin.

World War I

In the decaying Ottoman empire, the idea of the nation-state, imported from Europe, was not only the ideological argument for the Young Turk regime, which sought to found a state including all Turkish peoples, but also the foundation of struggles for autonomy among the Armenians, Assyro-Chaldeans, Kurds, and Arabs. On the eve of World War I, the British, French, and Russians deliberately used the politics of nationalism to win allies and weaken the Ottoman empire.

The Young Turks, who at first announced democratic reforms leading to equality for all peoples represented in the Ottoman empire, soon feared for their dominant position and championed instead the idea of a great Turkish empire from Russia to Central Asia. An agreement for the protection of the Christian millets in the Anatolian regions was established between Russia and the Young Turks. However, Russian interests and the politics of their national government worsened the situation. The Young Turk regime tried to maintain the cohesion of the empire and finally, with the help of Kurdish troops, acted against any effort for independence. Already well-known is the genocide of the Armenians, who were the target of massacres as early as 1894/6, as well as in 1909, and who eventually died by the hundreds of thousands during the deportations beginning in 1915. The West and East Syriac Christians suffered the same fate.

In 1907 an agreement between England and Russia divided the Persian-Mesopotamian region into Russian, neutral, and British spheres of influence. North-western Persia came under the control of the Russians, whose Cossack troops set up military posts in 1909 in Tabriz and Urmiyah, among other places. Consequently the Russian Orthodox mission among the East Syriac Christians, which had been operating since the nineteenth century, was strengthened, and many conversions occurred among their Assyrian fellow Christians. Eventually, as the Russian troops presented a strategic threat to the Young Turks, one of the first Near Eastern conflicts of World War I broke out in neutral Persia.

The Assyrian region of settlement lay on the line dividing the interests of Turkey and Russia. As late as 1914, Patriarch Benjamin Shimun XIX approached the Turkish provincial governor to negotiate for the security of his East Syriac tribes. The governor offered two separate guarantees, but Kurdish-Turkish attacks on Christians soon followed, because the Christians were seen as allies of Russia. On the one side, the Turkish and Kurdish troops proclaimed a "jihad" (holy war), while on the other, the Russians supplied the Christians with weapons. However, in January 1915, because of the military situation in the Caucasus, Russia had to withdraw its troops temporarily from north-western Persia. Turkish troops and Kurdish volunteers subsequently massacred the Assyrians, and peace returned only when the Russians advanced to Van. From here, they established contact with Patriarch Benjamin Shimun XIX in Kotchannes in the Hakkari mountain region. The news of the massacres of Christians and the hope for support from the Russians eventually led to the patriarch's officially declaring war on Turkey in the name of his nation (Millet) on May 10, 1915.

Shortly thereafter the strategic situation changed. The Russians had to withdraw from Van; the Kurds attacked the Assyrians and forced them higher into the mountains. Many East Syriac villages and churches were destroyed. These desperate straits led to the Assyrians' decision to evacuate all of their tribes from the Hakkari mountain region. Under the skillful leadership of their malik, 50,000 men, women, and children gathered together and reluctantly advanced toward Urmiyah, where they hoped to secure aid from Russian troops. On the plains they joined with the Assyrians they met. The "Mountain Nestorians" had left their homeland behind, and few would ever see it again.

Urmiyah lay in neutral Persia, where since 1915 starvation and epidemics had ravaged the large refugee population. The arrival of the East Syriac Christians from Hakkari exacerbated the situation. American aid workers and mission stations provided medical and other assistance; nevertheless, the death rate among the refugees may have reached one-third.

In Urmiyah the Russians recruited the battle-tested Assyrians to oppose the Turkish-Kurdish attacks. In January 1916 Patriarch Benjamin Shimun XIX traveled to Tiflis to meet with Tsar Nicolas, with whom he negotiated for an autonomous Assyrian settlement in their residential areas after the war. However, he had to bow to the general strategic situation. Due to the fatal conditions in Urmiyah, the patriarch was at least able to accomplish the transfer of 15,000 of his people into the Caucasus, where they founded a new home-land in the present-day states of Armenia and Georgia. Those Assyrians who remained behind were subsequently given military training by Russian officers, with the patriarch maintaining supreme command. At his side were placed his father, General David, and another Assyrian with excellent military training, Agha Petros de Baz.

In 1917 the British, who had captured Baghdad, had also been trying to establish relations with the Assyrians. In the battle against the Central Powers an alliance was formed between the Russians and British, which included the Assyrians, Armenians, and the Kurdish tribe of the Shekak. However, after the 1917 October Revolution, the Russian troops pulled out of the Urmiyah region and Turkey. According to British plans, the Assyro-Armenian-Kurdish troops were to form a collective front line to impede a Turkish offensive. While there were no problems between the Armenians and Assyrians, cooperation with the Kurds led to catas-trophe. On March 3, 1918, during talks in the village of Kohinsher, the Kurdish leader, Ismael Agha Simko, had Patriarch Mar Ben-jamin Shimun and his party murdered.

One month later the younger brother of the slain ruler was set up as the new patriarch in Salams. He adopted the name Mar Poulos Shimun XX. The military leadership of the Assyrians, however, was taken over by Agha Petros de Baz. Encouraged by the British, the Assyrian troops withstood the Turkish attacks on Urmiyah until June 1918, though they were surrounded and could no longer receive supplies. The Assyrians and their supporters then resolved to attempt a desperate breakthrough. In a forced march of some 500 kilometers, 70,000 people moved from Urmiyah through west-ern Iran to Hamedan (Ekbatana). Through hunger, epidemics, and Kurdish attacks, this undertaking left about a third of the people dead. In Hamedan the Assyrians found the British, who provided emergency care. In 1918, when the capitulation of Turkey became known, further transport in the direction of Baghdad followed, to a refugee camp near Bakuba. The opportunity to return the Assyrians to their homeland in the Hakkari region, which was at the time a real possibility, was wasted. The camp claimed numerous additional victims among the Assyrians, many of whom died from the strain of the experience. Among the casualties was the respected metropolitan Mar Isaac Khnanisho, who died in 1919. In 1920 the young patriarch Mar Poulos Shimun XX died of tuberculosis, a few months after he had been transferred from the Bakuba camp to the Syrian Orthodox (!) monastery of Mar Mattai near Mosul.

With the loss of the Hakkari region during World War I, the Assyrians lost not only their homeland but also more than half their population. From an estimated 150,000 before World War I, only about 70,000 left Urmiyah, and of these, a mere 50,000 made it through to the British in Mesopotamia. Among the victims were two patriarchs, the metropolitan, many bishops, and the majority of priests. This had a catastrophic effect on the church's situation; the Apostolic Church of the East appeared to have been entirely wiped out. However, the common struggle of World War I caused the particular interests of the Assyrian tribes to give way, in part, to a sense of solidarity. In place of ecclesiastical union, greater support developed for an Assyrian national movement, which would represent as a "nation" the interests of Assyrians and Chaldeans, as well as Syrian Orthodox, Syrian Catholics, and the respective Reformed churches, regardless of their particular confessions. As early as 1915, the Assyrian National Union of America was founded by Assyrian immigrants in the USA. In 1918, in the Babuka camp, an Assyrian National Council was established.

Postwar diplomacy and the question of an Assyrian state

The allied victory awakened among Christian Assyrians the hope for their own autonomous state or at least a return to their traditional homeland. At negotiations with the Assyro-Armenian troops regarding defense of the Urmiyah line, British, Russian, and French diplomats offered assurance of Assyrian autonomy, sponsored by the British. However, neither this question, nor the return to their traditional homeland was explicitly addressed at the Versailles peace talks. It soon became clear that return to the Hakkari region was impossible, and the Assyrians had to remain in Iraq as refugees.

The Assyrians, the "smallest ally," were not, however, the only ones to whom the British and French made promises which were not kept. The Armenians, Kurds, and Arabs had similar experiences. Plans for the Assyrians, Armenians, and Kurds each to have their own state were stymied by their overlapping territories. At the start of World War I the Arabs, under the leadership of Sherif Hussain of Mecca, a member of the Hashemite dynasty, were also promised by the British that following a victory over the Ottomans, they would receive support for the establishment of an independent Arab state. Like the Assyrians and Armenians, the Arabs fought as allies of the Entente. But as early as 1916, the British, French, and Russians had divided the Near East among themselves with the so-called Sykes-Picot Agreement. Following this, in 1917, the British foreign minister Arthur J. Balfour informed the French Baron Rothschild that his government had resolved, again without Arab involvement, to found a homeland in Palestine for the Jewish people. In 1919 Faisal, Hussain's son, made a triumphant entry into Damascus, and many of his supporters saw him as king of an Arab empire stretching from Antioch to Sinai. Nevertheless, at the peace talks following World War I, the Sykes-Picot Agreement – without the Russians, who had pulled out on account of the 1917 October Revolution – was carried out: Syria and Lebanon went to the French; Palestine, Jordan, and Iraq with Kuwait to the British. Many peoples believed they had been cheated out of political promises which had placed a vision of independence before their eyes. Thanks to British intervention, Faisal was nominally tolerated as king of Syria but found himself unprepared to act as a puppet for the French. For this reason, he was forced out of Damascus in 1920. The British subsequently gave Faisal the throne of Iraq. This state was founded in 1921 and stood under British mandate in order to keep open the lines of communication with India and protect British interests in the oilfields of Mesopotamia.

In the partition of the Near East and the securing of European power interests, the question of the Assyrians was but a small detail. At this time the Assyrians were divided into two groups: one stood under the leadership of the patriarchal family, the other under that of Agha Petros. They decided to send a joint representative to the peace negotiations and finally agreed upon Surma, the sister of the two deceased catholicoi, who had been educated by Anglican missionaries. Surma spent 1919/20 in England but failed to obtain permission to participate in the talks at Versailles.

In 1920 Surma's 11-year-old nephew became the new patriarch: Mar Eshai Shimun XXI. Despite the hereditary succession, a formal election was held in the Mendan refugee camp, north-east of Mosul, where a large group of Assyrians had been placed. In 1919, under new British promises, Assyrian troops were again recruited in Iraq to quell Arab and Kurdish uprisings. These so-called Iraqi aid troops (Iraqi Levies) enabled the Sunni Faisal to hold on to his throne in the face of opposition from the Arab Shiites of Iraq, but as foreigners and colonial mercenaries, they earned the hatred of the native population.

The 1920 peace treaty of Sèvres provided for the foundation of an autonomous Kurdish state, in which the Assyro-Chaldeans and smaller ethnic and religious minorities would be guaranteed protection and security. Since in the succeeding years the overall strategic situation and the interests of the victorious powers changed, no autonomous Kurdistan was established. The Assyrian question was also cleared out of the way. In Turkey the troops of Mustafa Kemal Atatturk achieved victory. In 1923 Atatturk proclaimed the Turkish republic, and in 1924 he abolished the caliphate in Istanbul. By the time of the Lausanne Conference (1923), Turkish sovereignty had, for all practical purposes, been reestablished. Turkey had already entered into treaties with France and the Soviet Union. As a consequence, the Kurdish question (and with it the Assyrian question) received scant attention in Lausanne, and Armenia, which had been a signatory power at Sèvres, was not even invited. In the Lausanne treaties the individual peoples were not even named but were merely referred to collectively as "non-Muslim minorities."

The Assyrians had to eke out an uncertain life in Iraq. With no solution in sight and the closing of the Babuka and Mendan camps in 1920, 6,000 mountain and Urmiyah Assyrians attempted, under the leadership of Agha Petros de Baz, to return to their former homeland. The operation failed, a group perished in the mountains, and Agha Petros had to go into exile in France.

Nonetheless, between 1922 and 1923 many Assyrians gradually returned to their former villages in Hakkari. The borders were not yet fixed, and the Turkish state not quite firmly established. In this way, some 8,000 succeeded in returning to their homeland. Most, however, remained as refugees in the plains surrounding Mosul and Kirkuk and set their hopes on the Mosul question, left open at Lausanne.

England, Iraq, and Turkey tussled over the Mosul region. Because of its oil deposits and agriculture, the area had great economic as well as military significance. The borders were not yet firmly established, and the British believed an Assyrian buffer state would have a calming effect on the region. At the 1924 conference of Constantinople, the English representative advocated shifting Iraq's border to the north and settling the Assyrians there. However, the negotiations were broken off. The Turks moved into northern Iraq. Kurds and regular troops attacked Assyrian villages and slaughtered women, children, and elderly people. The population fled by the thousands back into Iraq. In 1925 the archbishop of Canterbury appealed to the British public not to forget the promises made to the Assyrians. Nevertheless, an investigation by a commission of the League of Nations led to the creation of the so-called "Brussels line" dividing Turkey and Iraq, which placed the major region of Assyrian settlement conclusively in the Turkish state. The Assyrian settlement problem, which had existed since World War I, remained acute.

The end of the British mandate in Iraq

The British mandate in Iraq lasted over twelve years. During this time the Assyrian question could not be resolved. The people themselves were without a unified leadership as the young patriarch Mar Eshai Shimun had been living under the care of the archbishop of Canterbury in England, where he was receiving his education. In addition, the Assyrian aid troops were identified by the Muslim Iraqis as Christian supporters of the foreign occupation. Again and again the British thoughtlessly ordered the Iraqi Levies to oppose uprisings of Arab and Kurds. The hatred which built up among the native population made clear that the Assyrians could not be left behind unprotected after Iraq gained its independence.

At the 1927 Anglo-Iraqi negotiations regarding ending the mandate, a common Assyrian position could not be agreed upon. Only about half the Assyrians stood behind the patriarchal family. Other groups rejected the leader, who had returned from England. His position in the eyes of both the Assyrians and the Iraqi authorities was further weakened by his lack of practice in the East Syriac dialect and ignorance of Arabic. Some bishops' families desired the abolition of the hereditary patriarchate and the reintroduction of patriarchal elections, in hope of increasing the prestige of their own families and tribes.

Since the Assyrians recognized that British support would not be provided to the extent that been promised, both the pro- and the anti-patriarchal parties inundated the League of Nations with a flood of petitions between 1930 and 1933. At a 1931 assembly held under the direction of Mar Shimun, an "Assyrian National Pact" was adopted, calling for the recognition of the Assyrians in Iraq as "Millets," not only as a religious minority, and for their return to the Hakkari region. Additionally, the secular and religious leadership of the patriarch was emphasized. Their demands concluded with a declaration of loyalty to King Faisal. In 1932 Mar Eshai Shimun traveled to Geneva to bring the Assyrian concerns to the attention of the League of Nations. Nevertheless, it became clear that a settlement of the Assyrians as a collective ethnic group in a homogeneous and autonomous region was out of the question since Iraq wanted a centralized Arab state rather than a federal structure.

The Iraqi government proposed that the patriarch ought to relinquish the political and worldly power which he had held for centuries by virtue of the social structure of his people. In the course of this debate, the patriarch was placed under house arrest in Baghdad. The tensions with Iraq, which in 1932 was accepted into the League of Nations as an independent state, steadily increased. The perilous situation gradually increased Assyrian sentiment in favor of emigration.

In 1933 the British mandate in Iraq ended, and a group of Assyrians negotiated with the French for their families to be permitted into Syria. The Iraqi interior minister was informed of this peaceable intention. Some 800 men appeared at Little Khabur on the only recently established boundary between Syria and Iraq. The French judged the boundary crossing to be illegal; because they lacked refugee status, the men were sent back. On the Iraqi side, a clash broke out with the government troops who had taken up positions there; 530 Assyrians fled back to Syria, where they were interned. Those who were taken prisoner by the Iraqis were killed, and only a few were able to make it back to their families.

This border incident and the accumulating aggression against the Assyrians led in 1933 to the so-called massacre of Semile. A rumor spread among the Iraqis that the Assyrians were going to plunder northern Iraq. In response, Kurdish and Arab tribes were stirred up against the Assyrians. Sixty out of sixty-four villages were destroyed. Under the leadership of the Iraqi military, the Assyrians were gathered together, and all males over the age of ten were shot. What happened in Semile was a gruesome slaughter by Iraqi troops, which was celebrated by Iraq as a great victory, the defeat of an uprising and the liberation of the country from a great danger. In Semile alone, the dead numbered 350; the total accounting of Assyrian dead during this time reached 3,000.

The patriarch, who was being held in Baghdad, attempted through petitions to inform the diplomatic representatives and the League of Nations of the dramatically intensifying events. This led to the deportation of the 26-year-old leader from Iraq in August 1933; he was taken by British military aircraft to Cyprus. In the same year he again presented the concerns of his people to the League of Nations in Geneva. Excluding the metropolitanate of Trichur in India, there was at this time hardly an Apostolic Church of the East to speak of. The people had been terribly decimated, and the survivors were homeless, the patriarch expelled, the church leaderless. Of the 20–30,000 Assyrians remaining in Iraq, nearly all wanted unreservedly to leave.

In 1933 the League of Nations appointed a committee to resolve the Assyrian question. Various governments were asked to accept the Assyrians. Several remarkable resettlement plans – including such destinations as Brazil, East Africa, Latin America, Canada, and others – were proposed for this old and established mountain people of the Near East. They failed mostly due to lack of financial resources, but also because of immigration problems in the nations suggested.

Emigration and diaspora

While on Cyprus, Patriarch Eshai Shimun submitted numerous documents and petitions in an attempt to make the League of Nations aware of his people's fate. However, even among the Assyrians themselves, opinion regarding his status as a secular leader was divided. He was expelled from Iraq and denied entry into Syria. Eventually – after sojourns in Cyprus, Geneva, Paris, and London – he migrated in 1940/1 to the United States to join his diaspora community there. The center of the American Assyrian diaspora was Chicago, where some 30,000 Assyrians lived. As early as the mid-nineteenth century, the influence of American missionaries around Lake Urmiyah had led to isolated cases of migration to America. However, most migrated in response to the pressures of events during World War I. With the help of the American Episcopal Church, the Church of the East could again be consolidated. Over the course of the following years, churches were established in Gary, Indiana; Flint, Michigan; Yonkers, New York; New Britain,

Connecticut; Philadelphia, Pennsylvania; Turlock, California; and San Francisco. In 1950 in Chicago the theological center of the Apostolic Church was set up, and there selections from and translations of liturgical books were produced in English.

A solution for part of the Assyrians was found in Syria by the settlement committee of the League of Nations. In 1934 the men who had been interned since the 1933 border skirmish were given permits by the French mandate authorities allowing them to move to northern Syria. Beginning in May 1936, 9,000 Assyrians were taken from Iraq and settled in the desolate, entirely uncultivated region of Khabur in the plains of Jezireh. They were divided between thirty-four villages according to their tribal affiliation, with some others settling in the cities of Qamishli, Hassake, and Aleppo, as well. They attained Syrian citizenship in 1941. In the 1950s a few Assyrians migrated from Iraq or Syria to Lebanon, where they settled primarily in Beirut.

In Iran prior to the events of World War I the Assyrians lived almost exclusively in the area around Urmiyah. At that time some 9,000 Assyrians lived in the city itself, with another 30,000 in the surrounding countryside. After World War I and the emergency flight to Mesopotamia, a minor reverse migration began in 1922. About 7,000 Assyrians returned to Urmiyah, which had been named in honor of Shah Reza Pahlavi Rezaye. In some seventy outlying villages the Assyrians established scattered settlements. During World War II, Iranian Assyrians fought alongside Azerbaijanis for an independent republic. Since about 20,000 Assyrians lived in the Soviet Union, mostly in the Caucasus, the prospects for Russian support looked good. However, in 1946, with Stalin's approval, only the Kurdish "Republic of Mahabad" was established, and it collapsed after just a few months. Iranian troops, who marched on Azerbaijan, carried out pogrom-like attacks on Assyrians. Patriarch Mar Eshai Shimun then turned to the United Nations, while at the same time assuring the shah of his loyalty. Due to these events, in the 1950s many Assyrians moved to Teheran or migrated to the United States. Others settled in the province of Khuzistan or in Kuwait, where they found work in the oil industry.

In the mid-1960s the Assyrian community in north-western Iran was, in any case, extremely lively and active. The region around Urmiyah contained fifty-five churches. Many of those Assyrians who had, during the decline of their church, sought refuge in the Anglican, Presbyterian, Chaldean, or Baptist Churches, returned to their church in the 1950s. In 1965 the total number of Assyrians living in Iran ("Nestorians") reached 40,000; of these, most lived in Urmiyah and about 15,000 in Teheran.

At the beginning of World War II the 20,000 or so Assyrians who had remained in Iraq lived in scattered settlements in the north of the country. Thus they had lost their ethnic unity and were, as a "nation," leaderless. The church leadership had been reduced to Mar Yosip Khananisho. The main areas of settlement were Mosul, Irbil, and Kirkuk, but also the capital Baghdad. Beginning in 1961 the Assyrians became entangled in the struggles of the Kurds in northern Iraq. In this matter the Assyrians relied on the treaty of Sèvres, which guaranteed the Assyro-Chaldeans protection and security inside an autonomous Kurdish region. Over the course of the fighting, many Christian villages and churches were destroyed by the Iraqi troops. In June 1969 the monastery of Rabban Hormizd near Alqosh also fell victim to plundering. Mar Eshai Shimun again appealed to the United Nations, as well as to the World Council of Churches. He organized aid committees and public protests against the Iraqi government. Nevertheless, in the West attention was paid almost exclusively to the problems of the Kurds. The ten-year struggle led in 1970 and 1974 to promises of Kurdish autonomy from the Iraqi government, promises President Saddam Hussein has never fulfilled. In the course of the Iran–Iraq war (1980–8) more than 1,200 Kurdish villages were destroyed systematically by the government forces of Iraq.

The events of the first half of the twentieth century almost led to the complete disappearance of the Apostolic Church of the East. The drama began with the exodus from the Hakkari mountain region to Urmiyah. Some fled to the former Soviet Union, especially to the Caucasus. From Urmiyah, the path of suffering led further to Mesopotamia, to the camps of Iraq; from there to Syria, where most settled in Khabur. Many migrated to the United States, where they established their center in Chicago on Lake Michigan. Small groups also moved to France and England, the former mandate holders, as well as to Cyprus and Australia. Aside from the India metropolitanate, the Apostolic Church was fractured, its people spread across the lands of the Near East and uprooted in the diaspora.

Ecclesiastical reorganization and patriarchal schism

In the United States, through persistent efforts, Patriarch Mar Eshai Shimun succeeded in reorganizing his church and rebuilding it on a modest scale. The chief problem for the church was the shortage of priests and the reestablishment of an ecclesiastical hierarchy which had been nearly annihilated in the first half of the twentieth century. The church membership in the 1950s was about 3,200. In the USA the patriarch appointed a bishop for the newly created Diocese of America and Canada. Patriarch Mar Eshai Shimun maintained a connection with his congregations and dioceses in the diaspora by making numerous visits to Iran, Lebanon, and Kuwait. In 1954 the patriarch and his family clan transferred his residence to San Francisco. In addition to building up the organization of the church, he also devoted himself to the translation and publication of the literature of the fathers of his church.

Beginning in 1958 Iran was also established as a diocese and placed under the leadership of Bishop Mar Dinkha Khnanaya, who had been consecrated by Patriarch Mar Eshai Shimun. In 1962 he transferred his seat from northern Iraq to Teheran. The patriarch's access to Iran was good, due to his relationship with Shah Reza Pahlavi of Persia – beginning in 1964 the Assyrians were even represented by a member in parliament – so it was possible for him to visit the bishopric of Iran in the same year. The patriarch had hoped to travel afterwards to Iraq but was unable to obtain an entry permit.

In Iraq since the exile of the patriarch, his uncle and teacher, Metropolitan Mar Yosip Khnanisho, had held the leadership of the church. His diocese lay in the Persian–Turkish border region. In 1963 Mar Khnanisho transferred his see to Baghdad and exercised his office as patriarchal vicar over all the other dioceses of the Near East. In the 1960s additional bishops were ordained for Irbil, Kirkuk, Basra, and Baghdad. Patriarch Eshai Shimun could not return to his homeland until 1970, thirty-seven years after his expulsion. At that time he was again recognized by the Iraqi government as the religious head of his church. Nonetheless, the patriarch deemed the situation too uncertain to permit him to move his see back to Baghdad.

The communities of Khabur in Syria were left entirely to themselves for nearly thirty years. In 1948 Metropolitan Mar Yosip Khnanisho had visited the congregations there and thus reestablished a connection with the church, but they have remained until the present day poor and spiritually neglected. Interestingly, they were at this time cared for by the Syrian Orthodox Church. When in 1968 Mar Shimun sought to visit his congregations in countries of the Near East, he could not gain an entry permit for Syria. However, in Beirut the patriarch was able to ordain Mar Yohannan Abraham as bishop of Khabur, and Mar Narsai, who was originally from Khabur, as bishop of Lebanon.

In 1945 Metropolitan Mar Timothy Abimelech died in India. In the ensuing years, however, it was impossible for the patriarch to ordain a new metropolitan for the approximately 14,000 South Indian adherents of the Church of the East. Not until 1952 was the Syrian-born Mar Thomas Darmo consecrated in Chicago as metropolitan of India and Malabar with his see in Trichur. Nevertheless, in 1960 unrest rocked the Church of the East. Metropolitan Mar Thomas Darmo published a document opposing the hereditary succession of the patriarchate. Mar Eshai Shimun used a stay in India on the occasion of the third general assembly of the World Council of Churches in New Delhi in 1961 to visit the metropolitanate in South India and reestablish order. However, the peace resulting from the patriarch's subsequent reforms was short-lived.

In March 1964 Eshai Shimun issued a decree to his metropolitans and bishops, in which he announced some changes in his church. These included in particular the introduction of the Gregorian calendar, the shortening of Lent, and liturgical reforms. These novelties, which were seen as "Western," aroused opposition among some in the countries of the Near East, which was also tied up with various tribal rivalries. In Baghdad the opposition coalesced around the priest Ishaq Nwiya, who, despite the warnings of Metropolitan Mar Khnanisho and the bishop of Baghdad, Mar Joseph Sarkis, maintained the old Julian calendar and finally named himself head of the "Ancient Church of the East." The group supporting Ishaq Nwiya criticized in particular the more than thirty-year absence of the patriarch, the hereditary patriarchate, and the reforms which had not received synodal approval. The opposition won followers especially from the tribe of Tiari. To remedy the shortage of priests, they turned to the Indian metropolitan Mar Thomas Darmo; in 1965 the Nwiya party placed themselves under his jurisdiction. Mar Eshai Shimun subsequently dismissed the Indian metropolitan. In 1968 Mar Thomas Darmo traveled to Iraq and consecrated three bishops: Mar Poulos and Mar Aprem from Trichur, as well as Mar Addai from Baghdad. Shortly thereafter these three elected Mar Thomas Darmo patriarch of the Church of the East and they deposed Mar Eshai Shimun. Thus there was a duplication of the hierarchy and a patriarchal schism developed. After Mar Thomas died in 1969, the metropolitan of Baghdad, Mar Addai II Giwargis, was elected as his successor. At the beginning of the 1970s the

Figure 5.1 Parish Church of the East Syriac Metropolitanate of Trichur, Kerala (India). Photo: courtesy of Dietmar Winkler.

Apostolic Church of the East was split into two jurisdictions of roughly equal size.

The second crisis after this schism befell the church in the 1970s. In late 1972 Mar Eshai Shimun decided to resign the patriarchate; in 1973 he married. In the same year seven Assyrian bishops from Iran, Iraq (Irbil, Kirkuk, Basra, Baghdad), Lebanon, and Syria assembled in Beirut to discuss the resignation and marriage of the patriarch. The most significant outcome of the synod was the abolition of hereditary succession and the reintroduction of canonical election of the patriarch. Another synodical meeting concerning this difficult question for the Assyrian church took place in Beirut 1975. The problem of the patriarchate was supposed to be solved at a synod in Seattle, Washington. In 1975, however, Mar Eshai Shimun was assassinated. An estranged relative, who wanted to reestablish the family's honor, shot the patriarch on November 6 in San Jose, California.

In spite of this tragic end, the contributions of Patriarch Mar Shimun are difficult to overestimate. He worked hard for his church, led it for fifty-five years and consolidated it despite its near collapse.

The patriarchate of Mar Dinkha IV Khnanaya and ecumenical efforts

With the death of Mar Eshai Shimun, the hereditary succession of the patriarchate came to an end. On October 17, 1976, in London, five Assyrian bishops, two Italian bishops who had been consecrated by Mar Eshai Shimun, and representatives of Mar Khananisho of Iraq elected Mar Dinkha Khnanaya as the new patriarch and 120th successor to the seat of Seleucia-Ctesiphon. Present were also three bishops of the Anglican Church. At the age of thirty-three, Mar Dinkha had been appointed by Mar Eshai Shimun as metropolitan of Teheran and Iran – thus becoming the nineteenth bishop in his family. Even before his birth, this Iraqi native had been designated for the office of bishop, and when he was 11 years old, his education was entrusted to Metropolitan Mar Yosip Khnanisho. As bishop in Iran he spoke out publicly about Assyrian concerns, instituted ecumenical worship services in Teheran on religious holidays, and established a seminary, in which the candidates not only attended high school but also were educated in the Syriac language, liturgy, and church history.

Until the Iran–Iraq war (1980–8), Mar Dinkha had his see in Teheran; thereafter he transferred it to Chicago. The two wars in the Persian Gulf region brought renewed hardship to the Christian minority. In Iran the Persian empire under Shah Reza Pahlavi had been destroyed by the Islamic Revolution and the return of the Ayatollah Khomeini from his exile in France; a program of Shiite Islamicization ensued. In Iraq Saddam Hussein sought to institute a plan of Arabization, affecting in particular the Kurds and Christians in northern Iraq, who were violently expelled. In 1988 Saddam Hussein advanced on northern Iraq because the Kurds had supported Iran during the Iran–Iraq war. In the process, many Christian villages, churches, and monasteries were destroyed, and a wave of Kurdish and Christian refugees fled to Turkey, Iran, Jordan, and Syria. Despite the military clashes in northern Iraq, the Gulf War (1990–1) drew the world's attention to Kuwait in the south. The 1991 United Nations ceasefire resolution made no reference to northern Iraq. In 1992, West European and American initiatives led to the creation of a kind of "buffer zone" north of the 36th parallel, though this was not recognized under international law. The Kurds hoped for their own state within Iraq. The Assyrians were once again the forgotten segment of the region's populace. Since the end of the Gulf war in 1991 more than 10,000 Christians (Assyrians, Chaldeans, Armenians, etc.) leave Iraq each year because of the UN embargo against the regime of Saddam Hussein, because of the hopeless economic situation and the fear of a new war.

Catholicos-Patriarch Mar Dinkha IV sought to lead the Assyrians out of their isolation and neglect by focusing particularly on ecumenical engagement. As early as 1948 (or 1950) the Apostolic Church of the East was a member of the World Council of Churches (WCC). However, only Patriarch Mar Eshai Shimun regularly participated in its sessions at that time since in many countries his church had no contact with the ecumenical movement due to difficult political and personnel situations. The clergy first had to revitalize itself; theological formation was not possible. Besides the lack of qualified participants, the accusation of "Nestorianism" also stood in the way of involvement of the Assyrian Church in bilateral ecumenical dialogues. Within the WCC the Assyrian Church has participated in multilateral dialogue with Catholic, Orthodox, Oriental, Anglican, Reformed, and Lutheran Churches. Apart from that it was only in the 1980s that the church became associated with additional ecumenical institutions.

In 1984, on the occasion of its fourth general assembly in Limassol (Cyprus), Mar Dinkha IV sought to gain admission to the Middle East Council of Churches (MECC). However, the request was denied, opposed in particular by the Oriental Orthodox Churches under the leadership of the Coptic Orthodox Church. Their reservations grew out of the fifth-century Christological disputes between Cyril of Alexandria and Nestorius of Constantinople. Only the participation in the 1990 fifth general assembly in Nicosia (Cyprus) of the seven Near Eastern churches which stood in union with Rome inspired new impulses. A separate dialogue committee was established, and several official and unofficial meetings, with the aim of clarifying theological concerns, took place in the following years. In 1994 the sixth general assembly of the MECC instructed the executive committee to proceed with the admission and integration of the Assyrian Church into the MECC. However, due to the continued opposition of the Coptic Orthodox Church, admission remained impossible for the seventh general assembly, held in April 1999. The Assyrian Church was invited as an observer only. The synod held a month earlier in Chicago under Catholicos-Patriarch Mar Dinkha rejected this observer status. While

Protestant/Episcopal or Oriental Catholic churches can be members of the MECC, this is currently not possible for one of the oldest churches of Christianity.

Only at the sixth general assembly of the MECC (1994) had progress been evident, and the Coptic pope Shenouda III had even invited an Assyrian delegation to bilateral ecumenical talks. These took place in January 1995 at the Coptic monastery of Amba Bishoy (Wadi Natrun, Egypt). A joint declaration on Christology was worked out, and put forth for consideration by their respective synods. The Assyrian Church ratified the declaration in the same year, but the Coptic synod rejected it. The dialogue was stopped by the Coptic Orthodox Church in 1996.

In contrast, the dialogue with the Roman Catholic Church achieved success. The first meeting between Mar Dinkha IV and John Paul II had already occurred, on the occasion of the pope's inauguration in 1978. In 1984 Mar Dinkha made an official visit to Rome, and the two ecclesiastical leaders initiated a process of

Figure 5.2 Catholicos Mar Dinkha IV Khnanaya and Pope John Paul II in Rome (1994). Photo: courtesy of *The Messenger*, journal of the Holy Apostolic Catholic Assyrian Church of the East, 11 (1995).

theological dialogue. Between 1984 and 1994 there were five informal meetings, which led to the historic "Common Christological Declaration" of Mar Dinkha IV and John Paul II on November 11, 1994. This was also the starting point of an official theological dialogue between the two churches. From October 1995 to October 1999 five working sessions took place. Following the declaration on Christology, work was begun on a joint statement on sacramental theology.

This official process received unofficial support from the "Syriac Dialogue" of the Pro Oriente Foundation (Vienna, Austria). In June 1994, before the signing of the "Common Christological Declaration," the first Syriac Consultation took place in Vienna on the invitation of Pro Oriente. This multilateral ecumenical dialogue included for the first time representatives of all the churches of the Syriac tradition: the Assyrian and the Ancient Church of the East, the Oriental Orthodox Churches (Syrian Orthodox from Antioch, Malankara Orthodox from India), and the Oriental Catholic Churches (Chaldean, Syrian, Maronite, Syro-Malabar, and Syro-Malankara Catholic Churches) – supported by internationally recognized experts on the history, language, and theology of these churches. At this consultation the establishment of a coordinating body, the "Commission on Dialogue within the Syriac Tradition" (or "Syriac Commission"), was proposed, and in 1994 in Kaslik (Lebanon) it was finally constituted. This commission also organized the second, third, fourth, and fifth Syriac Consultations (Vienna in 1996, Chicago in 1997, Vienna in 2000 and 2002). In this way, controversial issues of history and Christology, as well as sacramental theology, have been discussed and could be successfully handled.

A positive consequence of the second Pro Oriente Syriac Consultation (1996) was the start of an official dialogue between the Assyrian and Syrian Orthodox Churches, which was initiated in the same year by the patriarchs Mar Dinkha IV and Ignatios Zakka I Iwas. However, in 1998 the Coptic Orthodox Church insisted that the so-called Oriental Orthodox Churches of the Middle East should only take part in ecumenical dialogues as a family. This was also manifested in a joint document of the Near Eastern patriarchs of the Coptic Orthodox, Armenian Apostolic, and Syrian Orthodox Churches. Because of this, official bilateral discussions between the Assyrians and the Syrian Orthodox were temporarily suspended. Pro Oriente has provided the only forum in which these churches could engage in ecumenical dialogue, at least on an unofficial level.

On the basis of the "Common Christological Declaration" of Mar Dinkha IV and John Paul II, the two East Syriac sister churches, the Assyrian Church and the Chaldean Catholic Church began their own dialogue. In 1996 the patriarchs, Mar Dinkha IV and Mar Raphael I Bidawid, inaugurated this official process of cooperation on pastoral and practical levels.

In 1994 in Sydney, as a structural measure for this multifaceted ecumenical engagement of the Assyrian Church, the synod created a "Commission on Inter-Church Relations and Educational Development." The dynamic and theologically well-educated bishop Mar Bawai Soro was named its general secretary. The synod also turned renewed attention to reunion with the "Ancient Church of the East" led by Patriarch Mar Addai II Giwargis, especially because there were no theological grounds for the division. As early as 1984 the two patriarchs had agreed on a reunion, but it had not yet happened for political and tribal reasons. In Chicago 1999 the Assyrian synod under Mar Dinkha recognized all previous ordinations and ecclesiastical orders from Reader to Patriarch of the "Ancient Church of the East" under Mar Addai II. In the same year there was also another meeting of the patriarchs in Chicago.

In the meantime, individual congregations and priests had returned to the jurisdiction of Mar Dinkha, with the Indian metropolitanate of Trichur representing the largest group. In November 1995 Metropolitan Mar Aprem, who had been ordained by Mar Thomas Darmo in 1968 and subsequently belonged to the opponents of Mar Dinkha, joined, along with all his congregations, with Mar Dinkha. In January 2000 the catholicos-patriarch visited the metropolitanate in India, which is once again united with the larger church.

Present situation and structure

There are no accurate statistics about the number of Christians in the Middle East. However, the following figures may give at least an idea of the size and spread of the Church of the East. At the beginning of the twenty-first century, the "Holy Apostolic Catholic Assyrian Church of the East" under Catholicos-Patriarch Mar Dinkha IV has approximately 385,000 members. The "Ancient Church of the East" under Patriarch Mar Addai II Giwargis (Baghdad) has two metropolitans in Iraq (Mosul, Kirkuk) and three bishops (Syria, Iraq, United States). It numbers perhaps 50–70,000 faithful in total.

Some 400,000 members belong to the Chaldean Catholic sister church, whose patriarch Raphael I Bidawid (since 1989) has his see in Baghdad. It has nine dioceses in Iraq, three in Iran, and one each in Turkey, Lebanon, Syria, Egypt, and the United States, as well as three vicariates in Europe and one each in Canada and Australia. The Indian Catholics who follow the East Syriac rite, the Syro-Malabar Church, are by far the largest group. They have about 3.8 million members. Their head since 1999 is Archbishop Major Varkey Cardinal Vithayatil, whose see is in Ernakulam.

Despite the unions with the Catholic Church, the political events of the twentieth century, and its present split into two jurisdictions, the Assyrian Church of the East appears on the cusp of the twenty-first century to be once again stable and structured. The see of the catholicos-patriarch is in Chicago. The church has four metropolitans with seats in Baghdad, Beirut, and Trichur, as well as eight bishops, whose congregations are spread around the world:

UNITED STATES (APPROX. 100,000)

Patriarchal Diocese of the Eastern United States
Head: His Holiness Catholicos-Patriarch Mar Dinkha IV (Chicago)
Eight parishes: four in Chicago; one each in Detroit; Flint, Michigan; Yonkers, New York; New Britain, Connecticut

Diocese of the Western United States
Chancellery: Bishop Mar Aprim Khamis (Phoenix, Arizona)
Six parishes: Phoenix; Modesto, Ceres, Turlock, Tarzana, Fullerton (all in California)

Diocese of Western California
Chancellery: Bishop Dr Mar Bawai Soro (San Jose, California), General Secretary of the Commission for Inter-Church Relations and Educational Development of the Assyrian Church of the East
Four parishes: San Jose, San Francisco, Sacramento, Seattle

CANADA (APPROX. 20,000)

Diocese of Canada
Chancellery: Bishop Mar Emmanuel Joseph (Etobikoke, Ontario)
Four parishes: Toronto, Mississauga, London, Hamilton (all in Ontario)
One mission in Windsor, Ontario

AUSTRALIA AND NEW ZEALAND (APPROX. 25,000)

Diocese of Australia and New Zealand

Chancellery: Bishop Mar Meelis Zaia (Fairfield, New South Wales, Australia)

Four parishes: two in Sydney; Reservoir (Victoria, Australia); Miramar (Wellington, New Zealand)

One mission in Manurewa (Auckland, New Zealand)

EUROPE (APPROX. 30,000)

Diocese of Europe

Chancellery: Bishop Mar Odisho Oraham (Norsborg, Sweden, and London)

Eight parishes: Norsborg, Göteborg, Huskvarna, Linkoping, Skovde (all in Sweden); London; Brabrand, Denmark; Arnhem, The Netherlands

Two congregations without priests in Wiesbaden, Germany; and Vienna, Austria

IRAN (APPROX. 20,000)

Diocese of Iran

Chancellery (administration): Catholicos-Patriarch Mar Dinkha IV (Chicago)

Four parishes: two in Teheran, two in Urmiyah

LEBANON (APPROX. 5,000)

Diocese of Lebanon and Syria

Chancellery: Metropolitan Mar Narsai de Baz (Beirut), Patriarchal Vicar

Four dioceses with priests: three in Beirut, one in Zahle

SYRIA (APPROX. 25,000)

Diocese of Hassake

Chancellery: Bishop Mar Afram Athnael (Hassake)

Seven parishes: Hassake, Qamishli, Khabur region

Twenty missions in the Khabur region

IRAQ (APPROX. 45,000)

Metropolitanate of Iraq
  Chancellery: Metropolitan Mar Geevargese Sliwa (Baghdad)
  Auxiliary: Bishop Mar Joseph Sarkis (Baghdad)
  Seven parishes in Baghdad

NORTHERN IRAQ, RUSSIA, ARMENIA, GEORGIA (APPROX. 90,000)

Diocese of Dohuk
  Chancellery: Bishop Mar Isaac Joseph
  Northern Iraq (approx. 40,000): four congregations with priests:
two in Dohuk, Sarsank, Mosul
  Russia and Armenia (50,000): one congregation with a priest in
Moscow; missions in Erewan (Armenia) and Georgia

INDIA (APPROX. 25,000)

Metropolitanate of India
  Chancellery: Metropolitan DDr Mar Aprem Mooken (Trichur)
  Twenty-eight parishes in the states of Kerala, Tamilnadu, and
Karnataka, and in Mumbai and New Delhi.

6

LANGUAGE AND LITERATURE OF THE CHURCH OF THE EAST

SYRIAC LITERATURE

Dietmar W. Winkler

In its scope and extent, Syriac literature represents the most important type of Oriental Christian literature. For the period of ancient Christian literature (the Patristic period), its notable translations, as well as its many original creations, can withstand comparison to contemporary Greek and Latin writings.

Language

As a Semitic language, Syriac belongs to Aramaic as a North-West Semitic language; it is the local Aramaic dialect of Edessa. This became the written language of Aramaic-speaking Christianity primarily through the translation of the Bible in the second century. In the fourth century, through the liturgy and its extensive literature, Syriac spread across the Persian empire and eastern provinces of the Roman empire and accompanied the missions of the Church of the East to India, and to Central and East Asia.

Because of political, geographic, and ecclesiastical divisions, the language began to diverge in East and West Syriac in the fifth century. Under the influence of Greek, West Syriac changed more significantly than East Syriac; thus the latter represents a more archaic step in the development of the language. This is clearly evident in pronunciation. The differences between classical East and West Syriac are not, however, particularly significant.

Beginning in the seventh century, as a consequence of the Arab conquest, Syriac was gradually displaced as a colloquial language, but it maintained an important position as a liturgical and literary language until the fourteenth century. Even today classical Syriac is used as a liturgical language in both the East and West Syrian traditions.

As a spoken language, classical Syriac continued to develop and lives on today through Modern Syriac or Modern Aramaic dialects in several linguistic enclaves. For example: the Eastern and Central Modern Syriac is spoken by Assyrians and Chaldeans in Iran (Urmiyah), Syria (Khabur), and Iraq (Mosul), while Modern West Syriac is used in particular by the Syrian Orthodox Christians in the Tur Abdin (south-eastern Turkey). Through the emigration of Christians from the Middle East, the language is also found in western countries, where its continued existence is threatened.

Script

Syriac is first attested in quite a number of pagan inscriptions from the first to the third centuries. The oldest extant Syriac manuscript (British Museum Add. 12150) was written in 411, also in Edessa. The most important collections of manuscripts at present are found in the British Museum, the Vatican Library, Paris, Berlin, Birmingham, Manchester, and Oxford, but also in Egypt, Iraq, Lebanon, Tur Abdin, and the United States.

Syriac is written right-to-left, consists of twenty-two consonants, and has three different forms: the old Edessan script, Estrangelo (from the Greek *strongyle*, "rounded"), was used until the thirteenth century, and is seen today in most academic texts. In the course of the eighth century the West Syrians developed the Serto ("character," "scratch") script, while later on the East Syrians developed a script from Estrangelo referred to by Western scholars as "Nestorian" or "Chaldean." The old Estrangelo script lacked vowel notation. For the East Syriac script – used by Assyrians and Chaldeans – a punctuation system was created to indicate vowels, while the West Syriac script – used by Syrian Orthodox and Maronites – beginning in the seventh century, added vowels deriving from Greek letters above and below the consonants. Syriac script was also used for other languages, such as Christian Palestinian Aramaic and Christian Arabic (Karshuni).

Literature

One can, in essence, divide Syriac literature into four major periods (cf. S. P. Brock).

From the beginnings to the fourth century

Syriac attained its significance as a literary language through translations of the Old Testament (Peshitta OT) and New Testament (Vetus Syra NT). The earliest Old Testament translations were done directly from Hebrew and can be traced back to the first century. The Syriac translation of the Gospels is preserved in the Curetonian (fifth-century parchment manuscript without the Gospel of Mark, British Library) and in Sinaiticus (fourth-century palimpsest, written over in the eighth century, held in the Sinai Monastery). The standard Syriac translation of the Bible, the Peshitta, was presumably completed in the fifth century. The Gospel harmony of Tatian (c.170), the Diatessaron, was also used in the Syriac churches.

Also from this early period are *The Book of the Laws of the Countries*, which was probably written by Philippus, a pupil of the Aramaean philosopher Bardaisan (154–222); the *Gospel of Thomas*, which presumably was written in Syriac around 150; as well as the *Odes of Solomon*, a collection of forty-two lyric poems. Into the apocryphal *Acts of Thomas* is incorporated the *Hymn of the Pearl*, a poetic fairytale, probably of Parthian origin.

The Golden Age: fourth to seventh centuries

This epoch represents the full flowering of Syriac literature and produced two extraordinary writers: Aphrahat and Ephrem. Aphrahat, called the "Persian Sage" was the first Syriac writer outside the Roman empire from whom a significant work has survived. He was the author of twenty-three *Demonstrations*, dating from 337 to 344 and addressing a variety of religious themes (faith, prayer, fasting, circumcision, care for the poor, Sabbath, etc.). With Ephrem the Syrian († 373), the beginning and zenith of Syriac poetry were achieved simultaneously. He was lauded as a poet and theologian by Jerome, Palladius, and Sozomen. However, Ephrem was also one of the most important Syriac prose writers. In addition to his outstanding hymns and verse homilies, he authored biblical commentaries and refutations of false doctrines.

Little has been preserved of the works of two other important writers. Balai († 431) was a writer of verse homilies and liturgical hymns. He favored a five-syllable meter, which has been named the meter of Mar Balai. From Cyrilliona's (c.400) major works, only six verse texts based on episodes from the Gospels have survived.

Beginning in the fifth century, through the political-geographical division on the one hand, and the theological-ecclesiastical on the other, separate East and West Syriac literatures developed. For East Syriac literature the theological school of the Persians in Edessa, which achieved fame through Ephrem, was most important at first. Presumably there the anonymous *Teaching of Addai* (*Doctrina Addai*), recounting the correspondence between Jesus and King Abgar and the conversion of Edessa, was produced. Following the closure of the school of Edessa by Emperor Zeno in 489, the school of Nisibis became influential for the Church of the East. One of the most outstanding teachers of this educational center was Narsai, the most important East Syriac poet-theologian of the fifth century. Some eighty verse homilies have survived. Through the translation projects of the schools of Edessa and Nisibis, some texts lost in the Greek original – because they were judged heretical – have been preserved. For instance, the original Greek writings of Theodore of Mopsuestia († 428) – exegetical works and catechetical homilies – were not only rescued by translation into Syriac but also became the most important foundation for East Syriac theology. For the Church of the East, Theodore serves as interpreter par excellence. Also dating from the fifth century is a rich treasury of hagiography, such as the *Acts* of the Persian martyrs under Shapur II.

Among the translators of the school of Nisibis, the future catholicos Aba is worthy of mention. He brought with him from his travels in the Roman empire the works of Nestorius, among others, and may have translated Nestorius' *Book of Heraclides* from Greek into Syriac. However, this project may have been the work of his student Cyrus of Edessa, author of six *Explanations* of the main dominical commemorations (Fast, Pascha, Passion, Resurrection, Ascension, Pentecost).

The generally free translations from Greek of the fourth and fifth centuries gave way in the sixth and seventh to increasingly literal approaches. Over the course of the sixth and seventh centuries, in addition to translations of Greek philosophical works, a small number of Middle Persian works were also translated into Syriac, among them the tales of *Kalilah and Dimnah*, which had Indian roots. Interestingly, the *History of Alexander the Great* of Pseudo-Kallisthenes may have been translated from Middle Persian into Syriac rather than from Greek.

The monastic renewal movement at the turn of the seventh century made important contributions to literature and spirituality. In this arena, the most significant representative of East Syriac theology is certainly Babai the Great (551–628). With his *Book of Union* he produced the definitive impulse behind East Syriac Christology. His reputation was so great in his own time that during the vacancy of the East Syriac patriarchal see, leadership of the Church of the East was entrusted to him.

Many graduates of the school of Nisibis were later important bishops or catholicoi of the Church of the East. One of the most notable was Ishoyahb III of Adiabene, who thoroughly reformed the liturgy of his church. Special note ought to be made of the redaction of the *Hudra* (lit. "cycle") a choral book for the daily offices, a joint project with the monk Henanisho. In his extensive collection of letters, which has been preserved, Ishoyahb combated the theology of another writer of his time, Martyrius Sahdona, author of a great *Book of Perfection.*

Finally, from the time of transition to the Arab period, the commentaries of Gabriel of Qatar and Abraham bar Lipeh represent valuable commentaries on East Syriac liturgy.

The Arab period until the Syriac Renaissance (seventh to thirteenth centuries)

The Arab conquest of the second half of the seventh century, which brought with it a political change in western Asia, did not interrupt the creation of Syriac literature. East Syriac literature was the mediator between the Greek heritage of the classical age and the Arab world, between Christianity and Islam. Beginning in the eighth century, Syriac was gradually eclipsed by Arabic, though it remained a literary and liturgical language.

During the Umayyad period (661–750), independent monastic literature continued to dominate at first. Dadisho of Qatar and Isaac of Nineveh were the most important representatives of this trend. Many of the works of Isaac of Nineveh written at the end of the seventh century were in the eighth and ninth centuries translated into Greek in Palestine, and thus gained significance in the West as well. In the twentieth century they influenced the monastic movement at Mount Athos and in the Egyptian desert. Likewise important in the West was the (anonymous) *Apocalypse of Pseudo-Methodius*, which was written around 700 in northern Mesopotamia, and in its Greek and Latin translations influenced other apocalyptic works.

In the eighth century John of Dalyatha and Joseph Hazzaya were highly influential figures in East Syriac monastic and spiritual literature. Around 792 Theodore bar Konai wrote his extensive *Book of the Scholion*, which not only introduced biblically based philosophy and theology but also presented Christianity over against Islam and refuted a number of heretical opinions. The vitality of intellectual life in East Syriac Christendom at this time is also shown by the letters of Catholicos Timotheos I (780–823). Abdisho bar Brika mentions the figure of 200 letters, of which 59 have survived.

Efforts toward greater understanding of the Bible interested two important representatives of East Syriac biblical exegesis: Isho bar Nun produced *Select Questions* on the Old and New Testaments, and Ishodad of Merv (mid-ninth century) commented on the entire Bible.

In the early ninth century Job of Edessa came to prominence, translating Galen's commentary on Hippocrates. In his *Book of Treasures* he referred to other works of metaphysics, psychology, astronomy, and medicine, which have unfortunately been lost. As a historical work, the extensive *Book of Superiors* (Abbots) of the monastery of Beth Abe by Thomas of Marga is of particular significance.

At the court of the Abbassid caliphs (750–1258) in Baghdad the East Syrians transmitted the intellectual heritage of antiquity to the blossoming Arab scholarship. Greek works of natural science, medicine, and philosophy were made available to Islam through the superb translations of scholars of the Church of the East. This is of paramount cultural and historical significance. As a consequence, Greek works translated into Arabic entered the Western world through Spain and Sicily even before the Greek originals were known in Europe. Not only East Syriac clerics produced literature, but also physicians and educated laypersons. One of the best-known translators was Hunain b. Ishaq († 873), who translated first from Greek into Syriac and then from Syriac into Arabic. Syriac Christians had already extensive experience translating complex Greek texts into Syriac, but at first none in translating directly from Greek into Arabic. For Hunain, the path from Syriac into Arabic, that is, within the Semitic linguistic family, was seen as easier. Some Greek works have only been preserved in their Syriac translations, such as the compendium of Aristotelian philosophy of Nicholas of Damascus.

In the tenth and eleventh centuries East Syriac literature experienced a decline. Dating from this period is the work of Elia bar Shinaya of Nisibis († 1046), which should be considered Christian Arabic, as well as Syriac, literature. Worthy of note is his world chronicle, written in Syriac and Arabic in parallel columns.

Likewise, Elia III Abu Halim († 1190) wrote in Arabic, though he also produced many Syriac liturgical texts for the morning office.

Syriac literature experienced a renaissance in the twelfth and thirteenth centuries. Especially significant among writers of poetry was Giwargis Warda, many of whose hymns were incorporated into the liturgy. At present, of his over 150 poems, only twenty-three have been edited. John b. Zobi was one of the most learned writers of this time and produced, in addition to his liturgical commentaries on baptism and the eucharist, a variety of grammatical and philosophical works.

The author of the anonymous *History of Yahballaha and Rabban Sauma* (after 1317), which was originally written in Persian and is preserved in Syriac, was eyewitness of many of the events of the journey of the two monks from China to the West. Timotheos II of Mosul († 1332) wrote on the ecclesiastical mysteries as well as Abdisho bar Brika († 1318), the last great East Syriac writer. Abdisho wrote in Arabic and Syriac, and his works included biblical commentaries, theological and canonical writings (e.g. *The Pearl, Nomocanon*), and writing in metrical form. Of particular importance is his catalog of Syriac writers, which is an invaluable source of information about Syriac authors and works.

Fourteenth century to the present

Because of the Mongol invasions under Tamerlane and epidemics of plague, East Syriac literature reached its nadir in the fourteenth century. Renewal began in the fifteenth century with Ishaq Qardahe Shbadnaya, author of several acrostics, and Sargis bar Wahle, author of a verse biography of Rabban Hormizd. Since then literary production has been continuous, if modest. However, this literature is little studied and minimally edited; only bits and pieces are well-known. For instance, from the end of the seventeenth and beginning of the eighteenth centuries, the Chaldean patriarch Joseph II († 1712) deserves mention.

As early as the start of the sixteenth century, works were also being written in Modern Syriac, particularly in the Alqosh dialect. It is folk poetry, which has mainly religious, but sometimes also secular or historical topics. Modern Syriac literature owed its success above all to the American missions at Lake Urmiyah, which promoted the use of Syriac as a written language. The most important witness to this linguistic revitalization was the nearly seventy-year run (1849–1918) of the missionary newsletter *Rays of Light*, in which questions of phonetics, dialects, and lexicology were discussed. Among the East Syrians the Chaldean metropolitan of Urmiyah, Toma Audo (1853–1917), was of outstanding significance on account of his compilation of an enormously valuable Syriac–Syriac dictionary.

In some areas attempts were made to revive classical Syriac. Today, for instance, it is the instructional language in the seminaries of the (West Syrian) Syrian Orthodox Church at the monastery of Mar Gabriel (Tur Abdin) and in Ma'arat Saidnaya (north of Damascus).

In the twentieth century the trans-confessional Assyrian nationalist movement championed the development of secular literature. Syriac was consequently used by authors for lyric poetry as well as for prose. The journal *Kokva* (*The Star*), founded in 1908 by the West Syrian Naum Fayeq (1868–1930), published pioneering work. In the twentieth century, Western secular literature was translated into Syriac. Examples of such translations include William Shakespeare's *Merchant of Venice*, translated by Benyamin Mushe Bet-Benyamin d-Ashita, born in Mosul in 1940; Jean Racine's play *Athalie*, by Abrohom Isu (Baghdad, 1978); and Niccolò Machiavelli's *Prince*, by Gabriel Afram (Sweden, 1995).

IRANIAN LITERATURE

Manfred Hutter

Iranian Christianity

In an inscription from the last quarter of the third century, the Zoroastrian priest Kartir indicated his enthusiasm for the spread of Zoroastrianism in the Sassanian empire, which had led to the persecution of other religions; among the Christians then living in the western Iranian region, Kartir distinguished between the Greek-speaking (*krestyane*) and Syriac-speaking (*nasraye*) communities. Almost a century later, the Syrian Acts of the martyrs present an already altered picture, as many of the Christian victims of Shapur II had Iranian names and some of the persecuted had converted from Zoroastrianism to Christianity. From these observations it is evident that beginning at the latest with the fourth century, attention must be paid to Iranian-speaking Christians. This is confirmed by a note in a work of John Chrysostom (cf. Patrologia Graeca 59.32), who mentions that during his time the Bible was translated into the language of the Persians. Somewhat later Theodoret of Cyrus also reports knowledge of the Bible among the Persians (cf. Patrologia Graeca 83.1045). When the Church of the East gained its jurisdictional independence as the "Persian Church" in the fifth century, it was advised to develop a separate Iranian Christian literature in order to underline with language the "Iranian" quality of Christianity (and thereby simultaneously its political separation from Byzantium) in the Sassanian empire. The *Chronicle of Seert* (cf. Patrologia Orientalis 7.117f), with its reference to Bishop Mana of Rewardashir, who is said to have translated the entire body of Syriac ecclesiastical literature into the Middle Persian vernacular at the end of the fifth century, indicates that active efforts were being made to translate works from Syriac into Iranian. It is also reported with regard to Catholicos Aqaq († 495/6) that he translated an account of Christian beliefs into Middle Persian for the Sassanian ruler Kawad I, in order to help him understand Christianity. However, the adoption or use of Middle Persian was not accomplished without controversy; in the autobiography of John of Dailam, for example, an account is given of a debate between Syriac- and Iranian-speaking monks over which language ought to be used in the liturgy. Likewise, as early as the fifth century, there was a metropolitan of the Church of the East in Samarkand, the central city in the East Iranian-Sogdian region.

Languages and scripts

As a result of the spread of Christianity, Iranian Christian literature was written in two languages: Middle Persian and Sogdian. West Iranian Middle Persian was written in the Pahlavi script, whose earliest beginnings may be traced back to the third century BC, when it was first adapted from Aramaic script for use on coins in the Persis. Beginning in the third century AD it became the dominant language for everyday use in the Sassanian empire and was even used for official inscriptions and stone monuments (especially in the third to fifth centuries) and in italics on papyri (sixth century); with the increasing Islamicization of Iran in the eighth century, this script was gradually replaced by the Arabic, and its last traces date from the eleventh century. As a "religious book script" the widely disseminated Pahlavi script enjoyed active use among both Christians and Zoroastrians; the Manichees, in contrast, adapted the Syriac script (probably in the form closest to the script used in Palmyra in Syria) for their Middle Persian literature. For East Iranian Sogdian the Christians used either East Syriac or Sogdian script, while the Manichees wrote their Sogdian texts in their own Manichean or Sogdian script. The Sogdian script is also a descendant and adaptation of the Aramaic script. The earliest certain examples of this script date to the third century AD, and beginning in the sixth century Sogdians became executives of the administration in Central Asia, thus making their language and script the trans-regional communication medium of the area. It is understandable that the Christians did not cut themselves off from this; it is, however, also worth noting that the Syriac texts were used more frequently in the Church of the East than the Iranian were and that Iranian Christian texts were largely dependent upon Syriac ecclesiastical literature. Beginning in the late first century, the linguistic variety of the Church of the East was further broadened in East Iranian and Central Asian communities by the addition of Old Turkish – used, for instance, on gravestones – whose script developed out of Sogdian.

Literature

Middle Persian texts

Although Middle Persian had been in liturgical use since the fourth century and was also known among Sogdian-speaking Christians as an "ecclesiastical language," only a few Christian texts have survived. The most extensive text is the Sogdian Turfan Psalter, found in Bulayiq (about 10 kilometers north of Turfan) in Chinese Turkestan (Sinkiang) at the beginning of the twentieth century along with almost the entire Iranian-speaking Christian corpus of writings, aside from individual inscriptions. The fragmentary manuscript includes Middle Persian translations of Psalms 94–9, 118, and 121–36, for which the textual model is the Syriac Peshitta. On linguistic grounds it is probable that these psalm translations were completed as early as the fourth century, though the manuscript at issue could only have been written in the sixth century at the earliest because one of the canons of Mar Aba († 552), head of the church in Persia, was inserted before the first verse of each psalm. Besides their consequences for the dating of the manuscript, these canons also indicate that the manuscript was produced in the East Syrian church and that it was intended for liturgical use and not for private readings of the Old Testament.

Besides these psalm translations, no Middle Persian Christian is

extant; only a few South Indian inscriptions with Christian references, dating from the ninth and eleventh centuries, remain to be
noted. A copper tablet from Quilon bestowed privileges upon the
church there, and the signatures of the witnesses are written in
Arabic, Middle Persian, and Jewish Persian. Likewise noteworthy
are a few crosses in South India bearing Middle Persian inscriptions
of their donors; up to now, at least six such crosses have been found
in Madras, Kottayam, and Travancore, as well as in Anuradhapura
in Sri Lanka. The material from these inscriptions offers no theological information, but it shows that Middle Persian was used, at
least on occasion, by Christians of the Church of the East until the
eleventh century.

Despite the relative dearth of extant Middle Persian literature, the
significance of this literature ought not be overlooked. This claim is
also indirectly supported by the Christian law book of Metropolitan Ishobokht of Rewardashir, originally written in Middle Persian but surviving only in its Syriac translation. Words borrowed
from Middle Persian appearing in Sogdian texts also demonstrate
that the original extent of Middle Persian sources must have been
incomparably greater, such that these texts were also translated into
Sogdian.

Sogdian texts

The majority of Christian Sogdian texts originated in the discovery
of Bulayiq in the Turfan oasis; a few additional texts (most important is a Christian book of oracles, less so some documents of everyday life) came from the so-called "Cave of the Thousand Buddhas"
in Tun-huang, farther to the east. A common characteristic of the
manuscripts from Tun-huang and Bulayiq shows that they were
predominantly translated directly from Syriac; a few, however, indicate a direct Middle Persian model. Based on evidence from paleo-
graphical observations – of both the more commonly used East
Syriac and the Sogdian scripts – all these manuscripts date from the
ninth and tenth centuries at the earliest, although even in the fifth
century Sogdia – beginning with Samarkand – had joined the
Church of the East. For our recognition of Samarkand as a center of
Sogdian Christianity we are indirectly indebted to a Sogdian
inscription from Ladakh, left by a Sogdian envoy to the Tibetan
ruler, though this clearly lies outside of the area Sogdian Christians
settled.

If one were to attempt to systematize Christian Sogdian literature, one could begin with biblical texts. Many books of New Testament pericopes have been preserved, most of these in a bilingual, East Syriac–Sogdian format, whose inclusion of two languages demonstrates that even in the Sogdian communities in Bulayiq, the dominant religious and liturgical language remained East Syriac. At present, the only Old Testament text known is the Sogdian translation of the Psalms: despite the limited extent of surviving texts, these two manuscripts enable a few interesting conclusions. In one manuscript, each psalm is given a Syriac heading; still more instructive is the section of text in which the Greek text from the Septuagint replaces the Sogdian version in the opening line of Psalm 32. It may be presumed that the transmission of knowledge of the Greek biblical text to the Sogdians was accomplished through their contact with the Melkites, who had had a catholicos in Tashkent since around 762. An indication that perhaps additional parts of the Old Testament existed in Sogdian translation can eventually be deduced from the numerous Old Testament citations in the *Antirrhetikos* of Evagrius Ponticus (346–99). That biblical texts fundamentally shape Christian texts is self-evident; it is nonetheless worth noting that Sogdian apocryphal texts are not unknown, such as a fragment about Simon Magus, originating from the *Acts of Peter*, as well as a collection of biblical puzzles and a small fragment regarding Mary Magdalene.

Some Sogdian texts stand directly in the Middle Persian tradition. Besides linguistic arguments, clues related to content support this claim. The most important texts with Middle Persian backgrounds in terms of content include above all the following: a biography of John of Dailam, who gained renown for, among other accomplishments, the founding of monasteries in Persia at the end of the seventh or beginning of the eighth century; the *Acts* of the martyrs under Shapur II, including, for instance, the well-preserved version of the martyrdom of Pethion. Also mentioned is the legend of the missionizing of the city of Merv by Bishop Bar Shabba. Besides missionary successes, another recurrent motif in these texts is that the successful missionary and his followers had to justify their turning away from Zoroastrianism, the dominant religion in the Sassanian empire, or be persecuted on this account. Although for most of these Sogdian Christian texts Syriac or, in some cases, Arabic parallel texts are known, they can also stand as a separate group within this literature, as they reflect the (ecclesio-political) Persian background of the East.

In addition to hagiography, and also hymns, one final group of texts deserves note, whose content focuses on monasticism and asceticism. Besides the aforementioned *Antirrhetikos* of Evagrius Ponticus and fragments of the *Apophthegmata Patrum*, other texts – in some cases not yet identified – have survived, promoting such values as fasting, renunciation of the world, nocturnal waking, and the life of solitude. Monastic biographies and commentaries thereof have been preserved: for instance, that of Abba Ishaya (late fourth century) from Scetis in Egypt, as well as Dadisho's commentary on Abba Ishaya; a fragment of a letter from the Egyptian Makarios (fourth century); a detailed biography of the hermit Serapion or the ascetic Eugen. Since East Syriac Christians in the fifth century had little interest in ascetic or eremitic lifestyles, the adoption and preservation of these Egyptian traditions in the Sogdian "library" of Bulayiq reflect the result of a development within the Church of the East, which evidently must have lessened its anti-ascetic stance in the mid-sixth century, enabling the acceptance of texts from the Egyptian ascetic tradition. In the monastic context of Bulayiq – albeit in manuscripts from some four centuries later – this development of the Syriac Church of the East remains available to us.

Summary

As the East Syriac church grew out of the Persian regions of the Sassanian empire into Central Asia, it is natural that Syriac and Middle Persian were used as ecclesiastical languages in the Central Asian missions, with the latter increasingly established along the northern Silk Road through the Sogdian *lingua franca*. That in the end the church is considered to be of Syriac origin is accounted for by the fact that Iranian Christian literature remained almost exclusively a literature of translation. Nor did this change at the end of the first millennium, as Sogdian was largely eclipsed as the *lingua franca* by New Persian (and to a lesser extent Old Turkish). As a consequence of this shift, New Persian Christian texts were also produced, such as a bilingual edition of the Psalms in New Persian and Syriac, probably dating from the end of the ninth century and marking the beginning of the process of changing languages. In the same way, a handful of late Sogdian texts from Bulayiq display linguistic features suggesting that these manuscripts were products of writers whose mother tongue was not Sogdian but Old Turkish. Thus Iranian literature eventually vanished from the Church of the East.

TURKISH, UIGHUR, AND
CHINESE LITERATURE

Wilhelm Baum

"Nestorian" texts in Central Asia and China have also been preserved in the Old Turkish, Uighur, and Chinese languages.

In Old Turkish fragments of *The Martyrdom of St George*, presumably modeled on a Syriac original, and an apocryphal text regarding the birth of Jesus and the adoration of the prophets have been preserved. An additional fragment, which defies categorization, contains a Christian explanation for the origins of fire worship and is thus of particular value for the history of religions. Likewise, the "Nestorian crosses" of the Onguts and Keraits bear Turkish inscriptions.

In Uighur, a fragment of the book of prophecies is so far known. In the eighth and ninth centuries the Turfan oasis was the capital of an Uighur empire. However, in the East Syriac monastery of Bulayiq there, mostly Sogdian writings (see above: "Iranian literature") were discovered.

Texts which presumably can be traced back to the monk Alopen extend back to the earliest period of the Christianization of China. Two writings ought to be mentioned: the *Jesus the Messiah Sutra*, dating from between 635 and 641, and the approximately contemporary *Treatise on Monotheism*, containing echoes of the "golden rule" of Confucius and an account of the spread of Christianity up to 641. Around 800 a Buddhist list of instructional texts from Xian mentioned that in 782 the Indian scholar Prajna, with help from the Persian monk and future bishop Adam (King-tsing), translated texts from Uighur. A register of books and people from around 800 includes those writings which had already been translated into Chinese. In 1908 King-tsing's translation of the "Gloria" from Syriac was found by Paul Pelliot in the monastery of Tunhuang in the "Cave of the Thousand Buddhas"; the *Mysterious Peace and Joy Sutra* and the *Radiant Religion of Ta-Tsin Sutra* were found there as well. However, the two sutras were dated to the period from 750 to 900. The famous and still extant "Nestorian stele" of Xian dates from after 781, and it recounts the early history of the Chinese mission. Among the Christian Onguts, Chinese poems were also produced, but one finds no Christian elements in them. The liturgical language remained, as a rule, Syriac.

A particularly valuable source for East Syriac Christianity is the anonymous *Chronicle of Chen-chiang*. The text describes the history of the monastery founded by Mar Sergis (Sarkis) and six other monasteries which can be traced to him. Finally, the names of various Christians are mentioned. The work belongs among the most influential documents of Christian literature in China. There were also Christians in China who produced works in Chinese, but these lack specifically Christian content.

Numerous gravestones of East Syriac Christians in the Mongol–Chinese region bear Turkish, Uighur, Sogdian, or Armenian inscriptions. In the monastery of Fang-shan, forty miles south-west of Peking, two inscriptions from 960 and 1355 were found.

For the (East Syrian) Christian communities in Central Asia and China, additional Chinese, Arabic, and Armenian sources were also significant. For instance, the imperial annals of the Mongol period, *Yuan-shih*, mention many Christian individuals. Among the Arabic authors, Suleiman, Abu Zaid, and Masudi are worthy of note; among Armenian authors, Hethum or Kirakos of Gantzag; among Persians, Rashid ad-Din should be mentioned.

APPENDICES

LIST OF THE CATHOLICOI OF THE CHURCH OF THE EAST*

Wilhelm Baum

SELEUCIA-CTESIPHON

Papa (310–17, † 329)
Shimun I (329–41)
Sahdost (341–2)
Barbahemin (343–6)
Vacant (346–63)
Tomarsa (363–71)
Qayyuma (377–99)
Isaac I (399–410)
Ahai (410–14)
Yahballaha I (415–20)
Maana (420)
Faraboht (421)
Dadisho I (421–56)
Babowei (457–84)
Akak (485–95/6)
Babai (497–502)
Silas (503–23)
Narses and Elisha (524–37)
Paul I (537–9)
Aba I the Great (540–52)
Josef (552–67, † 576)
Ezechiel (570–82)
Ishoyahb I of Arzun (582–96)
Sabrisho I (596–604)
Gregory I (605–8)

Vacant (609–28)
Ishoyahb II of Gdala (628–46)
Maremmeh (646–50)
Ishoyahb III of Adiabene (650–8)
Giwargis I (661–80)
John I Bar Marta (680–3)
Henanisho I (685–92/700)
John the Leper (692–3)
Vacant (700–14)
Saliba-Zakha (714–28)
Vacant (728–31)
Pethion (731–40)
Aba II (741–51)
Sourin (751)
Jacob II (754–75)
Henanisho II (775–80)

BAGHDAD

Timotheos I (780–823)
Isho bar Nun (823–8)
Giwargis II (828–31)
Sabrisho II (831–5)
Abraham II of Marga (837–50)
Theodosius I (Athanasius) (853–8)
Serge I (860–72)

* Based on Elias of Nisibis, the *Chronicle of Seert*, Masib. Sulaiman, and Barhebraeus, on which E. Tisserant's list also depends, and completed by the latest research of H. Murre-van den Berg.

Israel of Kashkar (877)
Enos I (877–84)
John II bar Narsai (884–92)
John III (893–9)
John IV bar Abgar (900–5)
Abraham III Abraza (906–37)
Emanuel I (937–60)
Israel I (961)
Abdisho I (963–86)
Mari II bar Tobi (987–99)
John V bar Isa (1000–11)
John VI Nasuk (1012–16)
Ishoyahb bar Ezechiel (1020–25)
Elias I (1028–49)
John VII bar Tagabi (1049–57)
Sabrisho III Zanbur (1064–72)
Abdisho II bar al-Arid (1074–90)
Makika I (1092–1110)
Elias II bar Molki (1111–34)
Barsauma I (1134–6)
Abdisho III bar Molki (1139–48)
Ishoyahb V Baladi (1149–75)
Elias III Abu Halim (1176–90)
Yahballaha II (1190–1222)
Sabrisho IV bar Qayyuma (1222–4)
Sabrisho V bar al-Masihi
  (1226–56)
Makika II (1257–65)
Dinkha I (1265–81)

MARAGHA

Yahballaha III (1281–1317)

ARBELA

Timotheos II (1318–32)

KARAMLES

Dinkha II (1332–64)

MOSUL

Shimun II
Shimun III
Elias IV († 1437)

JEZIREH

Shimun IV Basidi (1437–97)

Shimun V (1497–1501)
Elias V (1502–3)

RABBAN HORMIZD

Shimun VI (1504–38)
Shimun VII bar Mama (1538–51)
Shimun VIII Dinkha (1551–58)
Elias VI bar Giwargis (1558–91)
Elias VII (1591–1617)
Elias VIII Shimun (1617–60)
Elias IX Yuhannan Maraugin
  (1660–1700)
Elias X Maraugin (1700–22)
Elias XI Dinkha (1722–78)
Elias XII Ishoyahb of Alqosh
  (1778–1804)

SULAQUA-LINE (in communion with
Rome)

John VIII Sulaqa (1553–5), anti-
  patriarch of Shimun VIII
  Dinkha
Abdisho IV (1555–70)
Abraham (1570–7)
Yahballaha IV (1577–80)
Shimun IX Dinkha (1581–1600)
Shimun X (1600–38)
Shimun XI (1638–56)
Shimun XII (1656–62)
Shimun XIII Dinkha (1662–1700),
  Union ends 1672

DIYARBAKIR (in communion with Rome)

Joseph I (1681–96)
Joseph II Sliba Beth Marcuf (1696–
  1712)
Joseph III (1714–57)
Joseph IV (1759–81)
Joseph V (1781–1828), Union ends

MOSSUL/BAGHDAD (Chaldean
patriarchs, in communion with Rome)

John VIII Hormez (1830–8)
Nicholas I (1840–7), † 1855
Joseph VI Audo (1848–78)
Elias XIII Abolyonan (1879–94)
Abdisho V Khayyatt (1895–99)

Joseph Emmanuel II Thomas
(1900–47)
Joseph VII Ghanima (1947–58)
Paul II Cheikho (1958–89)
Raphael I Bidawid (since
1989)

KOTCHANNES (until 1920)

Shimun XIII Dinkha (1662–1700),
until 1672 in communion with
Rome
Shimun XIV Salomon (1700–40)
Shimun XV Michael Muktes
(1740–80)
Shimun XVI John (1780–1820)
Shimun XVII Abraham (1820–61)

Shimun XVIII Ruben (1861–1903)
Shimun XIX Benjamin (1903–18)
Shimun XX Poulos (1918–20)
Shimun XXI Eshai (1920–75), from
1940/1 on in Chicago and San
Francisco

BAGHDAD (Ancient Church of the
East)

Addai II Giwargis (since 1969)

CHICAGO (Assyrian Church of the
East)

Dinkha IV Khnanaya (since
1976)

LIST OF SOVEREIGNS

Dietmar W. Winkler

THE SASSANIANS (224–651)

Ardeshir I (224–41)
Shapur I (241–72)
Hormizd I (272–3)
Bahram I (273–6)
Bahram II (276–93)
Bahram III (293)
Narses (293–302)
Hormizd II (302–9)
Shapur II (309–79)
Ardeshir II (379–83)
Shapur III (383–8)
Bahram IV (388–99)
Yazdgird I (399–420)
Bahram V (421–38)
Yazdgird II (438–57)
Hormizd III (457–9)
Peroz (459–84)
Balash (484–8)
Kawad I (488–531)
Djamasp (496–8), *Usurper*
Chosroes I (531–79)
Hormizd IV (579–90)
Bahram Chobin (590–1), *Usurper*
Chosroes II (591–628)

628–32 Phase of unsettlement with
permanent change of rulers (term
of reign insecure)
Kawad II Shiruye (628)
Ardeshir III (628–9)
Boran (629–30)
Shahrvaraz (?)
Azarmdukht (?)
Hormizd V (630–2)

Yazdgird (632–51)

BYZANTINE EMPERORS (UP TO 641)

Constantine the Great (306–37),
Roman Emperor
Constantius II (337–61), from 353
Roman Emperor
Julian (361–3), Roman Emperor
Jovian (363–4), Roman Emperor
Valens (364–78)
Theodosius I (379–95), from 388
Roman Emperor
Arkadius (395–408)
Theodosius II (408–50)
Markian (450–7)
Leo (457–74)
Zeno (474–91)
Anastasius (491–518)
Justin I (518–27)
Justinian (527–65)
Justin II (565–78)
Tiberius (578–82)
Maurice (582–602)
Phokas (602–10)
Heraclius (610–41)
Constantine III (641)

THE FOUR PERFECT CALIPHS

Abu Bakr (632–4)
Omar (634–44)
Othman (644–56)
Ali (656–61)

THE UMAYYAD CALIPHS (661–749)

Muawiya (661–80)
Yazid I (680–3)
Muawiya II (683–4)
Marwan I (684–5)
Abdalmalik (685–705)
Walid I (705–15)
Sulaiman (715–17)
Omar II (717–20)
Yazid II (720–4)
Hischam (724–43)
Walid II (743–4)
Yazid III (744)
Ibrahim (744)
Marwan II (744–9)

THE ABBASID CALIPHS (UP TO 861)

Abul-Abbas (749–54)
Al-Mansur (754–75)
Al-Mahdi (775–85)
Al-Hadi (785–6)
Harun ar-Raschid (786–809)
Al-Amin (809–13)
Al-Mamun (813–33)
Al-Mutasim (833–42)
Al-Wathiq (842–6)
Al-Mutawakkil (847–61)

Between 861 and 1258 there are
twenty-seven more Abbasid
Caliphs, who cease to be
politically or historically
important

THE MONGOL GREAT KHANS

Genghis Khan (Temujin) (1162–
1227)
Ogdai (1227–41)
Kuyuk (1241–8)
Mongke (1250–60)
Kublai Khan (1260–94)

THE MONGOL IL-KHANS OF PERSIA

Hulagu (1256–8)
Abaqa (1265–81)
Taqudar-Ahmad (1282–4)
Argun (1284–91)
Gaichatu (1291–5)
Baydu (1295)
Ghazan (1295–1304)
Oljaitu (1304–16)
Abu Said (1316–35)

DYNASTIES OF CHINESE EMPERORS (618–1279)

Tang 618–907
  Kao-tsu (618–26)
  T'ai-tsung (626–49)
  Kao-tsung (650–83)
  Chung-tsung (684 and 705–10)
  Jiu-tsung (684–90 and
    710–12)
  Wu-hou (690–705), Empress,
    wife of Kao-tsung
  Hsuan-tsung (713–55)
  Su-tsung (756–62)
  Tai-tsung (762–80)
  Te-tsung (780–805)
  Shun-tsung (805)
  Hsien-tsung (806–20)
  Mu-tsung (820–4)
  Ching-tsung (824–7)
  Wen-tsung (827–40)
  Wu-tsung (841–6)
  Hsuan-tsung (846–59)
  I-tsung (860–74)
  Hsi-tsung (873–88)
  Chao-tsung (888–904)
  Ching-tsung (904–7)
The Five Dynasties in the North
907–60
The Ten Kingdoms in the South
902–79
Northern Sung 960–1127
Southern Sung 1127–1279
Liao (Kitan) 907–1125
Hsi-Liao (Karakitai) 1125–1211
Hsi-Hsia (Tanguten) 1038–1227
Chin (Dschurdschen) 1115–1234
Yuan, or Mongol, dynasty
1206–1368

From 1279 the Mongols controlled
the whole Chinese empire

BIBLIOGRAPHY

Brock, Sebastian, *Syriac Studies: A Classified Bibliography (1960–1990)*, Kaslik, 1996.

Hage, Wolfgang, "*Nestorian*ische Kirche," *Theologische Realenzyklopädie* 24 (1994): 272–6.

Internet: http://syrcom.cua.edu/hugoye
http://www.wlc.com/oxus/Bibliography.html

Sources

A Nestorian Collection of Christological Texts, 2 vols, ed. Luise Abramowski and Alan E. Goodman, Cambridge, 1972.

Abdisho bar Brika, *Collectio Canonum Synodicorum*, in Antonio Mai (ed.), *Scriptorum veterum nova collectio e Vaticanis codicibus*, Rome, 1838, T. X. 1.

Al-Masudi, *Bis zu den Grenzen der Erde*, ed. Gernot Rotter, Stuttgart, 1982.

Anonymi auctoris Chronicon ad A.C. 1234 pertinens, ed. Jean-Baptist Chabot, CSCO 81, 109 Syr. 36, 56.

Aphraat, *Unterweisungen*, vols I and II, trans. from the Syriac and intro. by Peter Bruns, Fontes Christiani 5/1 and 5/2, Freiburg, 1991.

Assemani, Josephus S., *Bibliotheca Orientalis Clementino-Vaticana*, vol. III, 1/2, Rome, 1725–8.

Ausgewählte Akten Persischer Märtyrer, with appendix, "Ostsyrisches Mönchsleben," trans. Oscar Braun, Bibliothek der Kircheväter 22, Munich, 1915.

Bardesanes, *Liber Legum Regionum*, ed. F. Nau, Patrologia Syriaca 2, Paris, 1907, 450–657.

Baum, Wilhelm and Senoner, Raimund, *Indien und Europa im Mittelalter*, Klagenfurt, 2000.

Braun, Oscar, "Ein Brief des Katholikos Timotheos I. über biblische Studien des 9. *Jahrhunderts*," *Oriens Christianus* 1 (1901): 299–313.

Budge, E. A. W. *Solomon of Basra: The Book of the Bee*, Oxford, 1886.

Chabot, J.-B. (ed.), *Histoire du Patriarche Mar Yahballaha III. Et du moine Rabban Cauma, Revue de l'Orient latin* 1 (1893): 567–610; 2 (1894): 73–304, appendix 566–643.

Chronicon anonymum ad A.D. 846 pertinens, ed. E. W. Brooks, CSCO 3 Syr. 3, Louvain 1904/1955; trans. J.-B. Chabot, CSCO 4 Syr. 4, Louvain. 1904/1955.

Chronicon anonymum Pseudo-Dionysianum, ed. Roberts Hespel, CSCO 507 Syr. 213, Louvain, 1989.

Chronique de Séert. Histoire Nestorienne inédite I. Arabe et français, ed. A. Scher and J. Périer, Patrologia Orientalis 4, Paris, 1907.

Das Buch der Synhados oder Synodicon Orientale. Die Sammlung der nestorianischen Konzilien, zusammengestellt im neunten Jahrhundert nach der syrischen Handschrift Mus. Borg. 82, trans. and commentary, Oscar Braun, Stuttgart and Vienna, 1900; repr. Amsterdam, 1975.

Die Chronik von Arbela, trans. Peter Kawerau, CSCO 468 Syr. 200, Louvain, 1985.

Die reiche Fracht des Pedro Alvarez Cabral. 1500–1501, ed. Johannes Pögl, Stuttgart, 1986.

Doctrina apostolorum, in W. Cureton (ed.), *Ancient Syriac Documents*, London, 1864.

Eliae Metropolitae Nisibeni Opus chronologicum, ed. E. W. Brooks, CSCO Scriptores Syr. III/7, Rome and Paris, 1910.

Ephraem, *Carmina Nisibena* I, ed. E. Beck, CSCO 218, 219 Syr. 92, 93, Louvain 1961, 1963.

Ephräm der Syrer: Reden über den Glauben. Ausgewählte Nisibenische Hymnen, Schriften der Kirchenväter 10, Munich, 1984.

Eusebius, *Historia Ecclesiastica*, German translation: *Des Eusebius Pamphili Bischofs von Cäsarea Kirchengeschichte*, trans. from Greek by P. Haeuser, Bibliothek der Kirchenväter 2, Munich, 1932.

Eusebius, *Vita Constantini*, German translation: *Des Eusebius Pamphili Bischofs von Cäsarea ausgewählte Schriften*, intro. A. Bigelmair, Bibliothek der Kirchenväter 9, Munich, 1913.

Fragmente syrischer und arabischer Historiker, ed. Friedrich Baethgen, Leipzig, 1884.

Gregorii Barhebraei Chronicon ecclesiasticum, vol. III, ed. Joannes Baptista Abeloos and Thomas Joseph Lamy, Paris, 1877.

Die Geschichte der Mongolen des Hethum von Korykos (1307) in der Rückübersetzung durch Jean de Long, ed. Sven Dörper, Europäische Hochschulschriften XIII, vol. 236, Frankfurt, Berlin, Bern, 1998.

Die von Guidi herausgegebene Syrische Chronik, ed. Theodor Nöldecke, Sitzungsberichte d. österr. Akademie der Wiss. 128, Vienna, 1893, 1–48.

Hunain ibn Ishaq über die syrischen und arabischen Galen-Übersetzungen, ed. G. Bergsträsser, Leipzig, 1925.

Ibn at-Taiyib, *Fiqh an-nasrânîya (Das Recht der Christenheit)*, ed. and trans. W. Hoenerbach and O. Spies, pt. 1, CSCO 161, 162 Arab. 16, 17, Louvain, 1956, 1957.

Isho'yahb Patriarchae III, *Liber epistolarum*, ed. Rubens Duval, CSCO 11.12 Syr. 11, 12, Louvain, 1955.

Johannes von Piano Carpine, *Die Mongolengeschichte*, ed. Johannes Gießauf, Graz, 1955.

Kaufhold, Hubert, *Syrische Texte zum islamischen Recht. Das dem nestorianischen Katholikos Johannes V. „bar Abgare" zugeschriebene Rechtsbuch*, Munich, 1971.

Les Lettres du patriarche nestorien Timothée I, ed. Raphael J. Bidawid, Studi e Testi 187, Vatican City, 1956.

Ludovico de Varthema, *Reisen im Orient*, ed. Folker Reichert, Fremde Kulturen in alten Berichten 2, Sigmaringen, 1996.

Marco Polo, *Il Milione. Die Wunder der Welt*, 6th edn, ed. Elise Guignard, Manesse Bibliothek der Weltliteratur, Zurich, 1994.

Maris, Amri and Slibae, *De patriarchis Nestorianorum commentaria. Ex codicibus vaticanis edidit ac latine reddidit H. Gismondi*, part 1: *Maris textus arabicus et versio latina*, Rome, 1899; part 2: *Amri et Slibae textus et versio latina*, Rome, 1897, 1899.

Narsai's Metrical Homilies on the Nativity, Epiphany, Passion, Resurrection and Ascension, ed. Frederick G. McLeod, Patrologia Orientalis 40, Turnhout, 1979.

[Narsai,] Martin F., "Homélie de Narsés sur les trois Docteurs nestoriens," *Journal Asiatique* 14 (1899): 446–92 (Text); 15 (1900): 469–525 (trans.).

Peregrinatio Aetheriae, *Die Pilgereise der Aetheria*, trans. from Latin by K. Vretska, Klosterneuburg, 1958.

Tabari, *Geschichte der Perser und Araber zur Zeit der Sasaniden*, ed. Th. Nöldeke, Leiden, 1973.

Terrae Incognitae, vol. II: *200–1200 n. Chr.*, ed. Richard Hennig, Leiden, 1937.

The Acts of Thomas, English trans. with introduction and commentary, ed. A. F. J. Klijn, NT Suppl. 5, Leiden, 1962.

The Monks of Kublai Khan Emperor of China, ed. E. A. Wallis Budge, London, 1926.

The Teaching of Addai, Syriac text and trans. George Howard, Texts and Translations 16, Early Christian Literature Series 4, Chico, 1981.

The Voyage of Pedro Alvares Cabral to Brazil and India, ed. William Brooks Greenlee, The Hakluyt Society II, 81, London, 1938.

Thomas of Marga, *The Book of Governors. The Historia Monastica of Thomas Bishop of Marga A.D. 840*, vol. I: *Syriac Text and Introduction*, ed. E. A. Wallis Budge; vol. II: *English Translation*, ed. A. Thompson and E. A. Wallis Budge, London, 1893.

Timothei Patriarchae I, *Epistulae*, ed. Oscar Braun, CSCO 74, 75 Syr. 30, 31, Louvain, 1953.

Timotheus I, *Les Lettres du Patriarche nestorien Timothèe I*, ed. Raphael Bidawid, Studi e Testi 187, Rome, 1956.

Vasco da Gama, *Die Entdeckung des Seeweges nach Indien*, 3rd edn, Stuttgart and Vienna, 1990.

180

Wilhelm von Rubruk, *Reisen zum Großkhan der Mongolen*, ed. Hans D. Leicht, Stuttgart, 1984.

General literature

Assfalg, Julius, and Krüger, Paul, *Kleines Wörterbuch des Christlichen Ostens*, Wiesbaden, 1975.

Atiya, Aziz S., *A History of Eastern Christianity*, 2nd edn, Millwood, 1980.

Atlas zur Kirchengeschichte, ed. Hubert Jedin *et al.*, Freiburg, 1987.

Badger, George Percy, *The Nestorians and their Rituals*, vols I and II, London, 1987 (reprint of 1852 edn).

Bauer, Johannes B., and Hutter, Manfred, *Lexikon der christlichen Antike, Unter Mitarbeit von Anneliese Felber*, Kröners Taschenausgabe 332, Stuttgart, 1999.

Brock, Sebastian, "The 'Nestorian Church': a lamentable misnomer," in J. F. Coakley and K. Parry (eds), *The Church of the East: Life and Thought, Bulletin of the John Rylands University Library of Manchester* 78/3 (1996): 23–35.

Brockelmann, C., Leipoldt, J., Finck, F.N., and Littmann, Enno, *Geschichte der christlichen Litteraturen des Orients*, Die Litteraturen des Orients in Einzeldarstellungen VII/2, Leipzig, 1907.

Coakley, J. F., and Parry, K. (eds), *The Church of the East: Life and Thought, Bulletin of the John Rylands University Library of Manchester* 78/3 (1996).

Fiey, Jean-Maurice, *Assyrie chrétienne*, 3 vols, Beirut, 1965–1968.

Fiey, Jean-Maurice, *Jalons pour une histoire de l'église en Iraq*, CSCO 310 Subs. 36, Louvain, 1970.

Gillman, Ian, and Klimkeit, Hans-Joachim, *Christians in Asia before 1500*, Ann Arbor, MI, 1999.

Hafner Forneris, Anna, *Schicksale und Erlebnisse einer Kärntnerin während ihrer Reisen in verschiedenen Ländern*, 2nd edn, Klagenfurt, 1995 (1st edn 1949).

Hage, Wolfgang, "Apostolische Kirche des Ostens (Nestorianer)," in Friedrich Heyer (ed.), *Konfessionskunde*, Berlin, 1977, 202–14.

Hage, Wolfgang, "Nestorianische Kirche," *Theologische Realenzyklopädie* 24 (1994): 264–76.

Handbuch der Orientalistik I/4: *Iranistik*, Leiden and Cologne, 1958.

Joseph, John, *The Nestorians and their Muslim Neighbors: A Study of Western Influence on their Relations*, Princeton, 1961.

Juckel, Andreas, "Eine ostsyrische Angelologie (Elija von Anbar, Ktaba d-Durrasa Memra IX), 1–20," in *Nubia et Oriens Christianus*, Festschrift for C. Detlef G. Müller, Cologne, 1988, 115–59.

Kawerau, Peter, *Ostkirchengeschichte*, vol. I: *Das Christentum in Asien und Afrika bis zum Auftreten der Portugiesen im Indischen Ozean*, CSCO 451 Subs. 70, Louvain, 1983.

Le Coz, Raymond, *Histoire de l'Église d'Orient. Chrétiens d'Irak, d'Iran et de Turquie*, Paris, 1995.

Leys, Roger, "Nestorianische Kirche, Nestorianer," in *Lexikon für Theologie und Kirche*, 2nd edn, 7.887f.

Mofett, Samuel Hugh, *Christianity in Asia*, vol. I: *Beginnings to 1500*, New York, 1998.

Müller, C. Detlef G., *Die orientalischen Nationalkirchen*, Die Kirche in ihrer Geschichte 1 D2, Göttingen, 1981.

Müller, C. Detlef G., "Nestorianer," *Evangelisches Kirchelexikon*, vol. 3, 3rd edn 1992, 666f.

Spuler, Berthold, "Die Nestorianische Kirche," in *Handbuch der Orientalistik*, vol. 8/2, Leiden, 1961, 120–69.

Spuler, Berthold, *Die morgenländischen Kirchen*, Leiden, 1964.

Tamcke, Martin, Schwaigert, Wolfgang, and Schlarb, Egbert (eds) *Syrisches Christentum weltweit. Studien zur syrischen Kirchengeschichte. Festschrift für Wolfgang Hage*, Studien zur Orientalischen Kirchengeschichte 1, Münster, 1995.

Teule, Herman, and Wessels, Anton (eds), *Oosterse christenen binnen de wereld van de islam*, Kampen, 1997.

Tisserant, Eugène, and Amann, Émile, "L'église nestorienne," *Dictionnaire de théologie catholique* 11 (1931): 157–323.

Trimingham, John Spencer, *Christianity among the Arabs in Pre-Islamic Times*, London, 1979.

Van Rompay, Lucas, "Past and Present Perceptions of Syriac Literary Tradition," *Hugoye Journal of Syriac Studies* 3/1 (2000).

Vine, Aubrey Russel, *The Nestorian Churches: A concise History of Nestorian Christianity in Asia from the Persian Schism to the Modern Assyrians*, London, 1937.

Wiesehöfer, Josef, *Das antike Persien. Von 550 v. Chr. bis 650 n. Chr.*, 2nd edn, Düsseldorf and Zurich, 1998.

Wiessner, Gernot, "Zur Auseinandersetzung zwischen Christentum und Zoroastrismus im Iran," *Zeitschrift der deutschen morgenländischen Gesellschaft*, Suppl. 1/2, Wiesbaden, 1969, 411–17.

Winkler, Dietmar W., and Augustin, Klaus (eds), *Die Ostkirchen. Ein Leitfaden. Mit Beiträgen von G. Larentzakis und Ph. Harnoncourt*, Graz, 1997.

Winkler, Dietmar W., *Ostsyrisches Christentum. Untersuchungen zur Christologie, Ekklesiologie und den ökumenischen Dialogen der Assyrischen Kirche des Ostens*, Hamburg, 2003.

Chapter 1: The age of the Sassanians
(Dietmar W. Winkler)

Abramowski, Luise, "Das Konzil von Chalzedon in der Homilie des Narses über die drei nestorianischen Lehrer," *Zeitschrift für Kirchengeschichte* 66 (1954/5): 140–3.

Abramowski, Luise, "Die Christologie Babai des Großen," in *Symposium Syriacum 1972*, Orientalia Christiana Analecta 197, Rome, 1974.

Abramowski, Luise, *Untersuchungen zum Liber Heraclidis*, CSCO 242 Subs. 22, Louvain, 1963.

Assfalg, Julius, "Zur Textüberlieferung der Chronik von Arbela," *Oriens Christianus* 50 (1966): 19–36.

Brock, Sebastian, "Christology of the Church of the East," in D. Afinogenov and A. Muraviev (eds), *Traditions and Heritage of the Christian East*, Moscow, 1996, 159–79.

Brock, Sebastian, *Studies in Syriac Christianity*, Collected Studies Series CS357, Hampshire, 1992.

Calvet, Yves, "Monuments paléo-chrétiens à Koweit et dans la région du Golfe," in *Symposium Syriacum VII*, Orientalia Christiana Analecta 256, Rome, 1998, 671–85.

Chabot, Jean-Baptist, "L'école de Nisibe. Son histoire, ses statuts," *Journal Asiatique* 10 (1896): 43–93.

Chaumont, Marie-Luise, *Christianisation de l'Empire Iranien des origines aux grandes persécutions du IVe siècle*, CSCO 499 Subs. 80, Louvain, 1988.

Chaumont, Marie-Luise, "Les Sassanides," *Revue de l'histoire des religions* 165 (1964): 165–202.

Chaumont, Marie-Luise, "L'inscription de Katîr à la 'Ka'bah de Zoroastre' (Texte, Traduction, Commentaire)," *Journal Asiatique* 248 (1960): 339–80.

Chediath, Geevargese, *The Christology of Mar Babai the Great*, Oriental Institute of Religious Studies 49, Kottayam, 1982.

Drijvers, Han J. W., "Edessa," *Theologische Realenzyklopädie* 9 (1982): 277–88.

Drijvers, Han J. W., "Addai und Mani. Christentum und Manichäismus im 3. Jh. in Syrien," in René Lavenant (ed.), *III Symposium Syriacum 1980*, Orientalia Christiana Analecta 221, Rome, 1983, 171–185.

Drijvers, Han J. W., *East of Antioch: Studies in Early Syriac Christianity*, Collected Studies Series CS198, London, 1984.

Drijvers, Han J. W., "Hatra, Palmyra und Edessa," *Aufstieg und Niedergang der römischen Welt* 2/8 (1977: 799–906.

Drijvers, Han J. W., "Nisibis," *Theologische Realenzyklopädie* 24 (1994): 573–6.

Engelhardt, Isrun, *Mission und Politik in Byzanz. Ein beitrag zur strukturanalyse byzantinischer Mission zur Zeit Justins und Justinians*, Miscellanea Byzantina Monacensia 19, Munich, 1974.

Fiey, Jean-Maurice, "Auteur et date de la Chronique d'Arebèles," *Orient Syrien* 12 (1967): 265–302.

Fiey, Jean-Maurice, "Les étapes de la prise de conscience de son identité patriarcale par l'église syrienne orientale," *Orient Syrien* 12 (1967): 3–22.

Fiey, Jean-Maurice, *Nisibe, métropole syriaque orientale et ses suffragants des origines à nos jours*, CSCO 388 Subs. 54, Louvain, 1977.

Gero, Stephen, *Barsauma of Nisibis and Persian Christianity in the Fifth Century*, CSCO 426 Subs. 63, Louvain, 1981.

Gero, Stephen, "Die Kirche des Ostens. Zum Christentum in Persien in der Spätantike," *Ostkirchliche Studien* 30 (1981): 22–7.

Hage, Wolfgang, "Die oströmische Staatskirche und die Christenheit des Perserreiches," *Zeitschrift für Kirchengeschichte* 84 (1973): 174–87.

Hage, Wolfgang, *Syriac Christianity in the East*, Môrân 'Eth'ô 1, Kottayam, 1988.

Hage, Wolfgang, "Die Kirche 'des Ostens': Kirchliche Selbständigkeit und Kirchliche Gemeinsamkeit im fünften Jahrhundert," in G. J. Reinink and A. C. Klugkist (eds), *After Bardaisan: Studies on Continuity and Change in Syriac Christianity in Honour of Prof. Han J. W. Drijvers*, Orientalia Lovaniensia Analecta 89, Leuven, 1999, 141–8.

Halleux, André de, "Autonomy and Centralization in the Ancient Churches: Edessa and Selucia-Ctesiphon," *Wort und Wahrheit* Supplementary Issue 4 (1978): 59–67.

Halleux, André de, "La première session du concile d'Éphèse (22 Juin 431)," *Ephemerides theologicae Lovanienses* 69 (1993): 48–87.

Halleux, André de, "Le symbole des évêques perse au synode de Séleucie-Ctésiphon (410)," in G. Wiessner (ed.), *Erkenntnisse und Meinungen II*, Göttinger Orientforschung. Syriaca 17, Göttingen, 1978, 283–94.

Halleux, André de, "Nestorius. Histoire et Doctrine," *Irénikon* 66 (1993): 38–51, 163–78.

Hermann, Th., "Die Schule von Nisibis vom 5. bis 7. Jahrhundert. Ihre Quellen und ihre Geschichte," *Zeitschrift für Neutestamentliche Wissenschaft* 25 (1926): 89–122.

Hirschberg J. W., "Nestorian Sources of North-Arabian Traditions on the Establishment and Persecution of Christianity in Yemen," *Rocnik Orientalistyczny* 15 (1939–49): 321–38.

Hutter, Manfred, "Shirin, Nestorianer und Monophysiten. Königliche Kirchenpolitik im späten Sasanidenreich," in René Lavenant (ed.), *Symposium Syriacum VII*, Orientalia Christiana Analecta 256, Rome, 1998, 373–86.

Krüger, Paul, "Die Lehrmeinungen über den Primat Petri und des Papstes im Frühnestorianismus in ökumenischer Sicht," *Oriens Christianus* 45 (1961): 54–69.

Labourt, Jérôme, *Le christianisme dans l'empire perse sous la Dynastie Sassanide (224–632)*, Paris, 1904.

Macomber, William, "The christology of the Synod of Seleucia-Ctesiphon AD 486," *Orientalia Christiana Periodica* 24 (1958): 142–54.

Maraval, Pierre, "Die neuen Grenzen. I. Persien [Dt. Fassung grundlegend bearb. u. erw. v. Peter Bruns]," in Charles and Luce Piétri (eds), *Das Entstehen der Einen Christenheit (250–430)*, Die Geschichte des Christentums 2, Freiburg, 1996, 1076–84.

Müller, Walter W., "Himyar," *RAC* 15 (1991): 303–31.

Sako, Louis R. M., *Le rôle de la hiérarchie syriaque orientale dans les rapports diplomatiques entre la Perse et Byzance aux Ve–VIIe siècles*, Paris, 1986.

Schwaigert, Wolfgang, *Das Christentum in Hûzistân im Rahmen der frühen Kirchengeschichte Persiens bis zur Synode von Seleukia-Ktesiphon im Jahre 410*, Marburg/Lahn, 1989.

Schwaigert, Wolfgang, "Katholikos Isaak (399–410 n. Chr.) und seine Zeit. Ein Beitrag zur nestorianischen Patriarchengeschichte," in M. Tamcke, W. Schwaigert, and E. Schlarb (eds), *Syrisches Christentum weltweit*, Münster, 1995, 180–9.

Schwaigert, Wolfgang, "Miles und Papa: Der Kampf um den Primat. Ein Beitrag zur Diskussion um die Chronik von Arbela," in René Lavenant (ed.), *V Symposium Syriacum 1988*, Orientalia Christiana Analecta 236, Rome, 1990, 393–402.

Tamcke, Martin, *Der Katholikos-Patriarch Sabrîshô (596–604) und das Mönchtum*, Frankfurt, 1988.

Vööbus, Arthur, *History of the School of Nisibis*, CSCO 266 Subs. 26, Louvain, 1965.

Vööbus, Arthur, "New Sources for the Symbols in Early Syrian Christianity," *Vigiliae Christianae* 26 (1972): 291–6.

Vööbus, Arthur, *The Statutes of the School of Nisibis*, Stockholm, 1962.

Vries, Wilhelm de, "Antiochien und Seleukia-Ktesiphon, Patriarch und Katholikos", in *Melanges E. Tisserant*, Rome, 1964, 429–50.

Vries, Wilhelm de, "Die syrisch-nestorianische Haltung zu Chalkedon," in *Das Konzil von Chalkedon I*, ed. A. Grillmeier and H. Bacht, 2nd edn, Würzburg, 1962, 603–35.

Wickham, Lionel R. "Nestorius/Nestorianischer Streit," *Theologische Realenzyklopädie* 24 (1994): 276–86.

Wigram, William A., *An Introduction to the History of the Assyrian Church or the Church of the East in the Sassanid Persian Empire 100–640 A.D.*, London, 1910.

Winkler, Dietmar W., *Koptische Kirche und Reichskirche. Altes Schisma und neuer Dialog. Mit einem Vorwort von Franz Kardinal König*, Innsbrucker theologische Studien 48, Innsbruck, 1996.

Winkler, Dietmar W., "Monophysitism," in Glenn Bowersock, Peter Brown, and Oleg Grabar (eds), *Late Antiquity: A Guide to the Postclassical World*, Cambridge, Mass., 1999, 586–8.

Witakowski, Witold, "Chronicles of Edessa," *Orientalia Suecana* 33–35 (1984–6): 487–98.

Chapters 2 to 4: The ages of the Arabs, Mongols, and Ottomans (Wilhelm Baum)

Aprem, Mar, "Codification of the Law by Mar Abdisho in 1290 A.D.," in *VI Symposium Syriacum 1992*, Orientalia Christiana Analecta 247, Rome, 1994, 371–80.

Athappilly, Andrew, "An Indian Prototype for Prester John," *Terrae incognitae* 10 (1978): 15–23.

Barthold, W., *Zur Geschichte des Christentums in Mittelasien*, Tübingen and Leipzig, 1901.

Balicka-Witakowska, Ewa, "Remarks on the Decoration and Iconography of the Syriac Gospels, British Library, Add. 7174," in *Symposium Syriacum VII*, Orientalia Christiana Analecta 256, Rome 1998, 641–59.

Baum, Wilhelm, *Die Verwandlungen des Mythos vom Reich des Priesterkönigs Johannes*, Klagenfurt, 1999.

Baum, Wilhelm, "The Syrian Christian Community and Its Contacts to Europe and the Mediterranean Area before the Arrival of the Portuguese," *Ephrem's Theological Journal* 5 (2001): 71–81.

Baum, Wilhelm, "Shirin, christl. Großkönigin v. Persien († 628)," *Bio-Bibliographisches Kirchenlexikon* 19 (2001).

Baum, Wilhelm, "Mari ibn Sulaiman, ostsyr. Theologe u. Geschichtsschreiber (12. Jhdt.)," *Bio-Bibliographisches Kirchenlexikon* 20 (2002).

Baum, Wilhelm, "Shimun XVII. (1820/25–1861), Katholikos," *Bio-Bibliographisches Kirchenlexikon* 20 (2002): 1331–6.

Bezzola, Gian Andri, *Die Mongolen in abendländischer Sicht (1220–1270)*, Bern, 1974.

Braun, Oscar, "Der Katholikos Timotheos I. und seine Briefe," *Oriens Christianus* 1 (1901): 138–52.

Briquel-Chatonnet, Françoise, *Manuscrits syriaques*, Paris, 1997.

Brockelmann, Carl, *Geschichte der islamischen Völker*, Munich and Berlin, 1943.

Brown, Peter, *Die Entstehung des christlichen Europa*, Munich, 1999.

Browne, Laurence E., *The Eclipse of Eastern Christianity*, Cambridge, 1933.

Cambridge History of China, The, vol. VI: Cambridge, 1994, 907–1368.

Cambridge History of Iran, The, vol. V: "The Saljuq and Mongol Periods," ed. J. A. Boyle, Cambridge, 1968.

Carswell, John, "The Excavation of Matota," *Ancient Sri Lanka* 9 (1990): 17–28.

Coakley, J. F., "The Archbishop of Canterbury's Assyrian Mission and the Consecration of Mar Abimalek Timotheus of Malabar," in *III Symposium Syriacum 1980*, Orientalia Christiana Analecta 221, Rome, 1983, 203–12.

Coakley, J. F., *The Church of the East and the Church of England: A History of the Archbishop of Canterbury's Assyrian Mission*, Oxford, 1992.

Dauvillier, Jean, *Histoire et institutions des Eglises au Moyen Age*, Collected Studies Series CS173, London, 1983.

Degen, Erika, "Daniel ben Maryam. Ein nestorianischer Kirchenhistoriker," *Oriens Christianus* 52 (1968): 45–80.

Dihle, Albrecht, "Indien," *Reallexikon für Antike und Christentum* 137 (1996): 34–56.

Fiey, Jean-Maurice, *Chrétiens syriaques sous les Abbassides surtout à Bagdad (749–1258)*, CSCO 420 Subs. 59, Louvain, 1980.

Fiey, Jean-Maurice, *Chrétiens syriaques sous les Mongols*, CSCO 362 Subs. 44, Louvain, 1975.

Fiey, Jean-Maurice, *Pour une Oriens christianus novus*, Beiruter Texte und Studien 49, Beirut, 1993.

Fitzgerald, C. P., *China. Von der Vorgeschichte bis zum 19. Jahrhundert*, Magnus Kulturgeschichte, Essen, 1975.

Flotz, Richard C., *Religions of the Silk Road*, Bloomsburg, 1999.

Franke, Herbert, "Westöstliche Beziehungen im Zeitalter der Mongolenherrschaft," *Saeculum* 19 (1969): 91–106.

Franke, Herbert, "Zu einigen christlichen Personennamen in Texten der Yüanzeit," *Zeitschrift der deutschen morgenländischen Gesellschaft* 148 (1998): 315–22.

Gollwitzer, Martin, "Sri Lanka: Drehscheibe des Handels," in St. Conerman (ed.), *Der indische Ozean*, Asien u. Afrika 1, Hamburg, 1998, 37–56.

Graf, Georg, *Geschichte der christlichen arabischen Literatur*, vol. II: *Die Schriftsteller bis zur Mitte des 15. Jahrhunderts*, Studi e Testi 133, Vatican City, 1947.

Gropp, Gerd, "Die Pahlavi-Inschrift auf dem Thomaskreuz in Madras," *Archäologische Mitteilungen aus Iran* NF 3 (1970): 267–71.

Grousset, René, *Die Steppenvölker*, Magnus Kulturgeschichte, Essen, 1975.

Gumilev, L. N., *Searches for an Imaginary Kingdom: The Legend of the Kingdom of Prester John*, Cambridge, 1987.

Haarmann, Harald, *Universalgeschichte der Schrift*, 2nd edn, Frankfurt, 1991.

Habbi, Joseph, "Les Chaldéens et les Malabares au XIXe siécle," *Oriens Christianus* 64 (1980): 82–107.

Hage, Wolfgang, "Crosses with Epigraphs in Medieval Central and East Asian Christianity," *The Harp* 8/9 (1995/6): 375–82.

Hage, Wolfgang, *Das Christentum im frühen Mittelalter*, Zugänge zur Kirchengeschichte 4, Göttingen, 1993.

Hage, Wolfgang, "Das Christentum in der Turfan-Oase," in *Synkretismus in den Religionen Zentralasiens*, Studies in Oriental Religion, Wiesbaden, 1987, 46–57.

Hage, Wolfgang, "Das Nebeneinander christlicher Konfessionen im mittelalterlichen Zentralasien," *Zeitschrift der deutschen morgenländischen Gesellschaft*, Suppl. 1/2 (1969): 517–25.

Hage, Wolfgang, "Der Weg nach Asien. Die ostsyrische Missionskirche," in Kurt Schäferdiek (ed.), *Kirchengeschichte als Missionsgeschichte II/1*, Munich, 1978, 360–93.

Hage, Wolfgang, "Einheimische Volkssprachen und syrische Kirchensprache in der nestorianischen Asienmission," in Gernot Wiessner (ed.), *Erkenntnisse und Meinungen*, vol. II, Göttinger Orientforschung 17, Göttingen, 1978, 131–60.

Hage, Wolfgang, "Kulturelle Kontakte des ostsyrischen Christentums in Zentralasien," *Orientalia Christiana Analecta* 221 (1983): 143–59.

Hage, Wolfgang, "Religiöse Toleranz in der nestorianischen Asienmission," in *Glaube u. Toleranz. Das theologische Erbe der Aufklärung*, Gütersloh, 1982, 99–112.

Hage, Wolfgang, "Yahballaha III," in *Gestalten der Kirchengeschichte*, vol. IV, ed. Martin Greschat, Stuttgart, 1983, 92–101.

Haussig, Hans Wilhelm, *Die Geschichte Zentralasiens und der Seidenstraße in vorislamischer Zeit*, 2nd edn, Darmstadt, 1994.

Hofstra, Johan D., "The Sources Used by Ishodad of Merw in His Commentary on St. John," ch. 1 in *Symposium Syriacum VII*, Orientalia Christina Analecta 256, Rome, 1998, 23–35.

Hollerweger, Hans, *Lebendiges Kulturerbe Turabdin. Wo die Sprache Jesu gesprochen wird. Unter Mitarbeit v. A. Palmer und mit einer Einleitung von S. Brock*, 2nd edn, Linz, 2000.

Holm, B., "Nasturiyyun," in *Encyclopedia of Islam*, vol. VII, Leiden and New York, 1993, 1030–3.

Hsü, C. H., "Nestorianism and the Nestorian Monument in China," *Asian Culture Quarterly* 14 (1986): 41–81.

Joseph, T. K., "The Malabar Christian Copper-Plates," *Kerala Society Papers*, Series 4, ND Thiruvanthapuram (1997): 201–4

Kaufhold, Hubert, *Die Rechtssammlung des Gabriel von Basra und ihr Verhältnis zu den anderen juristischen Sammelwerken der Nestorianer*, Abh. zur rechtswiss. Grundlagenforschung 21, Berlin, 1976.

Kawerau, Peter, *Christlich-arabische Chrestomathie aus historischen Schriftstellern des Mittelalters*, CSCO 385 Subs. 53, Louvain, 1977.

Kawerau, Peter, *Das Christentum des Ostens*, Die Religionen der Menschheit 30, Stuttgart 1972.

Kawerau, Peter, "Die nestorianischen Patriarchate in der neueren Zeit," *Zeitschrift für Kirchengeschichte* 67 (1955/6): 119–31.

Klein, Wassilios, "Christliche Reliefgrabsteine des 14. Jahrhunderts von der Seidenstraße," in *VI Symposium Syriacum 1992*, Orientalia Christiana Analecta 247, Rome, 1994, 419–42.

Klein, Wassilios, *Das nestorianische Christentum an den Handelswegen durch Kyrgyzstan bis zum 14. Jh.*, Silk Road Studies 3, Turnhout, 2000.

Klein, Wassilios, "Nestorianische Inschriften in Kirgizistan. Ein Situationsbericht," in René Lavenant (ed.), *Symposium Syriacum VII*, Orientalia Christiana Analecta 256, Rome, 1998, 662–9.

Lach, Donald F., *Asia in the Making of Europe*, 2nd edn, vol. I, Chicago and London, 1971.

Latourette, Kenneth Scott, *Geschichte der Ausbreitung des Christentums*, Göttingen, 1956.

Latourette, Kenneth Scott, *A History of the Expansion of Christianity*, vols I and II, Grand Rapids, 1970.

Lehmann-Haupt, Carl Friedrich, *Armenien einst und jetzt*, Bd. 1 (1910), repr. Hildesheim, 1988.

Lewis, Bernard, *Stern, Kreuz und Halbmond. 2000 Jahre Geschichte des nahen Ostens*, Munich and Zurich, 1977.

Lombard, Maurice, *Blütezeit des Islam*, Frankfurt, 1992.

Lüders, Anneliese, *Die Kreuzzüge im Urteil syrischer und armenischer Quellen*, Berlin, 1964.

Macomber, William F., "New finds of syriac manuscripts in the Middle East," *Zeitschrift der deutschen morgenländischen Gesellschaft*, Suppl. 1 (1969): 473–80.

Matuz, Josef, *Das Osmanische Reich. Grundliniern seiner Geschichte*, 2nd edn, Darmstadt, 1990.

Meinardus, Otto F. A., "Eine nestorianische Klosteranlage auf der Insel Kharg," *Ostkirchliche Studien* 35 (1986): 37–40.

Meinardus, Otto, "The Nestorians in Egypt," *Oriens Christianus* 51 (1967): 112–27.

Moule, A. C., *Christians in China Before the Year 1550* (1930), New York, 1977.

Müller, C. Detlef G., "Stellung und Bedeutung des Katholikos-Patriarchen von Seleukeia-Ktesiphon im Altertum," *Oriens Christianus* 53 (1969): 227–46.

Mundadan, A. Mathias, *History of Christianity in India*, vol. I, Bangalore, 1984.

Murre-van den Berg, Helene H. L., "A Syrian Awakening. Alqosh and Urmia as Centres of Neo-Syriac Writing," in *Symposium Syriacum VII*, Orientalia Christiana Analecta 256, Rome, 1998, 499–515.

Murre-van den Berg, Helene H. L., "The Patriarchs of the East from the Fifteenth to Eighteenth Century," *Hugoye* 2/2 (1999) http://syrcom.cua.edu/hugoye/Vol2No2.

Pigulewskaja, Nina, *Byzanz auf den Wegen nach Indien. Aus der Geschichte des byzantinischen Handels mit dem Orient vom 4. bis 6. Jahrhundert*, Berliner Byzantinistische Arbeiten 36, Berlin, 1969.

Podipara, Placid, *Die Thomas-Christen*, Das östliche Christentum NF 18, Würzburg, 1966.

Rao, Gopinatha T. A., "Three Inscriptions of Sthanu Ravi," in *Travancore Archaeological Series*, vol. II, Madras, 1916, 60–86.

Reflections on a Heritage. Historical Scholarship on Premodern Sri Lanka, part 1, History and Archaeology of Sri Lanka I, Colombo, 2002.

Rosenkranz, Gerhard, *Die älteste Christenheit in China*, 2nd edn, Berlin, 1939.

Rosenthal, Franz, *Das Fortleben der Antike im Islam*, Zurich and Stuttgart, 1965.

Sachau, Eduard, *Kurzes Verzeichnis der Sachau' schen Sammlung syrischer Handschriften*, Berlin, 1885.

Sachau, Eduard, *Verzeichnis syrischer Handschriften*, Die Handschriftenverzeichnisse der königlichen Bibliothek zu Berlin 23, Berlin, 1899.

Sachau, Eduard, *Zur Ausbreitung des Christentums in Asien*, Berlin, 1919.

Schöffler, Heinz Herbert, *Die Akademie von Gondischapur*, 2nd edn, Stuttgart, 1980.

Schwaigert, Wolfgang, "Die Theologenschule von Bet Lapat-Gundaisabur," *Zeitschrift der deutschen morgenländischen Gesellschaft*, Suppl. 4 (1980): 185–7.

Sciamani e Dervisci dalle Steppe del Prete Gianni, exhibition catalog, Venice, 2000.

Selb, Walter, *Orientalisches Kirchenrecht*, vol. I: *Die Geschichte des Kirchenrechts der Nestorianer*, Sitzungsberichte der Österreichischen Akademie der Wissenschaften, phil.-hist. Klasse 388, Vienna, 1981.

Sezgin, Fuat, *Geschichte des arabischen Schrifttums*, vol. I, Leiden, 1967; vol. III, 1970 (247–56 Hunain ibn Ishaq).

Sims-Williams, Nicholas, "Christian Literature in Middle Iranian Languages," in *Encyclopedia Iranica 5*, Costa Mesa, 1992, 534f.

Spuler, Bertold, *Die Goldene Horde. Die Mongolen in Russland*, 2nd edn, Wiesbaden, 1965.

Spuler, Bertold, "Syrisches Christentum in Vorderasien und Südindien," *Saeculum* 32 (1981): 242–54.

Stegensek, Augustin, "Eine syrische Miniaturenhandschrift des Museo Borgiano," *Oriens Christianus* 1 (1901): 343–55.

Subrahmanyam, Sanjay, *The Career and Legend of Vasco da Gama*, Cambridge, 1997.

Suermann, Harald, "Das arabische Reich in der Weltgeschichte des Johannan bar Penkaje," in *Nubia et Oriens Christianus, FS C. D. G. Müller*, Bibliotheca Nubica 1, Cologne, 1988, 59–71.

Suermann, Harald, "Timothy and his Dialogue with Muslims," *The Harp* 8 (1995/6): 263–75.

Suermann, Harald, "Der nestorianische Patriarch Timotheos I. und seine theologischen Briefe im Kontext des Islam," in Martin Tamcke and Andreas Heinz (eds), *Zu Geschichte, Theologie, Liturgie und Gegenwartslage der syrischen Kirchen*, Studien zur Orientalischen Kirchengeschichte 9, Hamburg, 2000, 217–30.

Tamcke, Martin, "Urmia und Hermannsburg, Luther Pera im Dienst der Hermannsburger Mission in Urmia 1910–1915," *Oriens Christianus* 80 (1996): 43–65.

Troupeau, Gérard, "Die Christenheit im Osten," in Gilbert Dragon et al. (eds), *Bischöfe, Mönche und Kaiser (642–1054)*, Die Geschichte des Christentums 4, Freiburg, 1994, 391–472.

Tubach, Jürgen, "Die nestorianische Kirche in China," *Nubica et Aethiopica. Internationales Jahrbuch für koptische, meroitisch-nubische, äthiopische und verwandte Studien* 4/5 (1999): 61–193.

Tubach, Jürgen, "Tarisappalli," *Orientalia Lovaniensia Periodica* 25 (1994): 69–79.

Übleis, Franz, "Marco Polo in Südasien," *Arbeiten zur Kirchengeschichte* 60 (1978): 268–304.

Van der Ploeg, J. P. M., "Mar Joseph, Bishop-Metropolitan of India (1556–

1569)," in *III Symposium Syriacum 1980*, Orientalia Christiana Analecta 221, Rome, 1983, 161–70.

Verghese, Paul (ed.), *Die syrischen Kirchen in Indien*, Die Kirchen der Welt 13, Stuttgart, 1974.

Von den Brincken, Anna Dorothee, "Eine christliche Weltchronik von Qara Qorum. Wilhelm von Rubruk OFM und der Nestorianismus," *Arbeiten zur Kirchengeschichte* 51 (1969): 1–19.

Von den Brincken, Anna-Dorothee, *Die "Nationes Christianorum orientalium" im Verständnis der lateinischen Historiographie*, Cologne and Vienna, 1973.

Vries, Wilhelm de, *Rom und die Patriarchate des Ostens*, Orbis Academicus III/4, Freiburg and Munich, 1963.

Vries, Wilhelm de, "Die Patriarchen der nichtkatholischen syrischen Kirchen," *Ostkirchliche Studien* 33 (1984): 3–45.

Weihrauch und Seide. Alte Kulturen an der Seidenstraße, exhibition catalog, Vienna, 1996.

Wiesehöfer, Josef, "Mare Erythraeum, Sinus Persicus und Fines Indiae. Der Indische Ozean in hellenistischer und römischer Zeit," in *Asien u. Afrika*, vol. I: *Der Indische Ozean in historischer Perspektive*, ed. Stephan Conermann, Hamburg, 1998, 9–36.

Willeke, Bernward, "Frühe Kontakte und christliche Mission in China," in *China (Forschung und Information)*, Berlin, 1980, 71–9.

Yule, Henry, and Cordier, Henri, *Cathay and the Way Thither*, vols I–III, London, 1913–15.

Chapter 5: The twentieth century
(Dietmar W. Winkler)

Anschütz, Helga, "Die Gegenwartslage der 'Assyrischen Kirche des Ostens' und ihre Beziehungen zur 'assyrischen' Nationalbewegung," *Ostkirchliche Studien* 18 (1969): 122–45.

Coakley, J. F., "The Church of the East since 1914," in J. F. Coakley and K. Parry (eds), *The Church of the East: Life and Thought, Bulletin of the John Rylands University Library of Manchester* 78/3 (1996): 179–97.

Hammerschmidt, Ernst, "Nestorianische Kirchen am Urmia-See," in Wilhelm Hoenerbach (ed.), *Der Orient in der Forschung. Festschrift für Otto Spies*, Wiesbaden, 1967, 254–78.

Hammerschmidt, Ernst, "Zur Lage der Nestorianer am Urmia-See," in Ernst Gräf (ed.), *Festschrift für Werner Caskel zum siebzigsten Geburtstag*, Leiden, 1968, 146–61.

Joseph, John, *The Modern Assyrians of the Middle East: Encounters with Western Christian Missions, Archaeologists, and Colonial Powers*, Studies in Christian Mission 26, Leiden, Boston and Cologne, 2000.

Kawerau, Peter, *Amerika und die orientalischen Kirchen. Ursprung und*

Anfang der amerikanischen Mission unter den Nationalkirchen Westasiens, Arbeiten zur Kirchengeschichte 31, Berlin, 1958.

Mäder, Horst (ed.), *Die Streitkräfte der Staaten des Nahen Ostens und Nordafrikas Teil B. Regionale Organisationen, Konflikte und ihre Ursachen*, Truppendienst Taschenbuch 34B, Vienna, 1995.

Madey, Johannes, "Die Kirche des Ostens in der Krise," *Der Christliche Osten* 25 (1970): 145–52.

Madey, Johannes, "Neue Beiträge zur Statistik der Alt-Orientalischen Kirchen," *Der Christliche Osten* 27 (1972): 136–8.

Madey, Johannes, "Zur Gegenwartslage der Orientalischen Kirchen," *Ostkirchliche Studien* 59 (1975): 169–84.

Malek, Y., *The Assyrian Tragedy*, Annemasse, 1934.

Malek, Y., *The British Betrayal of the Assyrians*, Fair Lawn, NJ, 1935.

Orthodoxia 1999–2000, Regensburg, 1998.

Pro Oriente (ed.), *Syriac Dialogue*, vols I–IV, Vienna, 1994–2000.

Spuler, Berthold, *Gegenwartslage der Ostkirchen in ihrer nationalen und staatlichen Umwelt*, 2nd edn, Frankfurt, 1968.

Strothmann, Rudolf, "Heutiges Orientchristentum und Schicksal der Assyrer," *Zeitschrift für Kirchengeschichte* 55 (1936): 17–43.

Surma d'Bait Mar Shimun, *Assyrian Church Customs and the Murder of Mar Shimun*, London, 1920.

Talay, Shabo, "Bericht über die Lage der Apostolischen Kirche des Ostens in Syrien," in Martin Tamcke and Andreas Heinz (eds), *Zu Geschichte, Theologie, Liturgie und Gegenwartslage der Syrischen Kirchen*, Studien zur Orientalischen Kirchengeschichte 9, Hamburg, 2000, 447–67.

Trummer, Peter and Pichler, Josef (eds), *Heiliges Land beiderseits des Jordan*, Innsbruck, 1998.

Vries, Wilhelm de, "Zur neuesten Entwicklung der Ostkirchen," *Ostkirchliche Studien* 2 (1953): 233–52.

Waterfield, R. E., *Christians in Persia: Assyrians, Armenians, Roman Catholics and Protestants*, London, 1973.

Wigram, W. A., *Our Smallest Ally*, London, 1920.

Winkler, Dietmar W., "Jüngste Entwicklungen in den ökumenischen Beziehungen der Assyrischen Kirche des *Ostens*," *Ökumenisches Forum. Grazer Jahrbuch für konkrete Ökumene* 18 (1995): 281–8.

Winkler, Dietmar W., "The Current Theological Dialogue with the Assyrian Church of the East," in René Lavenant (ed.), *Symposium Syriacum VII*, Orientalia Christiana Analecta 256, Rome, 1998, 159–73.

Winkler, Dietmar W., "Theologische Notizen zu den ökumenischen Dialogen mit der Assyrischen Kirche des Ostens," *Ökumenisches Forum. Grazer Jahrbuch für konkrete Ökumene* 17 (1994): 243–66.

Winkler, Dietmar W., "Zur Gegenwartslage der Christen im Nahen Osten," *Der Christliche Osten* 50 (2000): 34–44.

Yonan, Gabriele, *Assyrer heute. Kultur, Sprache, Nationalbewegung der aramäisch sprechenden Christen im Nahen Osten*, Hamburg, 1978.

Yonan, Gabriele, *Ein vergessener Holocaust*, Göttingen, 1989.

Chapter 6: Language and literature of the Church of the East

Syriac literature (Dietmar W. Winkler)

Albert, Micheline, et al., Christianismes orientaux. Introduction à l'étude des langues et des littératures, Paris, 1993.

Assfalg, Julius, "Die christlichen Literaturen des Orients," Kindlers Literaturlexikon 1 (1965): 65–77.

Baumstark, Anton, Geschichte der syrischen Literatur mit Ausschluss der christlich palästinensischen Texte, Bonn, 1922.

Brock, Sebastian, "An Introduction to Syriac Studies," in J. H. Eaton (ed.), Horizons in Semitic Studies: Articles for Students, Birmingham, 1980, 1–33.

Brock, Sebastian, "Bibelübersetzungen I. 4. Die Übersetzung ins Syrische," Theologische Realenzyklopädie 6 (1980): 181–9.

Brock, Sebastian, A Brief Outline of Syriac Literature, Môrân 'Eth'ô 9, Kottayam, 1997.

Brock, Sebastian, From Ephrem to Romanos: Interactions between Syriac and Greek in Late Antiquity, Collected Studies Series CS664, Hampshire, 1999.

Brock, Sebastian, "Syrische Sprache und Literatur," Lexikon für Theologie und Kirche 9, Col. 1213–15.

Desreumaux, Alain, and Briquel-Chatonnet, Françoise, Répertoire des bibliothèques et des catalogues de manuscrits syriaques, Paris, 1991.

Drijwers, Han J., and Healy, John F., The Old Syriac Inscriptions of Edessa and Osrohene, Leiden, 1999.

Duval, Rubens, La littérature syriaque, Paris, 1907 (repr. Amsterdam, 1970).

Wright, William, A Short History of Syriac Literature, London, 1894.

Iranian literature (Manfred Hutter)

Important text editions

Andreas, Friedrich C., and Barr, Kai, Bruchstücke einer Pehlevi-Übersetzung der Psalmen, Sitzungsberichte der Preussischen Akademie der Wissenschaften, phil.-hist. Klasse, 1933, Nr. 1, Berlin, 1933.

Gropp, Gerd, "Die Pahlavi-Inschrift auf dem Thomaskreuz in Madras," Archäologische Mitteilungen aus Iran 3 (1970): 267–71 and Table 118.

Hansen, Olaf, Berliner soghdische Texte 1. Bruchstücke einer soghdischen Version der Georgspassion (C 1), (Abhandlungen der Preussischen Akademie der Wissenschaften, phil.-hist. Klasse, 1941, Nr. 10 Berlin, 1941.

Müller, Friedrich W. K., Soghdische Texte II. Aus dem Nachlass herausgegeben von Wolfgang Lentz, Sitzungsberichte der Preussischen Akademie der Wissenschaften, phil.-hist. Klasse, 1934, Nr. 21. Berlin, 1934.

Sims-Williams, Nicholas, *The Christian Sogdian Manuscript C 2*, Berliner Turfantexte 12, Berlin, 1985.

Literature

Hansen, Olaf, "Die Christliche Literatur der Sogdier," in Ilya Gershevitch *et al.*, *Literatur. Lieferung 1*, Handbuch der Orientalistik, 1. Abteilung. 4. Band: Iranistik. 2. Abschnitt, Leiden, 1968, 91–9.

Sims-Williams, Nicholas, "Sogdian and Turkish Christians in the Turfan and Tun-Huang Manuscripts," in Alfredo Cadonna (ed.), *Turfan and Tun-Huang. The Texts. Encounter of Civilizations on the Silk Road*, Florence, 1992.

Sundermann, Werner, "Byzanz und Bulayïq," in Petr Vavrouöek (ed.), *Iranian and Indo-European Studies*, Praha, 1994, 255–64.

Turkish, Uighur, and Chinese literature (Wilhelm Baum)

Mehlhose, Robert, "Nestorianische Texte aus China," *Zeitschrift der deutschen morgenländischen Gesellschaft*, Suppl. 1/2 (1969): 442–9.

Moule, A. C., *Christians in China Before the Year 1550* (1930) New York, 1977.

Rosenkranz, Gerhard, *Die älteste Christenheit in China*, 2nd edn, Berlin, 1939.

Saeki, Yoshiro, *The Nestorian Documents and Relics in China*, 2nd edn, Tokyo, 1951.

Shimin, Geng, Klimkeit, Hans-Joachim, and Laut, Jens Peter, "Eine neue nestorianische Grabinschrift aus China," *Ural-Altaische Jahrbücher* NF 14 (1996): 164–75.

Internet

Homepage of the Assyrian Church of the East: http://www.cired.org

INDEX

195

Xindu 93f.

Yeh-lü Ta-shih, khan of the Karakitai
(† 1142) 79
Yeh-li-ya (Elias), son of Isa
(fourteenth century) 87

Yohanna Abraham, bishop 147
Mar Yonan (nineteenth century)
133
Yosip of Ada (nineteenth century)
133
Yosip Khananisho 146–8, 150

PEFC Certified

This product is
from sustainably
managed forests
and controlled
sources

www.pefc.org

PEFC™
PEFC/16-33-415

#0202 - 060116 - C0 - 216/138/12 - PB - 9780415600217